Confirm

2 Peter 1: 3 & 4

Presented To:

_____

By:

_____

Date:

_____

QUIET
MOMENTS
WITH GOD

DEVOTIONAL JOURNAL
for Teens

HONOR **HB** BOOKS

Inspiration and Motivation for the Season of Life

An Imprint of Cook Communications Ministries • Colorado Springs, CO

2 3 4 5 6 7 8 9 10 11 Printing/Year 08 07 06 05 04

Quiet Moments with God Devotional Journal for Teens
ISBN 1-56292-983-6
Copyright © 2001 by Honor Books, an imprint of
Cook Communications Ministries, Colorado Springs, CO 80918
Cook Communications, Paris, Ontario
Kingsway Communications, Eastbourne, England

Developed by Bordon Book

QUIET
MOMENTS
WITH GOD

DEVOTIONAL JOURNAL

for Teens

Introduction

In today's world, we are busier than ever. You probably wake up, rush through breakfast, race to school, try to chat with friends at lunch and in between classes. Then there is homework, baseball, volleyball, cheerleading, drama, band, and an endless list of activities. You might try to squeeze in a television show or a few moments on the computer chatting with a friend. In the midst of your life race, it's important to spend a few minutes with God. It's all about relationship with Him.

Quiet Moments with God Devotional Journal for Teens makes it easy to capture those precious quality moments and reflect on your relationship with Him. Just a few minutes each day, take time to reflect on the important role your Creator has in your life. It'll change your day!

Life can get downright busy between school, friends, family, activities, and work. How do you make it slow down? Take a few quiet moments—for personal meditation, for fellowship with God. We need both in order to live balanced lives while meeting the complex demands we face every day.

As our world moves and swirls past us with great speed and intensity, it's tempting to put those quiet times aside and regard them as luxuries rather than necessities. But the truth is—moments of tranquility are critical. They help us define our relationships, our roles, our priorities, and ourselves. Without them, we become slaves to our lifestyles rather than the masters of them.

We hope you will find that the devotionals in this book help you make your quiet moments productive and inspiring. We have made them short enough to fit easily into your special time, yet long enough to provide a solid kickoff for your day. As you read, we hope that they will draw you closer to God.

Wake-Up Call

> Awake to righteousness, and sin not.
>
> I CORINTHIANS 15:34 KJV

Steven sought his independence and pressed against his parents' rules and strict guidelines at an early age. Steven told his best friend, Matt, "Going into the service means freedom. I know boot camp will be tough, but I can handle it. Besides, boot camp lasts only six weeks. After that I'm free!"

That first morning Steven woke to his sergeant's yells and quickly stood face-to-face with the reality that Mom, Dad, and all his teachers clumped together couldn't compare to all he was about to experience. *Six weeks may as well be an eternity*, Steven thought. He began to regularly write his family and even included the first thank-you notes his parents had ever received from him. He expressed appreciation for what his teachers had done for him.

Steven immediately began to recognize the importance of being prepared and learning how to handle what could attack a soldier in war. The sergeant trained the young recruits to anticipate the enemy's strategy, and made certain they knew the enemy lurked nearby, ready to attack without warning. He taught them the enemy's tactics. Steven played his sergeant's words repeatedly in his mind, "The enemy is cunning. He watches and waits for your weakest, most vulnerable time to attack."

Steven remembered his father had said something like that. The Bible tells us to awake to righteousness and to prepare ourselves, so we will not sin. God has provided the right armor and training required to defeat the enemy. We become soldiers for Christ when we join His family. God's enemies are our enemies, and the battle is over the most precious of God's creations: the human soul.

Steven realized his parents had raised him in safety with boundaries and rules so that he would be prepared to face the world. The boundaries and rules his parents set, like God's commands, were established to protect him from error, failure, and pain. Steven's correspondence to his family allowed them to realize Steven had experienced his wake-up call.

Are THERE RULES MY PARENTS OR GOD'S WORD SET IN MY LIFE THAT I DON'T TAKE SERIOUSLY?

God takes notice of clean hands, not full hands.

Can-Do Attitude

Jesus said unto him, "No man, having put his hand to the plough, and looking back, is fit for the kingdom of God."

LUKE 9:62 KJV

I am

DETERMINED
TO CHANGE
MY ATTITUDE
FROM CAN'T
TO CAN. WHAT
ARE SOME OF
THE THINGS
I STRUGGLE
WITH?

Walter E. Isenhour wrote a clever poem that appeared in *The Wesleyan Youth* many years ago. Written for teens, its message remains timeless and for all ages and circumstances.

Watch Your Can'ts and Can's

If you would have some worthwhile plans
You've got to watch your can't's and can's;
You can't aim low and then rise high;
You can't succeed if you don't try;
You can't go wrong and come out right;
You can't love sin and walk in the light;
You can't throw time and means away
And live sublime from day to day.
You can be great if you'll be good
And do God's will as all men should;
You can ascend life's upward road,
Although you bear a heavy load;
You can be honest, truthful, clean,
By turning from the low and mean;
You can uplift the souls of men
By words and deeds, or by your pen.
So watch your can't and watch your can's.
And watch your walks and watch your stands,
And watch the way you talk and act,
And do not take the false for fact;
And watch the things that mar or make;
For life is great to every man
Who lives to do the best he can.[1]

As you go through your day, keep in mind that your life goes in the direction you aim it. A popular saying in recent years sums up this idea succinctly: "Whether you think you can, or can't . . . you're right." Have an "I can" attitude today, and then pursue excellence with all your ability.

People can alter their lives
by altering their attitudes.

The Lord Directs My Steps

The mind of man plans his way,
but the LORD directs his steps.

PROVERBS 16:9 NASB

Katy's thirteenth birthday party was going well and she was thrilled that all of her friends came to celebrate with her. Each present was "just what she wanted." The last game to play was Pin-The-Tail-On-The-Donkey, and everyone seemed excited because the winner would receive a new CD. When Katy had her turn, she lost her footing and stumbled on top of several of her friends.

It was very funny, but Katy wasn't able to get her position right and she continued to try to pin the tail everywhere except near the game's paper donkey. When the scarf was removed from her eyes and she saw how far she was from where she needed to be, she said, "I certainly needed someone to direct my steps."

God has promised to direct our steps if we will allow Him to do so. The plan for our lives was laid before the beginning of time. Each morning we can go to the Lord and have a fresh look at the direction He would have us go that day.

Are you faced with a major decision? Do you need direction and guidance? Throughout Scripture there are promises that God will show us the right path. We do not have to stumble or grope around blindfolded. Our Heavenly Father is eager to give us wisdom. All we need to do is ask, and He will direct every step we take.

**I would rather walk with God in the dark
than go alone in the light.**

I know
GOD IS DIRECTING ME WHEN . . .

Enjoyment Without Winning? You Bet!

Shout for joy to the LORD.
PSALM 100:1

What KIND
OF ATTITUDE
DO I HAVE
WHEN THINGS
GO MY WAY?
WHAT ABOUT
WHEN THEY
DON'T GO
MY WAY? DO
I SEE THE
SITUATIONS
AROUND ME
IN A GOOD
LIGHT?
CONSIDER
SOME RECENT
SITUATIONS.

Tyler and Kent were acquaintances but not friends. In fact, you could easily consider them rivals. Tyler was the stereotypical young athlete who was stronger, taller, faster, and better than most of his peers. Kent was smaller and slower but filled with dogged determination and an intense desire to win. One evening during a baseball game, a most remarkable event happened.

Tyler had pitched a "no hitter" the previous week, and his team was leading by one run at the bottom of the last inning when Kent came up to bat. With runners on first and second base and two outs, Kent needed to get a base hit for his team to win. The encounter challenged both boys, with Tyler nearly hitting Kent with the first pitch. From that moment on, adrenaline surged, Kent proceeded to swing mightily at the next three pitches—missing each one and striking out.

But to the surprise of everyone watching, the final strike and the end of the game found Kent striding toward the mound, a goofy grin on his face and his bat forgotten in his left hand, with his right hand outstretched to shake hands with Tyler. Tyler came off the mound to meet him with his own hand outstretched and a small smile on his lips—not a smug grin of triumph but a warm, delightful smile of a secret shared.

What happened? For just a moment, the joy of participating in the game superseded the need to win the game. Life can be like that too. With the right approach, the joy of living can countermand the need to win because we begin to trust God with the outcome while we enjoy the process.

Your life is not determined by what life brings to you but by the attitude you bring to life; not what happens to you but by the way your mind looks at what happens.

Circumstances and situations do color life,
but you have been given the mind
to choose what the color shall be.

Bringing the Sunshine Back

> The LORD gives strength to his people;
> the LORD blesses his people with peace.
>
> PSALM 29:11

It was one of those wet rainy days at the end of winter, in that interlude between the cold weather and the warmth of spring, a time of daffodils peeking their bright yellow blossoms through the ground and offering promise of more to come.

In a small house on the corner, Rhonda, only fifteen, was fixing lunch for her three younger brothers while her mother worked at a local bakery. Their favorite sandwich was peanut butter and jelly. She brought the bread and peanut butter out of the cabinet and removed the blackberry jelly from the refrigerator. The lid on the jar of peanut butter seemed to be stuck tight. She tried and tried to open it, but the lid wouldn't budge.

Suddenly, Rhonda burst into tears. She had reached her limit. The baby had cried all morning with a stomach ache, the two-year-old was his usual "terrible twos" self; the rain meant the kids couldn't play outside, and now the dumb lid to the peanut butter jar wouldn't come off. Rhonda was beginning to resent her father. He had gone out of state to look for a job since he had been laid off.

At about that time, her five-year-old sister came into the kitchen. Kylie had been playing with dolls in her bedroom when she heard Rhonda crying. The little girl hugged her sister around her waist and said, "Don't cry, Rhonda. God will bring the sunshine back tomorrow."

Kylie's words put everything back into perspective for Rhonda. She knew that she had overreacted. Kylie was right. Tomorrow was another day. Her father had found a good job and they would all be together again soon.

Perhaps you felt you were at the end of your rope at some time or other. Sometimes the smallest incident causes us to spill over, making us believe we can't cope anymore. Whatever the situation, always remember that God—in the words of a small child—will bring the sunshine back tomorrow.

Have I BEEN DOWN LATELY? SOME POSITIVE THOUGHTS THAT BRING THE SUNSHINE BACK ARE . . .

For most men the world is centered in self, which is misery: to have one's world centered in God is peace.

Someone Who Cares

An anxious heart weighs a man down,
but a kind word cheers him up.

PROVERBS 12:25

Who

DO I REALLY
CARE ABOUT?

Maureen wearily rinsed out her coffee cup and stacked it in the nearly full dishwasher. Her life had been difficult for months. As her father's illness rapidly progressed, her sense of security waned, and a fear of losing him filled her heart. After a few weeks in the hospital, her mother was forced to put him in a nursing home. It seemed that Maureen couldn't stop crying. Her heart felt heavier after each visit.

At first, people asked if there was anything they could do to help. Others telephoned and visited her. But after a few weeks, the calls and visits dwindled as her friends got on with their lives. Sometimes it seemed they altogether avoided her. She was overcome with weariness, and joy seemed so remote.

One day before she left for her daily visit to the nursing home, she stopped by the mailbox. Usually most of the mail was for her mother, but this time there was a small "thinking of you" card addressed to her. It was signed, "Someone who cares." A ray of sunshine touched her heart as she read those simple words.

Someone really cares, she thought. She didn't know who it was, but she knew that someone was concerned about the situation that overshadowed her life. As the weeks and months passed, Maureen continued to receive greeting cards from this anonymous person. The signature was always the same. But no one ever confessed to being the sender. Only God knew who uplifted her spirit. And for the sender, that was enough.

Kindness is a language we can all speak.

Grace Tickets

"The one who comes to Me
I will certainly not cast out."
JOHN 6:37 NASB

A Bible teacher once talked about God's "Grace Tickets." She said God makes himself available to us no matter how many times we reach out for an extra Grace Ticket. His grace is available to us in liberal amounts. She even prayed that she would have the wisdom to know when to reach out and take another.

When the alarm goes off at 5:30 A.M., it is all too easy to slip a hand from under the covers and push that snooze button to allow for ten more minutes of sleep. You might repeat the same involuntary movement every ten minutes until 6 A.M., when the clock radio is programmed to come on.

The minute the announcer's voice is heard, you are immediately jolted from bed, realizing you have overslept and must do in twenty minutes what would normally take fifty.

We all need several of God's Grace Tickets for times in our lives when we attempt to put God and His timing on hold. Yet God has made himself available to us every minute of the day. We are privileged to call out to Him no matter how severe or minuscule our situation. His grace is sufficient for each of us—at all times. He never runs out. It is up to us to open our eyes each morning and reach out to the Giver of all Grace Tickets.

Grace comes into the soul as the morning
sun into the world: first a dawning,
then a light; and at last the sun in
his full and excellent brightness.

God
WAS GRACIOUS
TO ME
WHEN HE . . .

Savor the Moment

So teach us to number our days, that we
may apply our hearts unto wisdom.
PSALM 90:12 KJV

Something

IN MY LIFE
ONCE BORING
THAT I NOW
SEE AS
SPECIAL IS . . .

Sixteen-year-old Ann described a lesson she learned after the painful loss of her mother. A few weeks before the prom, her father opened her mother's closet door and lifted out a dress still covered with plastic from the department store.

"This," he said, "is something your mother loved." He discarded the plastic and handed the dress to Ann. It was exquisite silk, handmade and trimmed with a cobweb of lace. The price tag, bearing an astronomical figure, was still attached.

"Your mother bought this the first time we went to New York three years ago. She never wore it but took it out of the closet, looked at it and admired the fabric. She was saving it for a special occasion."

He slammed the closet door shut and turned to Ann. "Don't ever save anything for a special occasion. Every day you're alive is a special occasion."

She carried his words throughout her life. Ann thought about all the things that her mother had done without realizing they were special. The words her father spoke changed her life.

Ann now spends more time with her family and friends. Her family uses the good china and crystal for every special event . . . such as losing a pound, unclogging the sink, or spying the first camellia blossom of the season.

As you watch the breathless beauty of a sunset or the colorful splendor of a rainbow, savor the moment. Cherish the brilliance of the maple leaf nipped by frost and the white clouds floating across the crystal blue sky. Remember that every moment of every day is special.

So here hath been dawning another blue day;
think, wilt thou let it slip useless away?

In the Dark

> Then Jesus spoke to them again, saying,
> "I am the light of the world. He who follows Me
> shall not walk in darkness, but have the light of life."
>
> JOHN 8:12 NKJV

Do you ever go exploring through the woods? Following an unfamiliar path seems like an adventure until it gets dark. While hiking up a mountainous trail, you lose track of time and murky shadows creep in. The sound of twigs and leaves cracking under your shoes grows deafening. Your great adventure now turns frightening. Suddenly, you can't see the path in front of you. If only another person would come along with a lantern and lead you back home.

Today, many people walk in darkness. They are confused about their purpose in life and are searching for answers. They need someone to hold out a light and show them the way.

Psalm 18:28 NKJV says, *For You will light my lamp; the* LORD *my God will enlighten my darkness.*

In the darkness of hopelessness and lack of direction, God promises to bring hope to our situation with His brilliant light of wisdom and understanding. Often that wisdom comes through the words of people we know or strangers we meet. Have you walked down a difficult road? Then share what God taught you in that situation. Lead others out of the darkness into a life filled with meaning and purpose. Share God's light with someone who is searching for the truth.

Share your God-given gifts and let your heart illuminate the lives of others. By helping other people find meaning for their lives, you'll discover God's purpose for your own.

Christ has turned all our sunsets into dawns.

I can

SHARE

WITH . . .

Everyone Counts

These things I command you,
that ye love one another.
JOHN 15:17 KJV

I can SHOW
LOVE AND
APPRECIATION
BY . . .

Faith, like light, should always be simple
and unbending; while love, like warmth,
should beam forth on every side and bend
to every necessity of our brethren.

Daniel had a habit of ignoring others whenever he was particularly busy or interested in something he enjoyed doing. One afternoon his best friend, Derek, complained, "I feel like last weeks' trash sitting on the curb." Daniel told him that he was simply busy and didn't mean to treat him badly, but as he tried to fall asleep that night he thought about what Derek had said. Had he been ignoring him? Was what he was doing more important than his friendship with Derek or others?

He thought about his frantic schedule filled with homework, chores, tennis practice, and time he spent playing video games. He felt exhausted just thinking about it. Brushing off Derek's comment, he dropped into a deep sleep.

Then one day he discovered for himself just how Derek had felt. He dropped by the offices of a well-known organization to get some information for an upcoming school project. He had hoped to meet and talk with some of the volunteers, but to Daniel's surprise everyone was too busy to speak with him. Convinced that he was not welcome, he left in discouragement.

In our busy world, we often ignore one another. Perhaps you feel overextended and over-committed. It's easy to make a habit of ignoring others, including those we love the most. But we can make a difference in the lives of the people around us by taking the time to listen to them—by showing them that they are precious to God . . . and to us.

Jesus Christ said that the greatest commandment of all is to love one another, and that His followers would be known by their love . . . a deep and abiding love. So tomorrow, as you go about your day, take a moment from your busyness. Tell a friend that you think she's special. Offer assistance when you see that a classmate needs help. Not only will you brighten up your friend's day, you'll also speak volumes to a hurting and neglected world.

Coping Skills

> My times are in your hand.
>
> PSALM 31:15 NRSV

How we handle delays tells us a lot about ourselves. How do you handle a traffic jam when you left the house already late for school? What do you do when an outdoor sport is delayed because of bad weather? How do you respond when the register in your checkout lane runs out of tape just as you reach the front of the line? Can you take a deep breath and walk a little slower when someone in front of you is taking their time on the way to class?

Consider how one man handled a delay. Just as the light turned green at the busy intersection, his car stalled in heavy traffic. He tried everything he knew to get the car started again, but all his efforts failed. The chorus of honking behind him put him on edge, which only made matters worse.

Finally, he got out of his car and walked back to the first driver and said, "I'm sorry, but I can't seem to get my car started. If you'll go up there and give it a try, I'll stay here and blow your horn for you."

Things rarely go as smoothly as we would like, and we don't usually schedule ourselves any extra time "just in case" something goes wrong.

The ability to accept disappointments, delays, and setbacks with a pleasant, generous spirit is a gift of graciousness that comes from one who has received grace from others in pressured circumstances. Life is a series of choices, and no matter what situation we are in, we *always* have the freedom to choose how we are going to respond.

Refuse to get out of sorts the next time your schedule gets interrupted or turned upside down. Pray for strength to remain calm, cheerful, relaxed, and refreshed in the midst of the crisis. And always remember: God's plans for you are not thwarted by delays!

What AREAS OF MY LIFE DO I NEED TO BE MORE PATIENT IN?

God engineers our circumstances as he did those of his Son; all we have to do is follow where he places us. The majority of us are busy trying to place ourselves. God alters things while we wait for him.

End-of-School Prayer

In all your ways acknowledge Him.
PROVERBS 3:6 NKJV

A good TIME
FOR ME TO
OFFER A WORD
OF THANKS
WOULD BE . . .

Many people are quick to pray before a meal, before they begin a new project, before they attempt something for the first time, or before embarking on a long journey. They desire to start on the right foot, asking for God's help, protection, creativity, and blessing, but what about prayer at the end of a day of school, a journey, or a task?

Such a prayer is like a second bookend on a shelf of freestanding books—it brackets our work and brings us to full recognition that we have received from the Lord the very things we requested. Rather than a prayer of petition, such a prayer is an expression of praise and thanksgiving.

Simeon had lived his entire life waiting to see the Messiah—a promise the Lord had made to him (Luke 2:26 KJV). Upon seeing the infant Jesus in the temple, Simeon took Him in his arms, blessed God, and said, "Lord, now You are letting Your servant depart in peace, according to Your word; for my eyes have seen Your salvation" (Luke 2:29-30 NKJV). Simeon recognized that God had been faithful to His Word, and his heart was encouraged and filled with joy.

Simeon is a wonderful example of how we can end the events of our lives with prayer. When we reach the end of a day, haggard and weary, we can remember Simeon's prayer, "Lord, let Your servant depart in peace, according to Your Word."

Knowing God was with us today and He will be with us tomorrow, we can move on to the evening hours with freedom and a sense of satisfaction.

Let a man go away or come back: God
never leaves. He is always at hand and
if He cannot get into your life, still He
is never farther away than the door.

Listen for the Music

How shall we sing the Lord's
song in a strange land?
PSALM 137:4 KJV

George Gershwin was talking to a friend on the crowded beach of a resort near New York City when the joyous shrieks of voices pierced their conversation. Clanking tunes ground out from a nearby merry-go-round while barkers and hucksters shouted themselves hoarse. From underground came the deep roar of the subway; beside them crashed the relentless waves of the ocean.

Gershwin listened and then remarked to his friend, "All of this could form such a beautiful pattern of sound. It could turn into a magnificent musical piece expressive of every human activity and feeling with pauses, counterpoints, blends and climaxes of sound that would be beautiful. . . . But it is not that. . . . It is all discordant, terrible and exhausting—as we hear it now. The pattern is always being shattered."

So many confusing sounds and noises, so much unrest, so much rapid change. But somewhere in the midst of it, a pattern could emerge; a meaning could come out of it.

Our job is to hear the music in the noise.

Sometimes, finding the melodic line is a simple matter of listening selectively—mentally tuning out all but one sound for a while. That's what happens when we sit for a few minutes and listen intently to a classmate, parent, teacher, or close friend. Once we listen and truly hear the "tune" they're playing, their unique melody will always be distinct to us, even in the cacophony of busy days.

If we are intentional about what we hear, the conflicting chaos swirling around our own symphony will be weeded out; God's music will be easier to hear.

In the midst of a busy day, it takes effort to hear all the melodies of those around you which make up the symphony of your life. But as each strain becomes distinguishable, a pattern emerges, and you can rejoice in God's unparalleled creativity in His world.

Take time this afternoon to be a creative listener!

I need
TO LISTEN
MORE TO . . .

✠

I have shown you the power of silence,
how thoroughly it heals and how fully
pleasing it is to God. . . . It is by silence that
the saints grew. . . . It was because of
silence that the power of God dwelt in
them; because of silence that the mysteries
of God were known to them.

Heaven's Spot Remover

It is of the Lord's mercies that we are not consumed, because his compassions fail not. They are new every morning: great is thy faithfulness.
LAMENTATIONS 3:22-23 KJV

What

BLEMISHES
IN MY LIFE
DOES GOD'S
REDEEMING
POWER NEED
TO TOUCH?

"Let it snow, let it snow, let it snow." That's the cry of neighborhoods everywhere when winter weather finally arrives.

First, there's catching those early snowflakes on your tongue. After a few more flakes hit the ground, you can start making snowballs and have some terrific battles. Several inches later, it's time to build the snowmen and snow forts. And when the blanket of snow reaches a hefty thickness, the best thing to do is make snow angels.

You may really enjoy snow angels. You find a good patch of untouched snow, stand with your arms stretched out to the side, and fall backwards onto what feels like a cold, wet cloud. Stay on your back for a few moments and stare at the sky. When the cold starts getting to you, flap your arms and legs as if you're doing jumping jacks. Then, carefully get up and look at your handiwork.

Between the snowballs and snowmen, the forts and the angels, it isn't long before every square inch of clean snow has been used up. Patches of dead grass show through where someone dug down deep to roll a snowman's head. The once-pristine landscape is now trampled and rutted.

But something magical happens overnight. While you are sleeping, the snow falls again. You look out your window in the morning to find another clean white blanket covering all of the previous day's blemishes. All that was ugly is once again beautiful.

Don't despair when what began as a beautiful day turns into something ugly. Although your own efforts to "fix it up" or "clean it up" might be futile, it can still be redeemed. The God who turned the humiliation and shame of His Son's death on the Cross into the gift of salvation for all who believe in Him can take the tattered rags of our daily lives and make them like new again—every morning.

✢

If God maintains sun and planets in bright and ordered beauty He can keep us.

Rise and Shine

Take my yoke upon you and learn from me,
for I am gentle and humble in heart,
and you will find rest for your souls.

MATTHEW 11:29

Janie jolted awake at the sound of her alarm clock. This was the third day in a row that she woke up in the middle of the night . . . at least it felt like the middle of the night although it was actually early morning. She was not at all sure why she went through the trouble. It especially seemed vague and worthless the moments before her head settled back down onto the pillow.

"No!" She yelled at herself, waking up again with a start. She promised she would do this and she was going to, even if she went around for the rest of the day with a sleep-deprived, grumpy attitude. Janie stumbled to the bathroom, splashed some water on her face, and carefully traversed the steps. Downstairs, she stuck a mug of hot chocolate into the microwave and sat down at the kitchen table. She had originally started her devotions on the sofa, only to discover they lasted only the five minutes it took for her to fall asleep again. At the kitchen table, she took out her Bible, her notebook, and devotional. Her attitude brightened.

Once she was up, every moment was worth it. Meeting God in the early morning hours didn't make her grumpy as she always anticipated, but instead they revitalized her and brought her peace. The early morning moments gave her a chance to see the sunrise, to watch an occasional bird, to enjoy the silence of a world not yet awake. It took awhile to convince her body of the benefits of such early rising, but soon it became habit. After a while, the only time she experienced grumpiness was when she missed her morning meeting with God.

God's yoke *is* light; He *is* the rest for our souls that we think sleep should bring. Taking the time with our Savior in the early morning hours is better than fine cappuccino, the smell of omelettes and bacon. It is the best part of our day.

What

CHARACTERISTICS ABOUT ME HAVE CHANGED SINCE I BEGAN A DAILY SPECIAL TIME WITH GOD?

God is a tranquil being and abides in a tranquil eternity. So must your spirit become a tranquil and clear pool, wherein the serene light of God can be mirrored.

Do Your Best

And it will come about that whoever calls on the name of the Lord will be delivered.

JOEL 2:32 NASB

What THINGS
IN MY LIFE DO
I FEEL INADE-
QUATE ABOUT?
AM I WILLING
TO ALLOW
GOD TO HELP
ME WITH
THOSE
THINGS?

Do you ever feel inadequate? Unworthy? Most of us do from time to time. And we all know people who we *think* are too successful to have those same feelings.

Martin Luther, the sixteenth-century German preacher and Bible scholar who initiated the Protestant Reformation, sounds like the type of man who would be eminently sure of himself. Any man who would dare to publicly question the theology of his church—in a time when it could have cost him his life—could not be a man who had doubts about himself. Or could he?

In truth, Luther spent his early years obsessed by his presumed unworthiness. He periodically fasted and mistreated his body in an attempt to "earn" God's favor. On a pilgrimage to Rome, he climbed the Steps of Pilate on his knees, kissing each step. He wrote later that in those years he was constantly confessing his sins to God, yet he never felt he had done enough.

One day while reading the book of Romans, Luther realized he could not earn his salvation. The Bible says we *receive* salvation, we do not earn it (Romans 4:13-14). Those verses of Scripture liberated Luther, radically changing his opinion that it was his works that made him worthy of God's grace.

He recognized Jesus Christ had already done all the "earning" necessary for his salvation. He simply needed to receive by faith what Jesus had done—paid the price for his sin on the Cross.

On days when we fall flat on our faces in failure or just feel low, we need to remind ourselves that our mistakes are not the end of the world. Our inadequacy is not our doom. Our salvation doesn't depend on how well we manage to color inside the lines!

Perfection may be our aim, but when we realize we haven't arrived there, we need to relax and turn to the Lord, saying, "Forgive me for what I have done, and for what I have left undone. I trust You to be my Savior, my Deliverer, my Hope, and my Perfection." He is and He always will be!

The farther a man knows himself to be from perfection, the nearer he is to it!

The Trouble With Being Right

> Take heed to yourselves: If thy brother trespass against thee, rebuke him; and if he repent, forgive him.
>
> LUKE 17:3 KJV

Am I QUICK TO POINT OUT OTHERS' MISTAKES? DO I ADMIT MY OWN MISTAKES? HOW CAN I FORGIVE MORE EASILY?

Believe it or not, it's often harder to gracefully receive an apology than it is to issue one. As Christians, we know we are to forgive "seventy times seven" times (Matthew 18:22 KJV), but some of us can sincerely forgive and still project an air of superiority unbecoming to a child of the King.

If you're waiting for someone to realize they owe you an apology, use your break between classes or at lunch to think of a response that reflects genuine forgiveness and allows the transgressor to feel he has retained your respect. Consider this humorous little story:

A passenger on a dining car looked over the luncheon menu. The list included both a chicken salad sandwich and a chicken sandwich. He decided on the chicken salad sandwich, but absentmindedly wrote chicken sandwich on the order slip. When the waiter brought the chicken sandwich, the customer angrily protested.

Most waiters would have immediately picked up the order slip and shown the customer the mistake was his. This waiter didn't. Instead, expressing regret at the error, he picked up the chicken sandwich, returned to the kitchen, and a moment later placed a chicken salad sandwich in front of the customer.

While eating his sandwich, the customer picked up the order slip and saw that the mistake was his. When it came time to pay the check, the man apologized to the waiter and offered to pay for both sandwiches. The waiter's response was, "No, sir. That's perfectly all right. I'm just happy you've forgiven me for being right."

By taking the blame initially and allowing the passenger to discover his own mistake, the waiter accomplished several things: he allowed the passenger to retain his dignity, reminded him to be more cautious before blaming others, and created a better atmosphere for everyone in the dining car. Next time someone blames you for their mistake, don't get defensive, but find a creative way to make things right.

Forgiveness is a funny thing—it warms the heart and cools the sting.

A Gift of Love

Give, and it will be given to you. A good measure, pressed down, shaken together and running over, will be poured into your lap.

LUKE 6:38

Who DO I KNOW THAT NEEDS ENCOURAGE-MENT OR A FRIEND? SOMEONE AT SCHOOL, CHURCH, OR IN MY NEIGH-BORHOOD? I COULD SHOW THEM KIND-NESS BY . . .

✠

He who bestows his goods upon the poor shall have as much again, and ten times more.

Kids made fun of "old woman Smith."

"Everyone knows she's crazy!" they said.

"She's NOT crazy," Tessie defended repeatedly. "Maybe she doesn't have any family. Maybe she's just lonely."

"But she claims people try to steal her money."

"She's poor like us. Just look at her run-down house and the filth in her yard."

"And she's grumpier than my bulldog!"

But Tessie ignored their taunts and adopted Mrs. Smith as her own special project. All through the year, she picked up trash and pulled her neighbor's weeds. In spring she planted flowers in her yard. She visited the old woman several days a week.

Never once did Mrs. Smith say "thank you." And no one else seemed to care. There was only one time that Tessie noticed a stranger, a middle-aged man, at the widow's house.

On Christmas Eve, Tessie took Mrs. Smith a basket of fruit and a special handmade gift. When no one answered the door, Tessie cautiously peered in, calling out her name softly.

Mrs. Smith lay on the living room couch. She apparently had died in her sleep. In her lap was a small, unwrapped Christmas present.

Tessie, her mom, and one man attended the woman's funeral—the same man Tessie had seen at Mrs. Smith's house a few weeks earlier.

The man handed Tessie the box she had seen in the old woman's lap. "I'm Mrs. Smith's lawyer," he said.

Tessie opened up the box, and inside was a cashier's check to her for $100,000, along with a note: "For college education first. Then spend wisely—as you wish."

Henry Wadsworth Longfellow said, "Give what you have. To someone it may be better than you dare to think." Giving out of love may not make us wealthy, but the return investment will be more than we give away—always.

Light-Bearers

> "Let your light so shine before men,
> that they may see your good works
> and glorify your Father in heaven."
>
> MATTHEW 5:16 NKJV

Jenny grasped the hand of her big sister, Kate, as they followed a group of tourists through the great cathedral. As the guide explained the various parts of the structure—the altar, the choir, the screen, and the nave—the little girl's attention was intently focused on a stained glass window.

For a long time Jenny silently pondered the window. Looking up at the various figures, her face was bathed in a rainbow of color as the afternoon sun poured into the transept of the huge cathedral.

As the group was about to move on, she gathered enough courage to ask the tour conductor a question. "Who are those people in that pretty window?"

"Those are the saints," the guide replied.

That night, as Jenny prepared for bed, she told her sister proudly: "Kate, I know who the saints are."

"And just who are the saints?" Kate asked, amused.

Without a moment's hesitation Jenny replied: "They are the people who let the light shine through!"

As you look back over your day, have you allowed God's light to shine through? As Christians we are called to share the light of Jesus in a world of darkness. Like rays of light that break through gloom and darkness, we can bring hope and encouragement.

Remember, the light of your life gives those around you a glimpse of Jesus, the Source of eternal and constant light. As you let your light shine, it will grow brighter!

HOW CAN I BE
"LIGHT" IN
SOMEONE'S
LIFE TODAY?

Should first my lamp spread
light and purest rays bestow;
The oil must then from you,
my dearest Jesus, flow.

Angels in Disguise

Man looketh on the outward appearance, but the LORD looketh on the heart.

I SAMUEL 16.7 KJV

HOW DO I NEED TO CHANGE MY ATTITUDE IN ORDER TO SEE PEOPLE AS GOD SEES THEM?

Stacie and her mom, Karyn, decided to travel across America one summer to see the sights they'd read about for years. Traveling alone in a truck, with their camper in tow, they launched out on the journey. One afternoon in California's rush-hour traffic, the water pump on the truck blew, but no one seemed interested in helping.

Leaning against the trailer, mother and daughter finally prayed, "Please, God, send us an angel—preferably one with mechanical experience." Within four minutes, a huge Harley roared up, ridden by an enormous man sporting long hair, a beard, and tattooed arms. He jumped off and went to work on the truck.

They were too dumbfounded to talk—especially when they read the paralyzing words on the back of his leather jacket: "Hell's Angels—California." As he finished the task, they finally got up the courage to say thanks and carry on a brief conversation.

Noticing their surprise, the biker looked them straight in the eyes and said, "Don't judge a book by its cover. You may not know who you're talking to." With that he smiled, closed the hood of the truck, and straddled his Harley. With a wave, he was gone as fast as he had appeared.[2]

God has a way of opening our eyes, expanding our perspective, and showing us His greatest treasures—people—if we will look beyond our prejudices and preconceived notions. Allow Him to show you a few of His treasures today!

Do not judge men by mere appearances;
for the light laughter that bubbles on the lip
often mantles over the depths of sadness,
and the serious look may be the sober veil
that covers a divine peace and joy.

Talent Scout

Stir up the gift of God which is in you.

2 TIMOTHY 1:6 NKJV

When you hear the word *talent*, you probably think of great musicians, actors, and artists. But this perspective of talent can make you feel *untalented* if you aren't gifted in any of these areas. Talents come in as many shapes and sizes as people do, and God has given each of us one or more.

Compassion is one of the not-so-obvious talents. Do you feel kindness toward someone in a troubling situation? Then you have been given a talent! Use that feeling to offer a smile, a positive word, or write a note of encouragement to someone in need. Do you like to bring joy to people who may otherwise feel forgotten or left out? Then you are gifted! Don't bury that talent—use it to brighten another person's day.

Perhaps you have the gift of seeing something good in every individual. That is a gift everyone needs to cultivate. Affirm the good in someone, and then spread the "good news" about them. It usually takes someone else to point out the best in people. You may see a talent in a person that he or she doesn't even know about.

Whatever gift you have, use it in the name of Jesus and for the glory of God. As you exercise your gift, you'll see it "grow" the same way a muscle grows when it's exerted on a regular basis.

Now think again. What talents do you have?

God does not require that each individual shall have capacity for everything.

How CAN I BETTER USE MY TALENTS TO SERVE GOD AND OTHERS?

Hope in Hard Times

Be strong and take heart,
all you who hope in the Lord.
PSALM 31:24

When MY COURAGE IS TESTED, WHERE DO I LOOK FOR SUPPORT?

In *The Diary of a Young Girl*, Anne Frank wrote, "I simply can't build up my hopes on a foundation consisting of confusion, misery, and death."[3] She understood that hope originates somewhere beyond our immediate circumstances. In fact, hope—real hope—often stands alone in the darkness.

How was this young girl capable of courage and faith far beyond her years? She refused to allow the devastation of her times to shape her view of life. In her words, "It's really a wonder that I haven't dropped all my ideals. . . . Yet I keep them. I hear the ever-approaching thunder. I can feel the sufferings of millions and yet, if I look up into the heavens, I think that it will all come right."

We can't know what horrors Anne Frank and her family suffered during the Holocaust, but we do know that only her father emerged alive. Yet her words live on. Decades later, several generations have read and been touched by the diary of a young girl facing one of the darkest periods in world history—a girl who chose hope in the midst of hopelessness.

Life sometimes includes hardship. When tests come, we have the same choice Anne Frank had: hold on to our ideals or drop them. When life's circumstances sound like "approaching thunder," remember the simple truth in the life of a young Jewish girl. A foundation made of the right ingredients makes for an overcoming life. Holding tightly to one's ideals no matter the circumstance is a hallmark of character.

Hope not only bears up the mind under
sufferings but makes her rejoice in them.

The Master Teacher

The son said unto him, Father, I . . . am
no more worthy to be called thy son.

LUKE 15:21 KJV

A poignant scene from the British movie *Educating Rita* demonstrates just how difficult it is to accept the possibility of a new life. As Rita stands on the sidewalk, peering into the window of a beautiful home, she sees nicely dressed people chatting with one another. In her hand she clutches her own invitation to the party, but her "different-ness" keeps her standing on the outside, looking in.

Her professor, impressed with her academic abilities, had invited her to attend the party so she could meet others at the university. But Rita came from a lower-middle class family, and no one in her family had attended a university before her. She struggles with feelings of inadequacy and wonders how she will fit in.

With a sadness of the soul, she turns and slowly walks away. Still clutched between her fingers is the unused invitation. However, thanks to a persistent mentor who sees more in her than she sees in herself, she eventually accepts the invitation to join a new world. By the movie's end, this once modest woman excels as a scholar.

The invitation to become a follower of Christ is very real—and it is extended to each one of us. Once we accept His invitation, we are encouraged through the Scriptures and other believers to excel—to run the race of faith with all our might. The greatest joy, though, is in knowing that our Master Teacher always sees much more in us than we see in ourselves.

Have I PLACED LIMITS ON WHAT GOD CAN DO THROUGH ME?

God does not ask about our ability, but our
availability. God wants us to be victors, not
victims; to grow, not grovel; to soar, not sink;
to overcome, not be overwhelmed.

A Divine Compass

The mind of man plans his way,
but the LORD directs his steps.
PROVERBS 16:9 NASB

In WHAT AREA
DO I NEED
DIRECTION
FROM GOD
TODAY?

The birthday party was going well, and Katrina was glad all her friends could be there to celebrate with her. After all the presents were torn open, everyone jumped in the pool for a game of water basketball. Wanting to make a grand entrance, Katrina ran along the wet pavement, expecting to make a graceful dive into the pool. Instead, she slipped and landed in the water in a belly-flop, her knee scraping the side of the pool on the way in. She came up sputtering; everyone shrieked with laughter.

It was funny but (she had to admit) also very embarrassing. If only she'd followed the pool rules and walked instead of run, she could have saved herself some humiliation and a skinned knee.

God has promised to direct our steps if we will allow Him to do so. Sometimes we face not only embarrassment but heartbreak and even danger when we go our own way. The plan for our lives was laid before the beginning of time. Each morning we can go to the Lord and have a fresh look at the direction He would have us go that day.

Are you faced with a major decision? Do you need direction and guidance? Throughout Scripture there are promises that God will show us the right path. We do not have to stumble or grope around blindfolded. Our Heavenly Father is eager to give us wisdom. All we need to do is ask, and He will direct every step we take.

I would rather walk with God in
the dark than go alone in the light.

Living Water

My soul thirsts for God, for the living God.

PSALM 42:2 NASB

The need for a refreshing drink when we first wake in the morning is often so strong we find ourselves anticipating the taste before we ever get a glass in our hands. At that moment, nothing else will satisfy like ice-cold water.

Another thirst needs to be quenched when we first wake up: a thirst we often ignore until it is so great that everything else in our lives—our relationships, our growth as Christians, our joy and peace—begins to wither.

A source of Living Water is available to us any time of the day or night. It never runs out, it never gets contaminated, it never freezes over, and it is always as refreshing as that first sip we took when we said yes to God. It is up to us to drink deeply by reading the Word of God, taking time to talk to Him alone, and allowing His Spirit to live through us.

Hudson Taylor, a nineteenth-century missionary to China, said, "There is a living God; He has spoken in the Bible and He means what He says and He will do all that He has promised." He has promised to quench our thirst in such a way that we will never be thirsty again!

Are you anticipating a drink from God's cup of Living Water in the morning? God gives you permission to start sipping right now!

Every character has an inward spring:
let Christ be that spring. Every action
has a keynote: let Christ be that note
to which your whole life is attuned.

How WILL A QUIET MOMENT WITH GOD AFFECT THE REST OF MY DAY?

A Work of Art

We are His workmanship, created in Christ Jesus for good works, which God prepared beforehand that we should walk in them.

EPHESIANS 2:10 NKJV

What

SPIRITUAL AND PERSONAL GOALS WOULD I LIKE TO ACHIEVE IN THE NEXT YEAR?

Many centuries ago, a young Greek artist named Timanthes studied under a respected tutor. After several years of effort, Timanthes painted an exquisite work of art. Unfortunately, he was so taken with his painting that he spent days gazing at it.

One morning, he arrived to find his work blotted out with paint. His teacher admitted to destroying the painting, saying, "I did it for your own good. That painting was retarding your progress. Start again and see if you can do better." Timanthes took his teacher's advice and produced Sacrifice of Iphigenia, now regarded as one of the finest paintings of antiquity.[4]

Timanthes' teacher knew what many great artists know—we should never consider ourselves truly finished with our work.

When the legendary cellist Pablo Casals turned ninety-five, a reporter asked, "Mr. Casals, you are ninety-five and the greatest cellist who ever lived. Why do you still practice six hours a day?" Casals answered, "Because I think I'm making progress."

Maya Angelou applies that same logic to daily life. In her book, *Wouldn't Take Nothin' for My Journey Now,* she writes: "Many things continue to amaze me, even well into the sixth decade of my life. I'm startled or taken aback when people walk up to me and tell me they are Christians. My first response is the question 'Already?' It seems to me a lifelong endeavor to try to live the life of a Christian."

It's exciting to be a work in progress. With God's help, our possibilities are limitless!

What God does, He does well.

Faith in Action

> What is faith? It is the confident assurance that something we want is going to happen. It is the certainty that what we hope for is waiting for us, even though we cannot see it up ahead.
>
> HEBREWS 11:1 TLB

In *You Can't Afford the Luxury of a Negative Thought,* John Roger and Peter McWilliams offer a new description of faith. They use the word "faithing" to describe their proactive approach to confidence in life's outcomes.

In their thinking, faithing works in the present, acknowledging that there is a purpose to everything and life is unfolding exactly as it should. Faithing means actively trusting that God can handle our troubles and needs better than we can. All we must do is let them go, so that He can do His work. Consider the words of this poem:

The Two Boxes

I have in my hands two boxes
Which God gave me to hold.

He said, "Put all your sorrows in the black,
And all your joys in the gold."

I heeded His words, and in the two boxes
Both my joys and sorrows I store,
But though the gold became heavier each day
The black was as light as before.

With curiosity, I opened the black.
I wanted to find out why
And I saw, in the base of the box, a hole
Which my sorrows had fallen out by.

I showed the hole to God, and mused aloud,
"I wonder where all my sorrows could be."
He smiled a gentle smile at me.
"My child, they're all here, with Me."

I asked, "God, why give me the boxes,
Why the gold, and the black with the hole?"
"My child, the gold is to count your blessings,
the black is for you to let go."[5]

Can a faith that does nothing be called sincere?

In WHAT AREA OF MY LIFE DO I NEED TO PRACTICE "FAITHING"?

A Two-Way Street

A man who has friends must himself be friendly, but there is a friend who sticks closer than a brother.

PROVERBS 18:24 NKJV

Good

FRIENDS ARE GIFTS FROM GOD. IS THERE SOMEONE I NEED TO CALL TODAY?

The late Leonard Bernstein—conductor, composer, teacher, and advocate—may well be the most important figure in American music of the twentieth century. With his personality and passion for music, he inspired generations of new musicians and taught that music should be an integral part of everyone's life.

As a public figure, Bernstein was charming and persuasive. While his career progressed, he was constantly sought after for performances, lectures, and other appearances. But it's said that in his later years his friendships eroded. Eventually he had few close friends. After his death, a longtime acquaintance said of him, "You wanted to be his friend, but so many other people sought his attention that, eventually, the friendliest thing you could do was leave him alone."

Scientific evidence now shows us how important friendships are, not only to our emotional health, but to our physical and mental health as well. Relationships are a two-way street, however. As Ralph Waldo Emerson once said, "The only way to have a friend is to be one."

Being a good friend is more than loaning a favorite CD or talking on the phone when you don't feel like it. It involves practical as well as thoughtful gestures. For starters, be aware of your friends' likes and dislikes. Remember their birthdays. Take an interest in their hobbies. Express what you admire about each one. Serve your friends in thoughtful, unexpected ways. Most of all, talk to your friends about God. Ultimately, that is the kindest thing you can do for anyone.

The only way to have a friend is to be one.

Original Beauty

If we confess our sins, He is faithful
and just to forgive us our sins and to
cleanse us from all unrighteousness.

1 JOHN 1:9 NKJV

Famed photographer and conservationist Ansel Adams was known for his visionary photos of Western landscapes, inspired by a boyhood trip to Yosemite National Park. His love of nature's raw perfection was apparent in his stark, mysterious black-and-white wilderness photos.

In 1944, he shot a beautiful scene, later titled "Winter Sunrise: The Sierra Nevada, from Lone Pine, California." It portrayed the craggy Sierra Mountains in the bright morning sunlight, a small dark horse appearing in the foothills. The story is told that as Adams developed the negative, he noticed "LP" carved in the hillside. Apparently, some local high school teenagers had etched their initials on the mountain.

Intent on recapturing nature's original, he took a brush and ink and carefully removed the initials from his negative. The man who gave the Sierra Club its look believed in preserving, even perfecting, nature in life as well as in photography.[6]

Ansel Adams probably never gave a second thought to the unsightly scar on the mountain in his photo creation. In his mind's eye, he saw the beauty of the original and took steps to bring that beauty back into focus.

Someone once observed that "the purpose of the Cross is to repair the irreparable." Through the blood of Christ, we know that our sins have been forgiven—our scars erased—and that once removed, our sins are forgotten. The Lord remembers them no more. When we are willing to confess our sins, He takes joy in restoring us to our original beauty.

Forgiveness is the fragrance that the flower
leaves on the heel of the one who crushed it.

How DOES BEING A CHRISTIAN MAKE ME A BETTER PERSON?

Serendipity Moments

We are his workmanship, created
in Christ Jesus unto good works.
EPHESIANS 2:10 KJV

I will ASK
GOD TO
INSPIRE ME
CREATIVELY IN
THE FOLLOW-
ING AREAS . . .

Serendipity, according to Merriam-Webster's Collegiate Dictionary, is "the faculty or phenomenon of finding valuable or agreeable things not sought for." We sometimes call it an "accident, dumb luck, or fate," but serendipity has given us new products and better ways of doing things. Consider this example . . . .

While George Ballas was driving his car through a car wash, he had a moment of serendipity that made him a millionaire. As he watched the strings of the brushes cleaning his car, he turned his mind to his list of things to do, among them edging his lawn.

Suddenly an idea "popped" into his head. He took another long look at the strings on the rotating brush. The strings straightened out when turning at high speed but were still flexible enough to reach into every nook and cranny of his car to get it clean. He asked himself, *Why not use a nylon cord, whirling at high speed, to trim the grass and weeds around the trees and the house?* His idea—his serendipity—led to the invention of the Weedeater.

Where do we get new ideas? God is the Master behind serendipity! He may not always give you a million-dollar idea, but He will make you more creative. One expert gives this advice: Capture the ideas, jot them down quickly before they are gone, and evaluate them later. Take time to daydream with the Lord. Seek new challenges. Expand your perspective. Learn and do new things.[7]

**Whatever is worth doing at
all is worth doing well.**

Comfort Zone

I am with you and will watch
over you wherever you go.
GENESIS 28:15

Zach was having the time of his life on the hiking trip with his father and his two best friends. They had decided to hike to Blue Lake, four miles high into a wilderness area. The trail, as most mountain trails do, led upward by winding around tall pine trees. Occasionally, the trail broke out into small clearings and crossed crystal-clear streams.

He was determined to be the first person to the lake. The path was plainly marked and easy to follow, so he pushed ahead of the small group. The sounds of the group's chatter soon faded, and suddenly Zach found himself surrounded by stillness. He was alone. He was so far ahead of the group that he was out of sight and hearing distance.

The beautiful morning began to take on an ominous air. What if a bear crept out of the woods? What if a mountain lion decided it wanted a meal? What if . . .

Figuring he was safer with the group, Zach turned and headed back down the path to meet them. In just a couple of minutes, he was with them again. Safe!

Sometimes we get so anxious to be first that we run off ahead of everyone important to us. We can even get too far from God by relying on our own knowledge or skill and place ourselves in dangerous circumstances. At that moment we can always return to the safety of being with the Father.

God shall be my hope, my stay,
my guide, and lantern to my feet.

Have I RUN AHEAD OF GOD IN CERTAIN AREAS OF MY LIFE? HOW CAN I GET BACK ON TRACK?

Thorn in the Flesh?

There was given to me a thorn in the flesh.

2 CORINTHIANS 12:7 KJV

How WILL
I RESPOND
THE NEXT
TIME I'M DIS-
APPOINTED?

Phillip hobbled across the schoolyard, the jeers of the other boys loud in his ears. Born with what used to be called a "clubfoot," he felt like an outcast. Because of his deformity, his classmates often excluded him from their games.

The main character, Phillip, in the novel *Of Human Bondage*, is convinced that if he prays hard enough, God will heal his foot.[8] He daydreams about his classmates' reaction when he returns to school with a new foot; he sees himself outrunning the swiftest boy in his class. At last he goes to sleep knowing that when he awakens in the morning, his foot will be whole.

But the next day brings no change. He still has a clubfoot.

Although just one of many disappointments, this proves to be a pivotal point in Phillip's life. Drawing upon an inner strength he did not know he had, he discovers that his clubfoot does not determine his destiny. How he responds to it will make all the difference, however. If he views it as a crippling deformity, he will live a limited life. Instead, he begins to see his handicap as nothing more than an obstacle to overcome, and it no longer holds him back.

Life is filled with opportunities camouflaged as disappointments. For Phillip Carey, it was a clubfoot. For the apostle Paul, it was a thorn in the flesh. Whatever it is in your life, don't despair. With God's help, you too can turn your scars into stars, your handicaps into strengths.

Obstacles in the pathway of the weak become
stepping-stones in the pathway of the strong.

Clinging Vines

"I am the vine, you are the branches; he who abides in Me, and I in him, he bears much fruit, for apart from Me you can do nothing."

JOHN 15:5 NASB

Scuppernong vines are parasites that grow up and cling to the trunks of healthy, firmly rooted trees in the southern United States. This walnut-sized, dark-skinned wild grape is used to make jams and jellies, and some Southerners use the hulls to make cobbler pies. The fruit produced by these vines has served as an inexpensive treat to poor families in the South for many years. In recent years scuppernongs have become more popular and can be purchased at stores all over the South.

As beautiful, diverse, and tasty as the scuppernong is, it cannot survive on its own. It needs the life support of well-established trees to cling to and draw its nourishment from. Should the scuppernong vine be pulled away from its host tree, it will dry up and stop producing fruit.

Like the scuppernong, we cannot survive without total dependency on God. Without Him, we have no true life source, no lifeline, no nourishment, and we cannot produce good fruit.

We can, however, learn to cling to the Lord by surrendering ourselves to Him. We can draw nourishment through Bible study, prayer, worship, service, and heartfelt obedience. Like the scuppernong, clinging to our Source will help us grow healthy and produce much good fruit.

All we want in Christ, we shall find in Christ.
If we want little, we shall find little. If we want much, we shall find much; but if, in utter helplessness, we cast our all on Christ, He will be to us the whole treasury of God.

Have I
BECOME TOO
INDEPENDENT
FROM GOD?
HOW CAN I
DPEND ON
HIM MORE?

Growing Pains

Now he who plants and he who waters are one; but each will receive his own reward according to his own labor.

1 CORINTHIANS 3:8 NASB

What CAN I DO TO PROMOTE HEALTHY GROWTH IN MY RELATIONSHIPS?

One evening, several guys at a youth retreat spread Limburger cheese on the upper lip of a sleeping friend. Upon awakening, the young man sniffed, looked around, and said, "This room stinks!" His friends tried to muffle their laughter, wanting to prolong the joke.

He then walked into the hall and said, "This hall stinks!"

Stepping outside for some fresh air, he exclaimed, "The whole world stinks!"

How long do you think it took for that sleepy student to discover the problem was right under his own nose?

It is easy to find fault with others while remaining blind to the ways we contribute to the problem. Are there times when we're the problem?

When a gardener plants a tree, if it does not grow well he doesn't blame the tree. He looks for reasons why it is not doing well. The tree may need fertilizer, more water, or less sun. Yet if we have problems with our friends or family, we are so quick to blame the other person. How much better it would be if we nurtured those relationships as the gardener does the growing tree.

If you want to see your relationships "grow," avoid negative attitudes and self-righteous behavior. Protect those relationships from jealousy and anger. Pour on love and kindness, and watch what begins to happen. When we apply God's love and care to our dealings with the important people in our lives, our relationships will send down deep roots like the tree—and flourish.

Sow a thought and you reap an act;
Sow an act and you reap a habit;
Sow a habit and you reap a character;
Sow a character and you reap a destiny.

Deeply Rooted

He will be like a tree firmly planted by streams
of water, which yields its fruit in its season.

PSALM 1:3 NASB

"Grow up!" is a taunt often used by teenagers to their peers who aren't acting as mature as they should at the moment. But commanding a friend to grow up is like telling a tree to grow up. For growth to occur, a process must take place, and that process takes time. Every living thing requires certain elements in order to grow—good soil, the appropriate amounts of sunshine and water, and plenty of time.

People, like trees, need a good start in order to be rooted securely. Young saplings can't mature into tall shade trees without the right mixture of sun, water, soil, and space. As long as a tree is living, it never stops growing and never outgrows its need for nourishment. Some of your friends may not have received the same "nutrients" you have. You can look for clues in their home life, their sense of self, and their relationship with God. Conversely, others appear stunted from the start, yet reach far beyond everyone's expectations.

In God's perfect timing, we will indeed "grow up." Like a baby taking its first steps, we must be willing to let nature take its course. The growth process is a long one, and it is never really complete. Flourishing trees don't strain to grow. They merely follow the natural process God planted in them. And healthy trees don't decide to ignore the nourishment of sun, rain, and soil. Instead, they continually draw life from these things.

No matter what our "season" of life, growing up is a continuous process—and it all happens in God's time.

Am I TRYING
TO RUSH
GOD'S PLANS
AND FORCE
HIS HAND
IN MY LIFE?

Be not afraid of growing slowly;
be afraid of standing still.

Rise to the Challenge

Until we all reach unity in the faith and in the knowledge
of the Son of God and become mature, attaining
to the whole measure of the fullness of Christ.

EPHESIANS 4:13

What IS MY
KNEE-JERK
RESPONSE
WHEN FACED
WITH A
CHALLENGE?
HOW CAN I
CHANGE IT?

Professional golfer Tiger Woods is considered the top player in the world, with the potential to rank among the greatest of all time. Watching him line up a forty-foot downhill putt today paints a stark contrast to the little boy who appeared on the *Tonight Show* years ago.

At age three, Tiger was already showing a talent for the game, so a small putting surface was set up for him. A ball was placed in front of Tiger, about eight feet from the cup. He lined up the shot, putted, and missed.

Another ball was placed in the same position. He again prepared to putt—then picked up the ball, placed it six inches from the cup, and promptly sank the shot. Johnny Carson and the audience laughed and cheered to see a small child do what many golfers would like to do. Of course, if he did that today, he would be ejected from the tournament.

A resident of a small town was once asked by a tourist: "Have any famous people been born here?"

He replied, "No, only babies."

We all start out as "only babies," but our Creator has placed within us the greatest power in the universe: the ability to grow, day by day, as we respond to increasing challenges.

How will you meet your challenges today? You could grow to be more selfish, more materialistic, or more filled with hate. Or, with the help of God, you can grow to be more understanding, more giving, and more loving. What will you choose?

All growth that is not toward God
is growing to decay.

Memorial Garden

Grow in the grace and knowledge
of our Lord and Savior Jesus Christ.

2 PETER 3:18

The senior class project at Coleridge High was to plant a memorial garden for a classmate who had died that year. Together the students tilled the soil, preparing it for the bright vegetation that would grow there.

None of the flowers at the local nursery caught the students' eyes, so they begged their sponsor to let them order some unique varieties from a mail order catalog. Carefully, they selected each one, often choosing the most expensive plants. They were confident theirs would be the best garden ever.

The tender plants arrived in the mail, and the students began working immediately. They planted and watered, fertilized, watched, and waited. But nothing happened. One by one, the leaves turned yellow and wilted. By the end of spring, not one plant remained. They had all shriveled and died.

The students wrote a scathing letter to the mail order nursery demanding their money back. Two weeks later, they received a reply. "Your letter indicated you planted your flowers in a beautiful shady area and fed them the best nutrients possible. Your flowers failed to grow because you planted them in the wrong place. You ordered flowers that must face the sun. Although you took great care to prepare the soil, these particular plants will die without sunlight."

Our lives are like that. We may expend great care and money to make ourselves beautiful. But if we are not facing the Son, we will wilt and eventually die. No amount of expensive "additives" will take the place of adequate Sonlight in our souls.

From morning to night keep Jesus
in your heart, long for nothing, desire
nothing, hope for nothing, but to have
all that is within you changed into the
spirit and temper of the Holy Jesus.

Have I SPENT
TIME WITH
JESUS TODAY?

Battling Giants

In all these things we overwhelmingly conquer through Him who loved us.

ROMANS 8:37 NASB

HOW IS GOD "STRONG" IN MY WEAKNESS? DOES HIS STRENGTH REQUIRE SOMETHING OF ME?

David, a mere sheepherder, faced the biggest battle of his life when he stepped up to face the Philistine giant Goliath. Standing about nine feet tall, Goliath was well prepared to meet his enemy in battle—and he had fought many battles before. He relied solely on his size and ferocity to win the battle before weapons were even drawn. He was the Philistine army's icon of strength.

Mocking laughter could be heard all over the countryside when this powerful warrior stood there facing a boy. How could this be? Surely Goliath had the upper hand. He was the strongest and the best the Philistines had.

What did David bring to this battle? He was a boy, untrained in the weapons of warfare. He did not stand a chance. He was too young. For David's people, this seemed to be yet another disaster waiting to happen.

While Goliath mocked God, David worshipped the Lord. Goliath was smug in his sure victory; David asked God for a miracle. Goliath trusted his size and strength to save him; David relied on Someone far bigger and stronger. Though small, David trusted in a mighty God, and one tiny stone defeated the giant.

The poet Ralph Waldo Emerson once said, "Our strength grows out of our weakness." What weaknesses do you face today? God promises to be strong in our weakness, proving that He—not we—has the upper hand when all around us seems to spell defeat.

Our strength grows out of our weakness.

Fit for a King

No one has ever seen God; but if we love one another, God lives in us and his love is made complete in us.
1 JOHN 4:12

In Henry Van Dyke's classic, *The Other Wise Man*, Artaban plans to join his three friends as they follow the star in search of the newborn King. He has three jewels to offer as gifts to the Christ Child.

Before he arrives, Artaban finds a feverish Hebrew exile in the road. Torn between duty and desire, he ultimately stays and helps the dying man. By the time Artaban arrives at the Bethlehem stable, the other magi have left. A note encourages him to follow them through the desert. He returns to the city, sells one of his three jewels, and buys camels and food. In Bethlehem, a woman tells Artaban that Joseph, Mary, and the baby fled to Egypt to escape Herod's soldiers.

Artaban wanders for years seeking to worship the new King. He discovers no baby king but finds many poor, sick, and hungry to feed, clothe, and comfort. Many years later in Jerusalem, he hears about a king facing execution. He rushes toward Calvary to ransom the King with his last jewel. But instead he rescues a young woman from slavery.

He mourns because he wanted to take gifts to the King, yet he spent his fortune helping people in need. The Lord comforts him with these words: "Verily I say unto you, inasmuch as ye have done it unto one of the least of these my brethren, ye have done it unto me" (Matthew 25:40 KJV).

Worship is more than mere words or gifts; real worship is a way of life.

This is adoration: not a difficult religious exercise, but an attitude of the soul.

HOW CAN I WORSHIP GOD THROUGH MY ACTIONS TODAY?

Cheat Sheet

[Speak] the truth in love.
EPHESIANS 4:15 KJV

Have I BEEN
HONEST WITH
OTHERS—AND
GOD—TODAY?

"You know that what you did was wrong, don't you?"

The words echoed in Sandra's mind as she went home from school that evening. She was a good student who had never cheated in her life. Yet this last assignment had been more than she could do. In a moment of desperation, she copied the work of another student.

Her teacher, Mrs. Brook, had asked her to wait after class, and Sandra knew what was coming. Still, it was a shock when Mrs. Brook asked her if it was really her work.

"Yes," she said, then wondered why she had lied.

Looking her straight in the eye, Mrs. Brook said, "You know that what you did was wrong, don't you? Take tonight to think about your answer, and I will ask you again in the morning if this is your work."

It was a long night for Sandra. She was a junior in high school with a well-deserved reputation for honesty and kindness. She had never cheated before, and now she had compounded her mistake by deliberately lying—to someone she admired and loved. The next morning she went to Mrs. Brook's classroom and quietly confessed her misdeed. She received the appropriate consequences: a zero on the assignment and detention.

Oddly enough, Sandra often thinks about that experience and feels gratitude for Mrs. Brook's loving correction. She was willing to help Sandra make honest choices—even on the heels of making a dishonest one.

**Power can do by gentleness what
violence fails to accomplish.**

The Shape of Beauty

Blessed is the man you discipline, O Lord;
the man you teach from your law.

PSALM 94:12

In the ancient Chinese art of bonsai, shape, harmony, proportion, and scale are all carefully balanced, and the human hand works in tandem with nature. A tree planted in a pot is not a bonsai until it has been pruned, shaped, and trained into the desired shape. Bonsai are kept small by careful control of the plant's growing conditions. Only branches that are important to the bonsai's overall design are allowed to remain, while unwanted growth is pruned away. The bonsai roots are confined to a pot and periodically clipped.

Some bonsai have been known to live for hundreds of years, and the appearance of old age is much prized. The living bonsai will change through seasons and years, requiring regular pruning and training throughout its lifetime. And as time goes on, it will become more and more beautiful.

In truth, the bonsai would be nothing more than your average tree but for the discipline of the artist. The artist gives constant attention to the direction of growth, trims away what is ugly or unnecessary, and strengthens the most vital branches over time. The result is a work of art that brings beauty to its surroundings for many years.

In our own lives, that same discipline makes the difference between an average life and one that brings joy and beauty to its surroundings. With God's Word as our discipline, we too can become works of art. Allow Him to prune, shape, and strengthen you every day of your life.

What PART
DO I PLAY IN
GOD'S
PRUNING
PROCESS?

Faith and obedience are bound up in the
same bundle. He that obeys God, trusts God;
and he that trusts God, obeys God.

Trademark

Every tree is known by his own fruit.
For of thorns men do not gather figs,
nor of a bramble bush gather they grapes.
LUKE 6:44 KJV

Have I KEPT
MY PROMISES
TO OTHERS? IF
NOT, WHAT
CAN I DO TO
MAKE THINGS
RIGHT?

"What does it matter what other people think of me? I don't care about them anyway!" Rebecca blurted out to her mom. "Why are you so concerned that I finish the service project in Girl Scouts? I'm gonna quit Scouts next year anyway, and I already have plenty of badges."

"Scouting and badges are not the issue," her mother replied. "I'm concerned about you and what you are known for. You are very caring, compassionate, and trustworthy. You care deeply for the welfare of others. You made a commitment to the people at the assisted living facility, and many of them look forward to your visiting them. It's just hard for me to see you not keeping a promise."

"But I'm tired of going up there every Saturday," Rebecca whined.

Her mother suggested they try to find a way to reduce some of her time commitment without abandoning the promise. Before long, Rebecca felt hopeful again that she could complete the commitment without giving up all of her free time.

And her mother's words stuck. Later she commented to a friend that she hoped she would always live up to her mom's belief in her to be caring, compassionate, and trustworthy.

We are known more by what we do than by what we say. Sometimes commitments are overwhelming, particularly during the holidays or when pressures at school, home, church, or community seem to stretch us to the limit. Setting priorities and living by them—and most importantly, asking God for wisdom—will help us keep our promises without losing our hearts.

A good name is better than great riches.

Small Players

> Now you are the body of Christ,
> and each one of you is a part of it.
> I CORINTHIANS 12:27

For years, Michael dreamed of playing basketball. He practiced daily after school. His dad bought a backboard and goal, and together they shot hoops in the driveway.

In his freshman year of high school, Michael failed to make the basketball team. Discouraged, but refusing to quit, he kept practicing and attended all the games. He hung around after school and watched the guys practice. In his sophomore year, he tried out again. This time he made the team but sat on the bench most of the year. Still he kept on practicing.

As a junior, Michael finally got his break and became a regular on the starting lineup. Although he could make most of his shots, the coach told him always to pass the ball to Jim, the star player. Jim won the Most Valuable Player award every year for three years and received a complete scholarship to a nearby college.

Michael expected no scholarship. After all, he was just a garden-variety player. Then one day a coach from a prestigious university out of state called him, offering him a full scholarship.

"Why would you want me?" Michael asked.

"We're impressed with your team skills. Lots of guys can be a star. But it takes a team—and a team player—to win successive games."

We may feel like "garden variety" Christians, being used in only small ways. We wonder how we could make a difference. But God is not in the business of recruiting star players. What He wants is a faithful heart, willing to serve Him as heaven's team player.

HOW CAN I BE A MORE FAITHFUL "TEAM PLAYER" FOR GOD?

The secret of success is to do all
you can without thought of fame.

No Limits!

I can do all things through Him who strengthens me.
PHILIPPIANS 4:13 NASB

DO I REALLY
TRUST GOD
WITH MY
FUTURE—EVEN
MY "TODAY"?

Scientists say it can't be done; the aerodynamic theory is crystal clear: Bumblebees cannot fly.

The reason is because the size, weight, and shape of the bumblebee's body in relation to the total wing spread makes it impossible for it to fly. The bumblebee is simply too heavy, too wide, and too large to fly with wings that small.

However, the bumblebee doesn't know these scientific facts and goes ahead and flies anyway.

It was God who created the bumblebee and God who taught it how to fly. The bumblebee obviously didn't question God about the problem with aerodynamics. He simply flew. He didn't question whether God really knew what He was talking about. He simply flew. He didn't wonder if God really loved him when He gave him such small wings. He simply flew.

When God created us, He also equipped us for the life ahead. He says He knows the plans He has for our lives. Because He loves us, He has promised to be with us, to teach us, to carry us, to be our rock. All we have to do is trust and obey.

God is not limited by our understanding of how things happen. Just because we can't see something doesn't mean it's not real. Faith is, indeed, the substance of things not seen. Sometimes life is unexplainable, and the impossible happens. We can't always explain everything.

And just because we don't understand how something can be done, doesn't mean Almighty God can't do it.

When a man has no strength, if he leans
on God, he becomes powerful.

The First Valentine

We love, because He first loved us.
1 JOHN 4:19 NASB

Most people would be surprised to learn that Valentine's Day was not intended to celebrate romance with gifts of flowers and chocolate. It was a day to honor a different kind of love.

Valentine was a Christian priest who lived near Rome in a period when Christians were punished for rejecting the Roman gods. During this time of persecution, legends say that Valentine assisted Christians in escaping from prison. He was discovered, arrested, and sent to trial, where he was asked if he believed in the Roman gods. He called their gods false. He continued to say that the only true God was He, whom Jesus called "Father."

Valentine was imprisoned, but it did not stop him from continuing his ministry. Even the prison guards began to listen to his witness. He befriended a blind girl as she waited at the jail while her adoptive father worked.

When the Roman emperor heard of Valentine's persistent worship of his God, he ordered his execution. In the days before his death, Valentine offered to pray for the jailer's blind daughter, and her sight was miraculously restored when he died. As a result, the jailer's entire family—forty-six people—came to believe in the one God and were baptized.

Saint Valentine knew every step of the way that his activities would endanger his life. But he continued because he loved God and people. It was a love that deserves to be honored and modeled after every day of the year.

Love is like a rose, the joy of all the earth.

HOW CAN I TELL THE PEOPLE IN MY LIFE THAT I LOVE THEM?

A Seagull's Gift

"I am the living bread that came down from heaven.
If anyone eats of this bread, he will live forever. This bread
is my flesh, which I will give for the life of the world."
JOHN 6:51

Who CAN I
OFFER THE
BREAD OF LIFE
TO TODAY?

Captain Eddie Rickenbacker, a famous World War I pilot, was forced down into the Pacific Ocean while on an inspection trip in 1942. The plane stayed afloat just long enough for all aboard to get out. Amazingly, Rickenbacker and his crew survived in rubber rafts for almost a month.

After eight days at sea, all of their rations were gone or ruined by the salt water. They knew that in order to survive, they needed a miracle. According to Captain Rickenbacker, his pilot conducted a worship service, and the crew ended it with a prayer for deliverance and a hymn of praise. Afterwards, in the oppressive heat, Rickenbacker pulled down his hat and went to sleep.

"Something landed on my head," said Rickenbacker. "I knew that it was a seagull. I don't know how I knew, I just knew." He caught the gull, which was hundreds of miles from land. The gull seemed to offer itself as a sacrifice for the starving men—something the captain never forgot.

In his old age, every Friday evening at sunset, Captain Rickenbacker would fill a bucket with shrimp and feed the seagulls along the eastern Florida coast. After he fed the gulls, he would linger on the broken pier, remembering a time when a seagull saved his life.

Jesus offered himself as a sacrifice too. Just as Captain Rickenbacker never forgot what one seagull meant to him, let us never forget what Christ did for us. Share the Bread of Life with those who are hungry.[8]

If Jesus Christ is God and died for me,
then no sacrifice can be too
great for me to make for him.

The Right Recipe

An angel of the Lord said to Philip, "Go south to
the road—the desert road—that goes down
from Jerusalem to Gaza." So he started out.

ACTS 8:26-27

When Sara attempted to bake her first cake
from scratch, the finished product was inedible,
and she sobbed her frustration to her mother. "I
don't understand why it doesn't look like the
picture in the recipe book!" she cried.

"Did you follow the recipe?" her mother asked.

"Yes," Sara replied. "I had to make a few sub-
stitutions though. The recipe said to use baking
powder, but I only had baking soda, so I used that
instead. And I didn't have baker's chocolate, so I
used a candy bar. I only had half the amount of
flour, so I substituted extra sugar to make up the
difference. And I was running late for class, so I
took it out of the oven a few minutes early."

What Sara failed to realize was the importance
of following a recipe exactly as it is written. The
proper ingredients, oven temperature, and baking
time will yield a picture-perfect result. Anything
less invites disaster.

God has a recipe for each of our lives too.
Our recipe will be a little bit different from
another person's. One person may need more
"time in the oven" to mature than someone else.
One may need more sweet experiences in life.
Another may need more of the oil of the Spirit to
soften a hardened heart.

Ask God to show you what He wants you to
add to the recipe of your life. If you follow His
recipe exactly, the results of your life can be just
like the one He pictured for you.

All my requests are lost in one,
"Father, thy will be done!"

It TAKES
COURAGE TO
GIVE GOD THE
REINS TO MY
LIFE. AM I
WILLING TO
TRUST HIM?

A Grateful Heart

Give thanks in all circumstances, for this
is God's Will for you in Christ Jesus.
1 THESSALONIANS 5:18

What THREE
THINGS AM I
MOST THANK-
FUL FOR
TODAY?

Books on etiquette aren't exactly best-sellers these days, but saying thank you will never go out of style. Even those who are rough around the edges know how much those two little words can mean. Whether it's a phone call, a face-to-face greeting, an e-mail, or a note dropped in the "snail mail," expressing gratitude for a favor, gift, or invitation will always brighten someone's day. It has reverse benefits as well.

When we take the time to thank someone, we are actually taking time to dwell on the nature of the one who has done something for us. Quite often, because we have taken the time for that reflection, we find ourselves grateful for more than just one simple favor or gift.

The Bible says to be thankful to God "in all circumstances." We say thanks to God when we pray before meals. We may say thanks before we go to bed. But why not write a thank-you note to God? Thank Him for your family, your friends, the roof over your head. Thank Him for all the little things in life that so easily go unregarded.

When you finish your note, date it, sign it, and place it in the back of your Bible or a favorite book. You'll probably forget about it after a few weeks. But one day you'll find that note at just the right moment, and you'll be reminded to say thank you again for the great things God has done for you.

We should spend as much time in
thanking God for His benefits as
we do in asking Him for them.

Invasion

See to it that no one misses the grace of God and that no bitter root grows up to cause trouble.

HEBREWS 12:15

The Matthews' kitchen had been invaded. Not by ants or mice. Not by ravenous teenagers. But by moths. Just a few of them at first. But then ten, fifteen, twenty a day. Whenever someone opened a cupboard door, a moth inevitably flew out into the person's face. But where were they coming from?

Systematically, the family began pulling open drawers and cupboards, finding small weblike nests that they washed away with disinfectant. After they cleaned out all the drawers and cupboards, the moth invasion slowed but never stopped. The Matthews knew there must be another stronghold somewhere.

The family looked deeper, even checking behind the refrigerator and stove. But it wasn't until one of the kids saw a dead moth next to the dog's dish that they had their first real clue. They had recently purchased a new feeding system from a pet supply store, a container that held several pounds of dog food and distributed the food in measured servings. When they lifted the lid of the feeder and glanced inside, they knew they had finally found the source of the infestation.

The Bible says bad feelings can invade our lives like the moths invaded the Matthews' kitchen. An unkind word or action can trigger long-term bitterness between two people. Unless the root problem is removed, the relationship may suffer severe damage. But if we talk through the misunderstandings, we'll reap the benefit of a strengthened relationship. Open communication will help close the cracks of bitterness and rid us of the infestation of hard feelings.

The mind grows by what it feeds on.

Have I ALLOWED BAD FEELINGS TO POISON A RELATIONSHIP? WHAT CAN I DO TO RESTORE IT?

Hidden Beauty

O Lord, our Lord, how majestic
is your name in all the earth!

PSALM 8:9

What ITEM
DO I SEE
BEFORE ME
THAT REMINDS
ME OF GOD'S
BLESSINGS?

Only weeks after the New Year arrived, Sheldon noticed the clutter on his computer table. He thought of the Christmas celebration weeks earlier and how neat and sleek his workspace had been in preparation for the new semester.

Now life was back to normal. The crisp, clean feel of a fresh start was gone from his table and replaced with receipts, floppy disks, notebooks, and unfinished homework assignments. Contributing to the jumble was a box of unopened pens and an address book.

Sheldon picked up the address book and flipped through the pages. Each page was filled with names, addresses, and telephone numbers. He realized that this book represented family and friends, and he thought about how fortunate he was to have so many people who loved him. As he read the names, he offered up a prayer for each one. He prayed for their special needs and asked God to walk with them daily.

He picked up his gym shoes and thanked God for his health. Then he looked over the bills and thanked God for his part-time job and the support of his family while he was in college. One by one, he counted his many blessings.

At first glance, the things on Sheldon's computer table seemed to invade his dorm room, but as he looked at each item, he realized that each one served as a reminder of God's presence in his life.

If men thanked God for good things,
they wouldn't have time to
complain about the bad.

Perfect Perspective

The Lord disciplines those he loves,
as a father the son he delights in.
PROVERBS 3:12

"You just don't want me to have any fun!" Dell shouted as he slammed out of the house and stomped through the backyard.

Dell hated the control his parents exercised over him. His friends got to do whatever they wanted. They could stay out late and watch whatever movies they wanted, and some of them were dating already. At fourteen, Dell felt he should have the same privileges. Why didn't his parents trust him?

"Dell?" It was his dad. He turned around reluctantly.

"What?" he asked. He almost missed the football flying through the air and had to throw up his hands to block it. "Geez, Dad!"

He held the football for a second, tempted to toss it aside. But there was his father, waiting patiently, a smile on his face. Dell swallowed his anger and tossed the ball back. He supposed there could be worse things than having a father who tossed a football around with him, a dad who wanted to keep him on the right track in life.

How often do you find yourself storming away from God's presence, holding on to something that He has asked you to let go of? How often do you resist His authority because of what your friends are doing? Remember that the Father who corrects you does so because He loves you. He wants to keep your vision unclouded so He can lead you to the life He has set aside for you. Allow God's correction to be the greatest affirmation of His love and hope for your life.

Look upon your chastenings as God's chariots sent to carry your soul into the high places of spiritual achievement.

Have I ALLOWED BAD INFLUENCES TO TAINT MY PERSPECTIVE? HOW CAN I LEARN TO SEE THINGS GOD'S WAY?

Truth Be Told

"Watch and pray so that you will not fall into
temptation. The spirit is willing, but the body is weak."
MARK 14:38

In WHAT
AREAS COULD I
TAKE A STAND
FOR TRUTH
TODAY?

Stacie was sitting in the Saturday study detention classroom when she first heard the commotion.

"No way!"

"Check it out!"

"Who's got some quarters?"

Stacie got up from her desk and walked toward
the sound of money jingling. She rounded the
corner to discover three of her friends gathered
around the vending machine. They were inserting
change, picking out items, and receiving both the
snack and their money back. The machine was
giving out free food.

Stacie grinned. No breakfast that morning and
quarters in her pocket added up to one thought.
She pushed to the front and gave it a try. Three
quarters—some powdered donuts. Three quarters
back—a big cinnamon roll. Carrying her quarters
and her unexpected breakfast, she headed back to
her desk with a smile on her face.

It wasn't until she sat down that the guilt
settled heavily on her conscience. No matter that
everyone else seemed to be okay with it. No matter
that the vending machine guy was always grumpy
and never stocked the items she liked. This was
wrong. It was stealing, and she couldn't do it.

When the vendor came later, she dug into her
pocket and paid for all three items. Her friends
looked at her oddly, but she felt much better.

Today, take a stand for the little acts of truth, the
small steps of honesty and courage. Though some
may mock you, you will earn the respect of others,
and God will use that to draw them to His heart.

Tis one thing to be tempted,
another thing to fall.

Bond of Sisterhood

"This is my command: Love each other."

JOHN 15:17

Tanya and Mary fought constantly. Although now in their teen years, they still tormented each other like toddlers—a push here, a shove there, stolen makeup, disappearing shoes.

One afternoon, their mother reached her limit. She sat down both girls and looked from one to the other. "I've had enough of your fighting. For the rest of the day, I don't want to hear a single raised voice. I want you to love each other and be kind. End of story." She got up and went back to her tasks.

Tanya and Mary looked at each other. Love each other? How could they love each other just by being told, especially when the sight of the other brought to mind a long list of past errors? But they had never seen their mother quite so angry.

A few moments passed in silence until Tanya finally nudged Mary with her shoulder. "Want to go to the mall?"

Mary smiled. "Okay."

Of course, it's not always quite this easy, but it's not as hard as we might think either. Sometimes loving each other is simply a matter of letting go and making a fresh start. Decide that the past is gone; you have a future to mold.

God commands us to love one another. Can you think of someone you have refused to love? Is there something you can do to extend friendship to that person? Even if your friendship is rejected, God asks only that you do your part. He will see to the rest.

What IS MY PART IN EXTENDING FRIENDSHIP TO ANOTHER?

They are the true disciples of Christ, not who know most, but who love most.

In the Whirlwind

Cast all your anxiety on him because
he cares for you.

1 PETER 5:7

What AM I
MOST AFRAID
OF? HOW
CAN I TURN
THAT FEAR
INTO TRUST
OF GOD?

In March of 1975, a tornado raked an eight-mile path across Atlanta, snapping pine trees like toothpicks. Even today, Gloria remembers that day as though it were yesterday. She was a high school senior then and worked part-time at a donut shop. The shop was closed that Monday for remodeling.

That morning as Gloria got ready for class, she noticed the sky turn an ominous black. The wind picked up, and trees bowed like rubber. She watched metal garbage cans tumble down the street. Then the driving rain hit. The last thing on Gloria's mind, though, was a tornado.

On her way home from school, visibility was poor as the rain slanted in sheets across the road. The constant scraping of the windshield wipers grated on her nerves, so she turned on the radio to drown out the sound. The weather forecaster said a tornado had been spotted in the area. She accelerated, urging her car toward home.

Not until later did Gloria learn that the tornado had destroyed the donut shop. When she finally went back to survey the damage, she found everything in shambles. She trembled when she saw the collapsed concrete wall on top of the checkout counter where she rang up donut sales every afternoon.

What a blessing to know that God never sleeps. He promises to be with us even in the midst of a whirlwind. Look to Him when darkness blankets your world, and He will show you the way home!

The wise man in the storm prays to God, not
for safety from danger, but for deliverance
from fear. It is the storm within that
endangers him, not the storm without.

Apple Pie Problems

He who was seated on the throne said,
"I am making everything new!"

REVELATION 21:5

Marilyn's favorite apple pie rolled from her fingertips without a pause. The pie crust lay trimmed and ready in the pie pan, awaiting the seasoned filling. Everything looked just fine. Yet as she added a sprinkling of walnuts and placed the top crust in position, a heavy sigh escaped from her lips. Her mind was not on the pie but rather on a troubled relationship with a close friend.

As she slid the pie into the oven, Marilyn remembered hearing a speaker who encouraged her listeners to keep a prayer journal. The speaker said she usually prayed aloud as she wrote her concerns in a journal. She felt it helped her clarify her problems and keep track of God's answers.

Marilyn picked up a blank book she had been given for Christmas. Sitting at the kitchen table, she began to write a letter to God, pouring out her heart and her hurt about this troubled relationship. Before she knew it, the oven timer sounded, and she sniffed the familiar warm scent of apples filling the room.

Surprisingly, her heart felt lighter. She was struck by the similarity between the pie and the prayer journal. Wrapped between two piecrusts and left to time and the work of the oven, the apples had changed from tart and crisp to sweet and smooth. In the same way, Marilyn had wrapped her concerns between the covers of prayer. God needed time to work. He would change that soured relationship and make things sweet again.

Friendship is in loving
rather than in being loved.

Lord, I NEED
TO TALK TO
YOU TODAY
ABOUT . . .

Accepting Substitutes

Unto him that is able to do exceeding abundantly
above all that we ask or think, according to the
power that worketh in us.

EPHESIANS 3:20 KJV

Some

OF GOD'S

SUBSTITUTES

CAN LOOK

AT IN A

DIFFERENT

WAY ARE . . .

A woman moved to Wyoming. Clothing stores were in short supply, and her busy ranch life left little time for trips to larger cities to shop. Her situation was made more difficult because she was a hard-to-fit size. She began relying on a major store catalog that carried her size. The printed order forms sent by the store had this sentence at the bottom: "If we do not have the article you ordered in stock, may we substitute?"

She was hesitant to trust strangers to make an appropriate substitution, but she replied, "Yes," hoping it wouldn't be necessary.

One day she opened a package and found a letter, which read in part, "We are sorry that the article you ordered is out of stock, but we have substituted . . . " To her surprise she found an item of greater quality worth double the price she had paid!

After that, the woman wrote "YES" in large red letters at the bottom of the order form by the substitution question. She knew the store would provide her with the best they had.

When we pray, we can trust God to send us the perfect answer because, as our Maker, He knows what will fit us better than we do. Because He knows the future, He can answer in a way that goes beyond our highest expectations. Every time He sends "substitutes," we can be sure He is sending something much better than we could have ever imagined.

When life isn't the way you like,
like it the way it is.

Get UP and Go!

> God did not give us a spirit of timidity, but a
> spirit of power, of love, and of self-discipline.
>
> 2 TIMOTHY 1:7

Getting yourself out of bed in the morning is one thing. Feeling prepared to face whatever the day holds—exams, a zit the size of Connecticut, the year-end debate with a top-rated school—is another. Where do you turn for a confidence-booster?

Believe it or not, one of the best confidence-builders you can find is your own two feet. Researchers have discovered that regular exercise—thirty minutes, three or four times a week—boosts the confidence level of both males and females.

When you exercise, changes take place inside your brain. Endorphins, released as you exercise, are proteins that make you feel more exhilarated. When the heart rate increases during exercise, neurotrophins are also released, causing you to feel more alert and focused.

Are you feeling anxious about your day? Set aside time for a mini-walk or jog, or do some calisthenics on your bedroom floor. See if you don't feel a little more confident.

The human body is one of the most awesome examples of God's creative power—an example we live with daily. He has created us not only to draw confidence from reading His Word and experiencing His presence through prayer, but also from the use of our body.

Get your body pumping, and talk with God as you go! Not only will your body become more fit and your mind more alert, but the Holy Spirit will give you direction and peace about your day.

Let it be in God's own might
We gird us for the coming fight,
And, strong in Him whose cause is ours,
In conflict with unholy powers,
We grasp the weapons He has given,
The light and truth and love of heaven.

What CAN I
TALK TO GOD
ABOUT AS I
EXERCISE
TODAY?

Epitaphs

He has shown you, O man, what is good;
And what does the Lord require of you
But to do justly, To love mercy,
And to walk humbly with your God?
MICAH 6:8 NKJV

If I DIED TODAY, WOULD PEOPLE REMEMBER ME AS LOVING OR SELFISH?

A speech teacher once assigned her students to give a one-sentence speech titled "What I Would Like My Tombstone to Read." The class told her later that this assignment was one of the most challenging assignments they had ever received. In every case, the students saw a great discrepancy between the way they lived and the way they desired their lives to be perceived by others.

What are your personal ideals—the qualities you consider foremost in defining good character?

Here's what a famous man once said about his own ideals: "I have three personal ideals. One, to do the day's work well and not to bother about tomorrow. . . . The second ideal has been to act the Golden Rule. . . . And the third has been to cultivate such a measure of equanimity as would enable me to bear success with humility, the affection of my friends without pride, and to be ready when the day of sorrow and grief comes to meet it with the courage befitting a man."

Many of us make New Year's resolutions to "turn over a new leaf." We greet a new day with a determination to "do better" in a certain area of our life. But rarely do we give serious thought to what we consider the noblest pursuits in life.

Today, give some thought to the qualities of a respected life. What do you aspire to in your own character? As you identify these traits, you'll see more clearly what must change in order to live up to your ideals.

Fame is vapor, popularity an accident,
riches take wings. Only one thing
endures and that is character.

Good Thoughts

As he thinks in his heart, so is he.

PROVERBS 23:7 NKJV

What we think about determines what we do. Even more important, the Scriptures tell us that what we think about shapes our attitudes and how we live our lives.

The Greek city of Philippi was one of the places where the apostle Paul had a fruitful ministry. The Greeks were great thinkers. They loved a good debate, a lively conversation about philosophy, or a rousing speech that triggered the imagination. Paul wrote to the believers in Philippi:

Whatever things are true, whatever things are noble, whatever things are just, whatever things are pure, whatever things are lovely, whatever things are of good report, if there is any virtue and if there is anything praiseworthy meditate on these things.

PHILIPPIANS 4:8 NKJV

It's interesting to note that Paul wrote this immediately after addressing three other concerns. First, he tells two women who are arguing to be of "the same mind in the Lord." Paul wants them to be at peace with each other and to rejoice together in the Lord.

Second, Paul tells them to be gentle with everyone—that is, to be at peace with those who don't know the Lord. And, third, Paul advises them not to worry about anything, but to turn all their troubles over to the Lord. He wants them to have total peace of mind and heart.

By becoming God's "peace people" through our thoughts and actions, the result is that "the God of peace will be with you" (Philippians 4:9).

As we look for the good in others and meditate on the goodness of our Creator, we find the path toward peace with others and the peace that passes all understanding in whatever situation we find ourselves.

How CAN I BE A "PEACE PERSON" TO OTHERS TODAY?

The mind grows by what it feeds on.

Bred for Success

The horse is made ready for the day
of battle, but victory rests with the LORD.
PROVERBS 21:31

HOW HAS MY
CHARACTER
CHANGED FOR
THE BETTER
THROUGH MY
RELATIONSHIP
WITH GOD?

Lexington, Kentucky, is renowned for producing the finest thoroughbred racehorses in the world. But it's not just the beautiful acreage that draws serious breeders to the area. The Kentucky bluegrass contains something that cannot be found in such abundance anywhere else on earth—a particular type of limestone that lies just the right distance under the surface of the ground, continuously releasing vital minerals into the soil.

Plants grown in this soil, such as the grass the horses eat, are rich in minerals needed to build extremely strong but very light bones—ideal for racing. Thus, a colt eating Kentucky bluegrass spends his first two years eating exactly what will help him win the race of his life!

Along the same line, the older males of the Alaskan bull moose herds battle for dominance during the fall breeding season, literally going head-to-head with their giant antlers. The moose with the largest and strongest antlers almost always triumphs. Therefore, the battle fought in the fall is really won in the summer when they do nothing but eat. The one that consumes the best diet for growing antlers will be the heavyweight in the fall.

No, you're neither a racehorse or a bull mooose, but there's a spiritual lesson here for all of us. We develop faith, strength, and wisdom for difficult times by spending time with God today.

Steep yourself in God's Word, and spend time with Him in prayer. If troubles arise later, you'll be attuned to your Father's voice and better equipped for the battle!

I am sorry for men who do not read the
Bible every day. I wonder why they deprive
themselves of the strength and the pleasure.

Fruitful Lives

Meditate upon these things; give thyself wholly
to them; that thy profiting may appear to all.

1 TIMOTHY 4:15 KJV

Two brothers were out walking on their father's vast acreage when they came upon a peach tree, its branches heavy with fruit. Each brother ate several juicy peaches.

When they started toward the house, one brother gathered enough peaches for a peach cobbler and several jars of jam. The second brother cut a limb from the tree to start a new peach tree. When this brother got home, he tended the tree cutting until he could plant it outdoors. The branch took root and eventually produced healthy crops of peaches for him to enjoy year after year.

Hearing the Word of God is like the first brother. He gathered fruit from hearing the Word and had enough to take home with him to eat later. But that doesn't compare with having your own peach tree in the backyard. Memorizing the Word is like having the fruit tree in your backyard. It is there to nourish you all the time.

Scripture memorization is often considered a dull, burdensome task. But we could get highly motivated if we were given one hundred dollars for every Bible verse we memorized! The rewards of putting Scripture to memory may not always be monetary, but they are a far better treasure for life.

There are many different ways to memorize Scripture. Find the one that works best for you and begin hiding God's Word in your heart, so it may bring continual life and nourishment to you. This will produce fruit in your life which you can share with others.

HOW CAN I HIDE GOD'S WORD IN MY HEART?

Sin will keep you from this book.
This book will keep you from sin.

Tethered by Love

My yoke is easy, and my burden is light.
MATTHEW 11:30 KJV

HOW CAN I
LET JESUS BE
MY "KITE
STRING"
TODAY?

Some people believe the lie that God's ways will restrict their creativity and growth. They fear they won't reach their full potential if they are tied down by "religious restrictions." Others see His commands as "taking away all their fun."

Sadly, many people will never reach their full potential because they *aren't* tied to Jesus. The fact is, true and lasting joy comes through knowing Jesus and following Him.

Consider this: You have watched a kite fly in the wind. Would you say the string that holds it is burdensome? No, it is there to control the kite. The kite will not fly unless it is in partnership with the string. The string and the kite are yoked together. You cannot cut the string and expect the kite to soar. When the string is cut, the kite may fly freely for a moment, but it will soon crash to the ground.

The string gives the kite direction and purpose by sustaining its position against the wind and using the wind to its advantage. Without the string, the kite would end up trapped in a tree or falling to the ground.

In like manner, our daily surrender to the Lord Jesus is not burdensome, nor does it take away enjoyment in life. Like the kite string, He makes certain the wind is in our favor and we are always in position to get the most out of life.

The greatness of a man's power is
the measure of his surrender.

Taproots

> The Almighty . . . blesses you with blessings of the heavens above [and] blessings of the deep that lies below.
> GENESIS 49:25

The taproot of a tree is the part of the root system that goes deep into the soil to absorb essential minerals and huge quantities of water—sometimes several hundred quarts a day. Taproots grow deepest in dry, sandy areas where there is little rainfall. The root system of a tree not only nourishes the tree but provides stability, anchoring it securely into the ground so it cannot be blown over by strong winds.

The root system is a good analogy for the Christian life. Richard J. Foster wrote, "Superficiality is the curse of our age. . . . The desperate need today is not for a greater number of intelligent people or gifted people but for deep people."

How do Christians grow deep in their spiritual life? In the same way a taproot grows deep—in search of the nourishment that will cause it to grow. In modern culture, Christians have to seek out spiritual food that will result in spiritual maturity. Regular times of prayer and Bible study, individual and corporate worship, serving others, and Christian fellowship are just some of the ways Christians can grow deep roots.

What are the benefits of depth in our spiritual life? Like the tree,

we will be able to stand strong—"the righteous cannot be uprooted" (Proverbs 12:3).

we will be fruitful—"the root of the righteous flourishes" (Proverbs 12:12).

Seek the Lord daily, so you can grow deep in your faith and withstand the storms of life.

A bit of the Book in the morning, to order my onward way. A bit of the Book in the evening, to hallow the end of the day.

In WHAT WAYS HAVE MY SPIRITUAL ROOTS STARTED TO GROW? WHAT CAN I DO TO HELP THEM GROW DEEPER?

No Distractions

Do you not know that in a race all the
runners run, but only one gets the prize?
Run in such a way as to get the prize.
I CORINTHIANS 9:24

Have I
ALLOWED ANY-
THING TO
TAKE THE
PLACE OF GOD
IN MY LIFE?

On March 6, 1987, Eamon Coughlan, the Irish
world record holder in the 1,500 meter race, com-
peted in a qualifying heat at the World Indoor
Track Championships in Indianapolis. With only
two and a half laps left, he was tripped by another
runner. Coughlan crashed onto the track but
managed to get up and regain his stride. In an
explosive burst of effort, he caught the leaders and
held steady at third place—a position good enough
to qualify him for the finals.

Just then, Coughlan looked over his shoulder
to the inside. When he didn't see anyone, he
slowed his stride. To his great surprise another
runner, charging hard on the outside, passed him
only a yard before the finish line, eliminating him
from the final race. Coughlan's great comeback
effort was rendered worthless because he took his
eyes off the finish line and assumed his race could
be run without further challenge.

Today you will face many distractions that have
the potential to take your attention away from your
goals. Some of those distractions will be the small
bump-in-the-road variety. Others may be the
stumble-and-fall variety—those that seriously
threaten your progress if you don't pick yourself up
and move on. But the distraction that most seriously
threatens your goal is the one that looks as if it is no
threat at all: the I've-got-it-made-so-relax variety. It
compels you to look over your shoulder, slow your
pace, and take your eyes off the finish line.

He that perseveres makes every difficulty
an advancement and every contest a victory.

Making a Difference

> "There is joy in the presence of the angels
> of God over one sinner who repents."
>
> LUKE 15:10 NASB

A teenaged girl went on vacation to a seaside hotel with her family. During their stay a powerful storm arose, lashing the beach and sending massive breakers against the shore all night.

Before daybreak the wind subsided. The girl got out of bed to go outside and survey the damage done by the storm. She walked along the beach and noticed it was covered with starfish that had been thrown ashore by the massive waves. They lay helpless on the sandy beach. Unable to get to the water, the starfish faced inevitable death as the sun's rays dried them out.

Further down the beach, she saw a figure walking along the shore. Every now and then the figure would stoop and pick up something. As she approached she realized it was a young boy picking up the starfish one at a time and flinging them back into the ocean.

As the girl neared the young boy, she said, "Why are you doing that? One person will never make a difference—there are too many starfish to get back into the water before the sun comes up."

The boy said, "Yes, that's true," and then bent to pick up another starfish. "But I can sure make a difference to that one."

God never intended for an individual to solve all of life's problems. But He did intend for each one of us to use whatever resources and gifts He gave us to make a difference where we are.[9]

Small drops of water hollow out a stone.

HOW CAN I MAKE A DIFFERENCE IN SOMEONE'S LIFE TODAY?

Night Watch

I consider thy heavens, the work of thy fingers,
the moon and the stars, which thou hast ordained.
PSALM 8:3 KJV

What AN AWESOME THOUGHT: THE CREATOR OF THE UNIVERSE INVITES ME TO HAVE A PERSONAL RELATIONSHIP WITH HIM!

When was the last time you gazed up into the star-filled sky on a clear night? Writer Jamie Buckingham described a night like that in the snowy mountains of North Carolina: "I walked up the dark, snow-covered road toward Cowee Bald. The sky had cleared, revealing a billion stars twinkling in the clear, cold night. The only sound was the gurgling of a small mountain stream beside the road and the soft crunch of my shoes in the snow. All the other night noises were smothered, leaving me with the impression of standing alone on earth.

"I kicked the snow off my boot, and standing in the middle of the road, threw my head back and breathed deeply of the pine-scented air. Looking into the heavens I could see stars whose light had left there a million years ago, and I realized that I was just glimpsing the edge of space. Beyond that was infinity—and surrounding it all, the Creator.

"I remembered a quote from the German philosopher Kant. Something about two irrefutable evidences of the existence of God: the moral law within and the starry universe above. I breathed His name: 'God.'

"Then, overwhelmed by His presence, I called Him what I had learned to call Him through experience: 'Father!'"[10]

Tonight, contemplate the stars in the heavens. You will find there a glimpse of eternity.

The more I study nature, the more
I am amazed at the Creator.

Safe Passage

Now will I arise, saith the Lord; I will set him
in safety from him that puffeth at him.
PSALM 12:5 KJV

What
EFFECT DOES
COMPLETE
TRUST IN
GOD HAVE
ON MY LIFE?

Two teen girls boarded a ferry to cross the English Channel from England to France, where they planned to vacation with another family. About halfway through their journey, the ferry hit rough waters and was tossed about violently on the waves.

When it became apparent that the pitching of the boat was not going to abate, one of the girls decided to return to her assigned seat in the middle of the ferry. She soon fell sound asleep and experienced no more seasickness. Toward the end of the trip, after the ferry had moved into calmer waters off the coast of France, the other girl joined her. "That was awful," she exclaimed. "I was nauseous for two hours!"

"I'm sorry to hear that," said the second girl.

"Weren't you sick?" the first girl asked in amazement.

"No," her friend responded. "Here at our seats I must have been at the center of the boat's motion, and it was relatively calm. I simply imagined myself being rocked in the arms of God and fell asleep."

All around you today, life may be unsettling and stormy, your entire life bouncing about on rough waters. But when you return to the "center" of your life, the Lord, He will set you in safety. Let Him rock you gently to sleep, and trust Him to bring you through the rough waters tomorrow.

No sleep can be tranquil unless
the mind is at rest.

Tightrope Trust

I know whom I have believed, and am
persuaded that he is able to keep that which
I have committed unto him against that day.
2 TIMOTHY 1:12 KJV

If GOD
WERE THE
TIGHTROPE
WALKER,
WOULD I
TRUST HIM
ENOUGH TO
CLIMB ON HIS
SHOULDERS?

In the mid-nineteenth century, a tightrope walker named Blondin was going to perform his most daring feat yet. He stretched a two-inch steel cable across Niagara Falls and asked the crowd of onlookers, "How many of you believe I can carry the weight of a man on my shoulders across this gorge?"

The crowd shouted and cheered, believing that he could perform this difficult feat. Blondin picked up a sack of sand that weighed 180 pounds and carried it across the Falls, arriving safely on the other side.

Then Blondin asked, "How many of you believe I can carry a person across the gorge?" Again, the crowd cheered him on. "Which one of you will climb on my shoulders and let me carry you across the Falls?" Silence fell across the crowd. Everyone wanted to see Blondin carry a person across the gorge, but nobody wanted to put his life into the tightrope walker's hands.

Finally, a volunteer came forward. It was Blondin's manager, who had known the tightrope walker personally for many years.

As they prepared to cross the Falls, Blondin instructed his manager, "You must not trust your own feelings, but mine. You will feel like turning when we don't need to turn. And if you trust your feelings, we will both fall. You must become part of me." The two made it across to the other side safely.[11]

Jesus gives us the same instruction when we are asked to trust Him in difficult circumstances: "Don't trust your own feelings, trust Me to carry you through."

All I have seen teaches me to trust
the Creator for all I have not seen.

Anger-Busters

Be ye angry, and sin not: let not
the sun go down upon your wrath.
EPHESIANS 4:26 KJV

That mean girl in science class shoulder-bumps you as she passes you in the hallway; your mom blames you for something your little brother did—and he gets away with it; the drama coach cuts you from the play at the last minute.

Anger starts to boil inside you.

As Christians, we know that anger can be a terrible enemy. The beginnings of anger are subtle: petty irritations, ordinary frustrations, minor aggravations—things we experience daily. But when these small things add up, pressures build and turn into rage. Without relief, pent-up anger can turn violent, with devastating consequences.

How do we take control of our anger before it takes control of us? How can we defuse the "bomb" that makes us want to retaliate? There are several things we can do:

1. Yell at God first! He already knows you're upset.

2. Ask God to give you understanding about the situation, to show you the root of your anger, if that's the case.

3. Turn the situation over to God. Forgive those who have hurt you and let Him deal with them.

4. Don't do anything without having complete inner peace from His Spirit.

An old proverb says, "He who goes angry to bed has the devil for a bedfellow." The next time you feel anger boiling in you, try following the guidelines above. Then you'll sleep easily at night, knowing God can turn anything around to work for your good.

I was angry with my friend. I told my wrath,
my wrath did end. I was angry with my foe.
I told it not, my wrath did grow.

What
SITUATION DO
I NEED TO
TURN OVER TO
GOD TODAY?

No Compromise

"You are the salt of the earth. . . .
You are the light of the world."
MATTHEW 5:13-14 RSV

In WHAT
AREAS HAS MY
FAITH BEEN
CHALLENGED?
HOW DID I
RESPOND?

Standing in line with his squad in the communist Red Army, Taavi had already made up his mind what he was going to say. The officers made their way toward him, interrogating each soldier down the line with the same question: "Are you a Christian?" "No." Then to the next one: "Are you a Christian?" "No."

As the officers got closer to Taavi, who had been drafted into the Red Army during the Soviet occupation of his country, he thought about his life. Although only older people were permitted to go to church in his country, Taavi's grandmother had shared her faith with her grandson. He had accepted the Lord as his Savior and learned the Scriptures from his grandmother.

When the officers reached his place in line, they asked, "Are you a Christian?"

"Yes," Taavi said in a clear voice.

"Then come with us," ordered the commanding officers.

Taavi followed them immediately. They got in a vehicle and drove to the building that housed the kitchen and mess hall. Did they plan to shoot him there?

"We are taking you out of combat preparation," the officers said. "You are a Christian and you will not steal, so we will put you in the kitchen." The kitchen was the biggest black-market operation in the Red Army, with the smuggling and illegal sale of food to hungry soldiers. They knew Taavi's presence would reduce the amount of theft.

When you are challenged for your faith, rise up and boldly proclaim the truth. God will be with you, and He will reward you for your faithfulness.

If we are correct and right in our Christian
life at every point, but refuse to stand for
the truth at a particular point where the
battle rages—then we are traitors to Christ.

Morning Glory

You are a chosen people, a royal priesthood,
a holy nation, a people belonging to God, that
you may declare the praises of him who called
you out of darkness into his wonderful light.

I PETER 2:9

At the turn of the century, a city worker who had spent his teen years in evil living met God during a revival meeting. Soon after, he ran into one of his old drinking pals. Knowing his friend needed Jesus, he told him about the change in his life. His friend made fun of him for "turning pious."

"I'll tell you what," said the new Christian, "you know that I am the city lamplighter. When I go around turning out the lights, I look back, and all the road over which I've been walking is blackness. That's what my past is like."

He went on, "I look in front, and there's a long row of twinkling lights to guide me, and that's what the future is like since I found Jesus."

"Yes," said the friend, "but when you get to the last lamp and turn it out, where are you then?"

"Why, when the last lamp goes out, it's dawn," said the Christian, "and there's no need for lamps when the morning comes."

Darkness is a metaphor for many things: death, uncertainty, fear, evil. But in all of them, Jesus is the Light that brings illumination and comfort.

When light shines, not only is darkness eliminated, but fears are relieved. Not only does Jesus give you as much light as you need to proceed in faith, but because of His sacrifice at Calvary, you can be assured of His eternal dawn when the last lamp goes out!

Christ has turned all our sunsets into dawns.

HOW HAS THE LIGHT OF CHRIST CHANGED MY LIFE?

Letting Go

Forgetting those things which are behind, and
reaching forth unto those things which are before,
I press toward the mark for the prize of
the high calling of God in Christ Jesus.

PHILIPPIANS 3:13-14 KJV

What DOES
"LET GO AND
LET GOD"
MEAN TO ME
IN A REAL-
WORLD
SITUATION?

The spider monkey is a tiny animal native to South and Central America. Quick as lightning, it is a very difficult animal to capture in the wild. For years, people attempted to shoot spider monkeys with tranquilizer guns or capture them with nets, but they discovered the monkeys were nearly always faster than their fastest draw or quickest trap.

Then somebody discovered the best method for capturing this elusive creature. They found that if you take a clear, narrow-mouthed glass bottle, put one peanut inside it, and wait, you can catch a spider monkey.

What happens? The spider monkey reaches into the bottle to get the peanut, and he can't get his hand out of the bottle as long as it is clenching the peanut. The bottle is so heavy in proportion to his size that he can't drag it with him—and the spider monkey is too persistent to let go of a peanut once he has grasped it.

How many of us are like that? Unwilling to change a habit, try a new method, or give up something we know is wrong, we stubbornly cling to our way, even if it brings pain and suffering.

Today, don't cling to a negative situation. As the bumper sticker advises, "Let go and let God!"

Trust the Lord to lead you to the new opportunities He has for you. Have faith in Him to provide what you truly need to live a fulfilling life.

Finish every day and be done with it. You have done what you could.

Some blunders and absurdities no doubt have crept in; forget them as soon as you can.

Tomorrow is a new day; begin it well and
serenely and with too high a spirit
to be cumbered with your old nonsense.
This day is all that is good and fair. It is
too dear, with its hopes and invitations,
to waste a moment on yesterdays.

Recharge Your Battery

There remains, then, a Sabbath-rest for the people of
God; for anyone who enters God's rest also rests
from his own work, just as God did from his.
HEBREWS 4:9-10

How much oxygen does a person need throughout the day? Years ago, a scientist determined to find out. He was able to demonstrate that the average workman breathes thirty ounces of oxygen during a day's work, but he uses thirty-one. At the close of the day he is one ounce short, and his body is tired.

He goes to sleep and breathes more oxygen than he uses to sleep, so in the morning he has regained five-sixths of the ounce he was short. The night's rest does not fully balance the day's work!

By the seventh day, he is six-sixths or one whole ounce in debt again. He must rest an entire day to replenish his body's oxygen requirements. Further, the scientist demonstrated that replenishing an entire ounce of oxygen requires thirty to thirty-six hours, when part of the resting is done while one is awake and moving about.

Over time, failure to replenish the oxygen supply results in the actual death of cells and, eventually, the premature death of the person. But a person is restored as long as he or she takes the seventh day as a day of rest.[12]

Sound familiar? The God who created us not only invites us to rest, He created our bodies in such a way that they demand rest.

Most people think that "keeping the Sabbath" is just an act of devotion to God. But in turning your attention to God, He can offer you true rest and replenish every area of your life—spirit, soul, and body. He is not only our daily strength, He is our source of rest, recreation, and replenishment.

Take rest; a field that has rested
gives a bountiful crop.

What STEPS CAN I TAKE TO ALLOW GOD TO RECHARGE MY BATTERY TODAY?

Merciful Goodness

"If you forgive men when they sin against you,
your heavenly Father will also forgive you."
MATTHEW 6:14

Whom DO I
NEED TO
FORGIVE
TODAY? ON
THE FLIP SIDE,
HAVE I
WRONGED
ANOTHER
PERSON?

Just before he commenced work on his depiction of the Last Supper, Leonardo da Vinci had a violent quarrel with a fellow painter. Leonardo was so enraged he determined to use the face of his enemy as the face of Judas, taking his revenge through his art.

The face of Judas was one of the first he finished, and everyone recognized it as the face of the painter with whom he had quarreled. However, when he attempted to paint the face of Jesus Christ, Leonardo could make no progress. Something seemed to stifle him—holding him back and frustrating his efforts. At length, he came to the conclusion that painting his enemy into the face of Judas was the source of the problem.

When he painted over the face of his enemy in the portrait of Judas, he commenced anew on the face of Jesus. His depiction became a success that has been acclaimed through the ages. The moral of this story: You cannot paint the features of Jesus Christ into your own life and at the same time paint another face with the colors of hatred.

If you are harboring bitterness toward someone, forgive the person who wronged you and put him into God's hands. As you forgive, you will be forgiven and set free to live your life with inner peace.

He that demands mercy, and shows
none, ruins the bridge over
which he himself is to pass.

The Power of Love

> The wolf also shall dwell with the lamb,
> and the leopard shall lie down with the kid;
> and the calf and the young lion and the fatling
> together; and a little child shall lead them.
>
> ISAIAH 11:6 KJV

Who IS MOST IN NEED OF MY LOVE AND ACCEPTANCE TODAY?

The orange kitten weighed no more than ten ounces when he first slid under the fence into the grizzly bear's pen. The zoo worker who witnessed the kitten's foolhardy venture panicked—carnivorous bears make much larger animals a part of their diet.

Griz had come to the Oregon wildlife center in 1990 when he was just a cub. Hit by a train while foraging on railroad tracks in Montana, he suffered severe head injuries and was deemed unfit to return to the wild. The kitten, now called Cat, was one of four kittens abandoned at the center early in the summer.

Afraid to do anything that might alarm Griz, the man just watched, expecting the worst. As the 650-pound grizzly was eating his midday meal, something extraordinary happened. The bear gently picked out a chicken wing with his forepaw and dropped it near Cat.

From that moment on, Griz and Cat became something of a slapstick animal act. Cat would lie in ambush, then leap out and swat Griz on his nose. Griz would carry Cat in his mouth. Cat would ride on Griz's back, and sometimes Griz would lick Cat. Their friendly relationship defies both the patterns of nature as well as their own troubled life histories. Griz never took advantage of Cat's weaknesses, and each animal has accommodated the other's needs.[13]

We can help each other break free from the patterns of our past that keep us from loving each other. Never cease loving a person, and never give up hope for him; even the Prodigal Son could still be saved.

> The bitterest enemy and also he who was
> your friend could again be your friend; love
> that has grown cold can kindle again.

The Sympathetic Jewel

I say unto you, Love your enemies,
bless them that curse you, do good to them
that hate you, and pray for them which
despitefully use you, and persecute you.
MATTHEW 5:44 KJV

Am I AFRAID
OF REJECTION?
WHAT WILL
HAPPEN IF I
MAKE THE
FIRST MOVE
TOWARD
SOMEONE
WHO HAS
REJECTED ME?

A man visited a jewelry store owned by a friend. His friend showed him diamonds and other magnificent stones. Among these stones the visitor spotted one that seemed quite lusterless. Pointing to it, he said, "That stone has no beauty at all."

His friend put the gem in the hollow of his hand and closed his fingers tightly around it. In a few moments, he uncurled his fingers. The entire stone gleamed with the splendor of a rainbow. "What have you done to it?" asked the astonished man.

His friend answered, "This is an opal. It is what we call the sympathetic jewel. It only needs to be gripped with the human hand to bring out its full beauty."

People are very much like opals. Without warmth, they become dull and colorless. But "grasp" them with the warmth and love of God, and they come alive with personality and humor. Unlike chameleons, which simply adapt to their background, people who feel embraced by the love of God and His people come alive with colorful personalities all their own.

It's difficult to embrace those who have rejected us. However, if we can look beyond the facade they have erected and see the potential inside them, we can be the healing hands of Jesus extended to them—and bring healing to ourselves in the process.

The safe and sure way to destroy
an enemy is to make him your friend.

Acts of Grace

> Then God saw everything that He had made,
> and indeed it was very good.
>
> GENESIS 1:31 NKJV

When we think of a hippopotamus, the word graceful rarely comes to mind. Rather, we think of the words *fat, ugly,* and *awkward.* There is little to admire in the way a hippo looks or acts—or so we think.

Visitors to a new exhibit at a popular zoo are learning otherwise, however. A large glass aquarium gives visitors an opportunity to watch hippos from a different vantage point—underwater.

They are surprised to discover that even with its short fat legs, bulky body, and oversized head, the hippopotamus is a graceful, strong swimmer, capable of staying underwater for long periods of time. The tiny eyes of the hippo are better adapted to the underwater murkiness of African rivers than to bright sunlight. Indeed, the hippo spends much of its time foraging along the bottoms of rivers.

The main function of the hippo in the natural order appears to be that of "channel clearer." Hippos eat enormous amounts of river grasses that grow along the banks of rivers, thus keeping the river free of blockages that might cause floods.

Ugly? Yes. But hippos are gifted in unusual ways and have a valuable role to play. Every day you will encounter people who may seem awkward, different, ugly, or without much purpose. Look again! God has created each element of nature—plant, mineral, bird, fish, and animal—to fulfill a specific purpose and to do so with unique talents and abilities. There is an element of beauty, gracefulness, and goodness in everything He creates.

Have I JUDGED SOMEONE BY OUTWARD APPEARANCES RATHER THAN BY WHAT'S IN THEIR HEART?

Everywhere I find the signature,
the autograph of God.

Words of Life

Thou hast lifted me up, and hast not
made my foes to rejoice over me.

PSALM 30:1 KJV

Have I
REACHED OUT
TO SOMEONE
IN NEED OF
A FRIEND?

A convict had just been released from prison. He had spent three long years in prison for embezzlement, and though he wanted to return to his hometown, he was concerned about being rejected by the townsfolk. Still, he was lonesome for his home and decided to risk the worst. He had barely set foot in town when he ran into the mayor himself.

"Hello!" greeted the mayor. "I'm glad to see you! How are you?" The man appeared ill at ease, so the mayor moved on.

Years later, the former mayor and the ex-convict accidentally met in another town. The latter said, "I want you to know what you did for me when I came out of prison."

"What did I do?" asked the mayor.

"You spoke a kind word to me and changed my life," replied the grateful man.

We cannot always know how important the seed of a kind word may be to the one who receives it. More often than we know, words of encouragement or recognition provide a turning point in a person's outlook on life.

Just as Jesus spoke with love and acceptance to the hated tax collector Zacchaeus, the mayor set the tone for others' contacts with the ex-convict by addressing him as a neighbor. People watch those they respect for cues regarding their own relationships with certain people.

Genuine, kind words cost the giver nothing but can mean the world to the one receiving them.

Be kind; everyone you meet
is fighting a hard battle.

The Language of Love

You were called into the fellowship
of his Son, Jesus Christ our Lord.
I CORINTHIANS 1:9 NKJV

A student working on her doctoral thesis spent a year on a reservation living with a group of Navajo Indians. As the student did her research, she became part of a Native American family. She slept in their home, ate their food, worked with them, and generally lived their lifestyle.

The grandmother in the family did not speak English, yet she and the student were able to form a close bond of friendship. They spent much time together, forging a relationship that was meaningful to each one, yet difficult to explain to anyone else. The two shared experiences together although they could not talk with each other.

Over the months each one of them worked to learn phrases in the other one's language. When the year ended, it was time for the student to return to campus to write her thesis. The tribe held a going-away celebration in honor of her.

As the student climbed into her pickup truck to leave, the old grandmother came to say good-bye. With tears flowing down her cheeks, she put her hands on either side of the student's face and said: "I like me best when I'm with you."

Good friends are the ones around whom we "like ourselves best" because they have a way of bringing out the best in us.

All the best stops in our nature are
drawn out, and we find music
in our souls never felt before.

Who COMES TO MIND WHEN I THINK OF BEING "MY BEST" AROUND THEM?

Sweet Revenge?

If thine enemy hunger, feed him; if he thirst, give him drink: for in so doing thou shalt heap coals of fire on his head. Be not overcome of evil, but overcome evil with good.
ROMANS 12:20-21 KJV

How CAN I
EXTEND GRACE
TO SOMEONE
WHO HAS
WRONGED ME?

A young, hot-tempered officer in the Army struck a foot soldier. The foot soldier felt the insult deeply, but military discipline forbade him to return the blow. "I will make you repent it," he said to the officer.

One day in the heat of battle, the foot soldier saw an officer who was wounded and separated from his company. He forced his way through enemy lines to the officer, whom he recognized as the one who had insulted him. Nevertheless, he supported the wounded man with one arm as the two fought their way back to their own lines.

The officer grasped the hand of the soldier. "Noble man! What a return for an insult so carelessly given!"

The young man smiled and said, "I told you I would make you repent it." From that time on they were as brothers.

John Wesley found another positive way to settle quarrels. In his journal he wrote of a disagreement that took place in a church gathering. Fourteen people were expelled from the group as a result. Wesley called the entire group together to try to bring about reconciliation.

Prior to the service, Wesley recalls, "I willingly received them all again; requiring only one condition of the contenders on both sides, to say not one word of anything that was past." Healing took place in the group when the recounting of old wounds was eliminated.

Extending God's grace to those who have wronged us can repair just about any broken relationship. Instead of returning anger with anger, kindness proves the best peacemaker.

By taking revenge, a man is but even with his enemy; but in passing over it, he is superior.

Secret Chambers

> Behold, I stand at the door, and knock: if any man
> hear my voice, and open the door, I will come in
> to him, and will sup with him, and he with me.
>
> REVELATION 3:20 KJV

A nurse on duty in a pediatric ward often gave the children an opportunity to listen to their own hearts with her stethoscope. One day she put the stethoscope into a little boy's ears. She asked him, "Can you hear that? What do you suppose that is?"

The little boy frowned a moment, and then he broke into a grin. "Is that Jesus knocking?"

Another story is told of a group of students who went to visit a great religious teacher. The wise teacher asked the young scholars a seemingly obvious question. "Where is the dwelling place of God?"

The students laughed among themselves. "What a thing to ask! Is not the whole world full of His glory?"

The learned old man smiled and replied, "God dwells wherever man lets Him in."

Imagine your life to be a house of many rooms. Each room represents a different aspect of your life. Some of the rooms are messed up, others are clean and tidy. The doors that are locked represent areas where you have not invited Jesus to enter.

Like the little boy, when we hear Jesus knocking at the closed doors of our lives, it is up to us to open the door and let Him in. Even those rooms that are dark and frightening are filled with light and understanding when Jesus enters.

You need not cry very loud;
He is nearer to us than we think.

IS THERE A "ROOM" OF MY LIFE THAT I HAVEN'T OPENED TO JESUS?

True to Yourself

The Lord looks on the heart.

I SAMUEL 16:7 NRSV

Am I MY TRUE
SELF AROUND
THOSE
CLOSEST
TO ME?

A father tells of his young daughter who, like many American girls, had a large collection of dolls. Modern dolls, he noted, are far different from their predecessors. Today dolls can walk and talk, drink and wink, slurp, burp, cry, sigh, and laugh—almost anything a real baby does, including wet itself and get diaper rash.

After years of buying the most expensive dolls for his daughter, the man wondered which was her favorite. To his surprise, he found she especially liked the small rag doll she had been given on her third birthday. The other dolls had caught her eye, but the rag doll had won her heart.

To the little girl, the rag doll was real, and she loved it just the way it was—missing both eyes and most of its hair. Through the years the doll was still what it had always been—just itself.

Within every person lies the innate desire to be loved, accepted, and pleasing to others. But if we spend all our energy trying to be something we are not, we will never know the joy of being loved for who we are.

Be yourself! Genuine love is not a reward for performance or achievement. People may like or admire you for what you can do, but they will love you for who you are.

Likewise, try to see past others' outer appearances and love them for who they are.

We are so accustomed to wearing
a disguise before others that we
are unable to recognize ourselves.

God's Masterpiece

Now we see through a glass, darkly; but then
face to face: now I know in part; but then
shall I know even as also I am known.

1 CORINTHIANS 13:12 KJV

French painter Claude Monet painted the world in a new way. In one of his most famous works, *Impression: Sunrise,* he used only color to create a composition. With no outlines, shapes were only suggested and blurred. His purpose was to catch a fleeting moment; moments later, the sun would be in another position, the small boat would have moved, and all would look different.

Working outdoors, Monet painted landscapes directly from nature. He had to work quickly, before the light changed, leaving little time to worry about fine detail. He wanted to catch just a glimpse of a particular moment in time. The altering light allowed him to see the same object in different ways. Monet often painted a series of paintings of the same subject to show these different appearances as the light changed.[14]

God's radiant light shapes our perspective of life. The struggles we face on earth are fleeting moments compared to spending eternity with God. Difficult situations can sometimes blur our ability to see God's best for us, because we are seeing only a small glimpse of what God is doing.

Staring at the unfinished canvas of our lives, we tend to miss the beauty of the masterpiece in progress. We may see only splashes of color without form or reason, never stepping back to visualize the entire spectrum of experiences that brought us to this point in our lives.

Spend time in God's illuminating presence. It will refresh your outlook and give you a different way of looking at life's daily problems, as the Master completes the composition within you.

DO I SEE MYSELF AS GOD SEES ME?

It isn't your problems that are bothering you.
It is the way you are looking at them.

Hidden Character

Finally, beloved, whatever is true, whatever is honorable,
whatever is just, whatever is pure, whatever is pleasing,
whatever is commendable, if there is any excellence and if
there is anything worthy of praise, think about these things.
PHILIPPIANS 4:8 NRSV

What

FORMED THE
PILLARS OF
CHARACTER IN
MY LIFE? DO I
BEAR ANY
RESEMBLANCE
TO MY HEAV-
ENLY FATHER?

Hidden beneath the Chihuahuan Desert in New Mexico lies one of God's great wonders, Carlsbad Caverns. Over the centuries, tiny drops of water built a startlingly beautiful monument forty feet high. Drop after drop, depositing particle after particle, a marble-like finger begins to grow. Ultimately, this process forms a great pillar; thus, the cavern's sculptures are created.

A similar process goes on inside each of us. As a single thought finds its way into our minds, it leaves sediment that sinks deep down within our souls, forming our own pillars—pillars of character. If we let immoral, selfish, and violent thoughts fill our minds, we form eroding pillars of evil and failure. If we fill our minds with truth and love, we form strong and beautiful pillars within our souls.

In Proverbs 23:7 KJV, King Solomon said, "For as he thinketh in his heart, so is he." Solomon understood that the things we dwell on determine the person we become. When we pursue God, we begin to reflect His character in our lives.

You can become the person God has designed you to be by renewing your mind daily in the Word of God. Just as the Carlsbad Caverns were developed over time, hidden from view, so our own true character is built.

The mind grows by what it feeds on.

Spin Cycle

This Book of the Law shall not depart
from your mouth, but you shall meditate
in it day and night, that you may observe
to do according to all that is written in it.
JOSHUA 1:8 NKJV

Have you ever watched a scary movie before going to bed and then had a frightening dream? The last thing we think about before we doze off settles deep within our subconscious mind. Like clothes in a washing machine on the spin cycle, thoughts spin around all night in our minds. They often return to our consciousness as the first thought we have in the morning.

King David said in Psalm 4:4 (NKJV), "Meditate within your heart on your bed and be still." Before you fall asleep, think about God's Word and what God is doing in your life. Ask yourself, *What is the condition of my spirit? Am I fulfilling God's plan for my life?* These questions will not only deepen your relationship with God, but also expand your knowledge of Him.

Meditate on God's Word as you lie in bed at night. By spending time going over and over a Scripture, you can draw from it the depth of its meaning. The Bible reminds us to be transformed by the renewing of the mind.

Tonight, read a passage or two of Scripture. As you drift off to sleep, meditate on it. When you wake, you will have "meditated" all night on God's Word, waking refreshed and renewed. Then in the morning, you can praise God as King David did: "My voice You shall hear in the morning, O LORD; In the morning I will direct it to You, and I will look up" (Psalm 5:3 NKJV).

HOW HAS
GOD'S WORD
CHANGED
MY LIFE?

Think often on God, by day, by night, in your business, and even in your diversions. He is always near you and with you; leave Him not alone. You would think it rude to leave a friend alone who came to visit you; why, then, must God be neglected?

Faithful Soldiers

Fight the good fight of faith.
I TIMOTHY 6:12 KJV

HOW DO I REACT WHEN THINGS DON'T GO MY WAY? AM I OPEN TO CHANGING MY ATTITUDE?

Joseph, a seventeen-year-old patriot of the American Revolution, clutched his musket to his chest and leaned into the bitter wind. Valley Forge was twelve miles away; he realized the Army had a long and painful march ahead of them.

This is how he described the circumstances: "We were literally starved. I did not put a morsel of victuals into my mouth for four days and as many nights, except a little black-birch bark which I gnawed off a stick of wood. I saw several of the men roast their old shoes and eat them.[15]

The last few miles to Valley Forge were uphill, and the weary soldiers struggled to keep going. Because of the lack of supplies and the barrenness of the surrounding countryside, the men were without adequate shelter, food, or clothing; they lived in crude huts built by their own hands. Many died of starvation and cold. This was one of the darkest periods of the American Revolution. Yet it was at Valley Forge in February 1778 that the Army was trained, disciplined, and reorganized. And despite all the hardships they suffered, these soldiers continued the fight for America's independence.

How many of us today would endure such extreme hardships for our beliefs? During hard times, we are trained and disciplined to endure the stresses of life and appreciate the blessings of God. Tonight, ask God for the stamina to help lead others to the kind of freedom that can be found only in Christ.

Adversities do not make a man frail;
they show what sort of man he is.

The White Cane

> Rise in the presence of the aged, show respect for
> the elderly and revere your God. I am the LORD.
>
> LEVITICUS 19:32

The first time Cathi saw Hank, a cantankerous old man, he was leaning over the receptionist's desk with his white cane raised high and yelling at the top of his lungs. Part of Cathi's job as a student volunteer for the state's social services division was to visit elderly residents in their homes with their caseworker, but Hank couldn't wait. He was letting the whole office know about his problems.

She was nervous the first time she accompanied the caseworker to Hank's house. He acted out with his usual yelling and cane-waving, probably just to see how fast they would run. But Cathi detected an undercurrent of sadness in the old man. Hank had outlived all his family and friends, including his wife. He had no children. Cathi thought of how lonely life must be for Hank. Maybe his cane-waving was a bid for attention, the way a two-year-old throws tantrums.

Over the course of the next year, Cathi and the caseworker visited Hank many times. They found him to be an intelligent man whose body had just gotten too old for him; he simply couldn't do the things he wanted to do.

We have much to learn from the elderly; they form a bridge from the past to the present and to the future. Do you have a "Hank" in your family or neighborhood? That person may suffer from loneliness, just as Hank did.

Nothing is more beautiful than
cheerfulness in an old face.

HOW CAN I
MAKE THE DAY
A LITTLE
BRIGHTER FOR
A LONELY
ELDERLY
PERSON?

Footsteps of Faith

Lift your drooping hands and strengthen your
weak knees, and make straight paths for your feet.
HEBREWS 12:12-13 NRSV

DO I KNOW
GOD'S PATH
FOR MY LIFE?
WHAT CAN I
DO TO STAY
ON COURSE?

John loved to run and walk in the park during the mild winter weather where he lived. So he was surprised one morning in mid-January when he discovered that the area had been covered with a blanket of snow during the night. Since he was up early anyway, John decided to go ahead and run on the graveled jogging trail in the park. No one had been out yet to leave footprints in the snow, but he had been on the trail often enough to know its general direction and its twists and turns. John forged a path along the trail, leaving the prints of his shoes in the snow. After several laps, other joggers joined him on the course, following in his footprints.

Later that day, John returned to the park to walk his dogs. As he walked around the jogging trail, he noticed that the melting snow showed the route of the graveled trail in many places. It differed from the path of footprints. Now that the path was partially visible, people followed it rather than the footprints in the snow.

John thought about the way he lived his life. Most individuals follow an established way rather than forging their own path. It is a unique person who breaks away and makes his own footsteps. Did he know God's pathway well enough to walk in it when faced with uncertain circumstances? Did he set a course so that those who followed him would not be misled?

All of us have doubts as we go through life, but if we study God's Word and keep our eyes on Jesus, we can follow in the footsteps of our faith. We can make footprints for those who come after us.

God made the moon as well as the sun;
and when he does not see fit to
grant us the sunlight, he means us
to guide our steps by moonlight.

MicroWave Friends?

> There are "friends" who pretend to be friends, but
> there is a friend who sticks closer than a brother.
>
> PROVERBS 18:24 TLB

DO I KEEP MY FRIENDS AT ARMS' LENGTH? HOW CAN I CULTIVATE REAL, LASTING FRIENDSHIPS?

When Sara was a little girl and went to visit her grandpa, he would set her on the kitchen counter and let her watch him make popcorn in the popcorn machine. Those special times with Grandpa and the popcorn machine were not to last. Grandpa discovered the convenience of microwave popcorn. It was easy, cheap, and quick.

Now when Sara visits him, Grandpa asks her to put a bag into the "micro" and "nuke" it. It only takes one person to stick a bag of popcorn into the microwave. Sara misses those precious moments of making popcorn with him.

Have we become a generation of microwave friends—friends who are here one minute and gone the next? We used to call this type of friend an acquaintance—someone to have lunch with, go shopping with, or see a movie with once in a while. It is enjoyable sharing our time with these people, but we know they are not the friends who would sacrifice themselves to help us in a time of need.

The individual we can count on and whom we would sacrifice our needs to help in all circumstances is our true friend. This is the person we have spent time with, cried with, and rejoiced with—the person we have a history with and have taken the time to discover who and what they are like. Friendship is a relationship that stays strong—no matter what.

Real friendship is shown in times of trouble;
prosperity is full of friends.

Tested by Trials

The fire will test each one's work, of what sort it is. If anyone's work which he has built on it endures, he will receive a reward. If anyone's work is burned, he will suffer loss; but he himself will be saved, yet so as through fire.
1 CORINTHIANS 3:13-15 NKJV

What ARE SOME "FIERY TRIALS" IN MY LIFE RIGHT NOW? HOW WILL TRUSTING GOD IN THE MIDST OF HARDSHIP CHANGE ME AS A PERSON?

On the slopes of the rugged Sierra Nevada, the giant sequoias inhabit a forest realm they have ruled for millennia. From the mists of the ancient past they have emerged—a symbol of an incredible will to survive. Over the years the sequoias have had to adapt to endure. The most important of these adaptations has to do with fire, since lightning storms are common in the foothills of the forest.

These trees have developed a thick, fire-resistant bark that burns poorly. Although a particularly hot fire may succeed in burning a tree and leaving a scar, a healing process begins almost immediately. New bark creeps over the wounds until the breach is covered and fully protected again.

Natural fires also provide optimum conditions for germination. Hot updrafts dry and open old cones, releasing seeds that shower the forest floor. The freshly burned floor, now cleared of undergrowth and competing trees, allows the seedlings access to sunlight and minerals in the soil.

The fires, or trials of life, that we endure also help to burn away the undergrowth and weeds that prevent us from maturing in the Lord. Weeds such as greed, pride, and ungratefulness must be removed in order for us to bear fruit in our lives.

Just as the seedlings need sunlight and minerals to survive, we thrive on God's light by entering His presence through prayer and receive nourishment by reading His Word. Although the trials of life are painful to bear, God is there to begin the healing process and protect us during those times.

Afflictions make the heart more deep,
more experimental, more knowing
and profound, and so, more able
to hold, to contain, and beat more.

Spotlight

> His anger is but for a moment; his favor
> is for a lifetime. Weeping may linger for
> the night, but joy comes with the morning.
>
> PSALM 30:5 NRSV

As a teenager, LuAnne entered a national beauty pageant. She'd won several other beauty contests, but this was the first time she would compete nationally. She wanted to win more than anything. Taking home a national title would boost her self-esteem, eliminating all her problems—or so she thought.

The night of the contest, LuAnne carefully applied her make-up and slipped into a pink chiffon evening gown. Onstage, she smiled and walked with elegance. For the talent portion, she sang better than ever. Later, the announcer read, "And the winner is . . . Miss Kentucky!" The applause roared in her ears. *Finally,* she thought, *I'm somebody!*

But when LuAnne returned home, she realized she still had problems just like everyone else. In fact, her life was filled with more stress than before the contest. She traveled around the country giving speeches while trying to maintain high academic grades. In addition, she had to meet deadlines for television and newspaper interviews.

After months of a hectic schedule, LuAnne felt drained of all energy. She looked forward to the day when her reign as a beauty queen would end and a new girl would take her place. She wanted her old life back so she could spend time with her friends.

Our stress-filled problems may seem to offer no solutions, but there is hope. We can find joy and peace and contentment by staying close to our Father. God promises not to give us more than we can bear.

Hope not only bears up the mind under sufferings but makes her rejoice in them.

Am I OVER-WHELMED IN SOME AREA OF MY LIFE? WHAT STEPS CAN I TAKE TO FIND REST IN GOD?

Forgive and Forget

"If you do not forgive men their sins,
your Father will not forgive your sins."
MATTHEW 6:15

Am I IN
BONDAGE TO
BITTERNESS
BECAUSE
OF UNFOR-
GIVENESS?

One day Corrie ten Boom visited a friend in the hospital. Though her friend was quite ill, Corrie noticed she also was quite bitter. The woman's husband had left her for a younger woman. "Have you forgiven him?" Corrie asked.

"Certainly not!" the woman replied.

Corrie remembered a time when she herself had been unforgiving. After World War II, she had recognized a nurse who was cruel to her dying sister at the Ravensbruck concentration camp. Memories flooded back, and she recalled how her sister suffered because of this nurse.

In that moment, Corrie knew she had not forgiven—but she also knew she must forgive. "Lord," she prayed, "You know I cannot forgive her. My sister suffered too much because of her cruelties." The Lord revealed Romans 5:5 to Corrie: "The love of God is shed abroad in our hearts by the Holy Ghost which is given unto us." Then she prayed, "Thank You, Father, that Your love in me is stronger than my bitterness."

When she finally met the nurse, Corrie told her that she loved her, in spite of the past. By the end of their conversation, the nurse accepted Jesus Christ as her Lord and Savior.[16]

Forgiving someone else is powerful. It is a blessing to the one forgiven, but it also releases the one forgiving from the bondage of bitterness. If you need to forgive someone today, ask God to show you how.

**Life lived without forgiveness
becomes a prison.**

The Highest Name

> My purpose is that they may be encouraged in heart and united in love, so that they may have the full riches of complete understanding, in order that they may know the mystery of God, namely, Christ, in whom are hidden all the treasures of wisdom and knowledge.
>
> COLOSSIANS 2:2-3

Joyce Girgenti, a Christian artist, shares her faith by painting the name of Jesus into her inspirational paintings. One year, Joyce was approached by an organization that wanted her to donate a Christmas card scene. Her first effort, a fireplace scene complete with a Christmas tree and nativity, was turned down. Undaunted, Joyce replaced the scene with another, and it was accepted. Later, Joyce realized why her original scene was rejected—God had other plans.

Joyce had used a photo of her own fireplace to paint the original scene. Working from the top of the canvas, she painted the Christmas tree, the nativity on the mantel, the roaring fire, and the stones that formed the fireplace. As she began to paint the bottom of the fireplace, she turned to her daughter. "Wouldn't it be neat to hide something in the fireplace that refers to Christmas?" she asked.

Before her daughter could answer, Joyce said, "What better than Jesus? He's why we celebrate Christmas." She then arranged the fireplace stones to spell out the name of Jesus. At her daughter's urging, she added a stone that resembled a heart.

After her first card was rejected, Joyce used it to send to clients and friends. The response was overwhelming. People were encouraged when they discovered the name of Jesus hidden in the artwork. Today, Joyce plants the "Name above all names" in each of her inspirational paintings. She also shares her faith with everyone she meets, saying, "If you forget me, you've lost nothing, but if you forget Jesus, you've lost everything."

Only when Jesus is revealed are we able to discern His hidden treasure for us—His gift of salvation.

What DOES THE NAME OF JESUS MEAN TO ME IN A PERSONAL WAY?

Sin separates, pain isolates, but salvation and comfort unite.

A Flash Prayer

Dear friends, since God so loved us, we also ought to love one another. No one has ever seen God; but if we love one another, God lives in us and his love is made complete in us.

1 JOHN 4:11-12

Who CAN I SAY A FLASH PRAYER FOR TODAY? HOW WILL PRAYER CHANGE THE WAY I FEEL ABOUT THIS PERSON?

At school, everyone seemed to feel as Jan did. No one smiled, and everyone seemed to be struggling through the day. She decided to at least change her own outlook. She smiled—not a forced smile, but a caring smile that radiated the love of God. For some, she whispered a "flash prayer" that their day would be blessed by the Father.

As she went about her day, her smiles brought blessings from God in the form of a classmate who rushed to her side to share a funny story, a teacher who privately complimented her reassuring presence in a room full of defiant teens, and a boy who allowed her to take his place in the lunch line.

Jan remembered how a smile began a friendship with a girl no one seemed to like. As they changed into their gym clothes one day at school, the girl returned Jan's smile.

"Hi," she said timidly, not wanting to venture anything more.

Every day Jan got a few more words out of the girl until they shared friendly conversations. As they departed in the hallway for their next classes, Jan whispered a "flash prayer" for this special child of God. "Lord, bless her," she whispered.

Sometimes the most unexpected encounters can teach us a lesson in humility, but the greatest lesson in humility is found in Jesus Christ.[17] Right now, whisper a "flash prayer" for someone you saw today.

As it is the business of tailors to make clothes and of cobblers to mend shoes, so it is the business of Christians to pray.

Starry, Starry Night

The heavens declare the glory of God; and
the firmament sheweth his handywork.

PSALM 19:1 KJV

Remember when you were a kid, lying on your back outdoors, staring up at the stars and moon? How relaxing it was to gaze at the shimmering lights and simply dream! Everyone needs a quiet time to be alone with God, without television or radio or the Internet. If you can't find quiet time, it's because you've given it away. But you can take it back now.

You are more special than all the other things God created. The psalmist wrote in Psalm 8:3-5, "When I consider thy heavens, the work of thy fingers, the moon and the stars, which thou hast ordained; What is man, that thou art mindful of him? And the son of man, that thou visitest him? For thou hast made him a little lower than the angels, and hast crowned him with glory and honour."

God has a special place in His heart just for you and wants you to know Him intimately. The Lord desires this relationship even more than you do. Having your friendship pleases Him. Don't listen to the lies of the enemy, who tells you that God is angry because you haven't read your Bible lately. As you spend time with God, you will be strengthened. This strength will keep you from throwing in the towel when times get tough.

Make your quiet time top priority. Consider it an appointment with God. Mark on your calendar now the time you plan to spend with God each day, and give it first place.

The Bible grows more beautiful as
we grow in our understanding of it.

Have I GIVEN AWAY MY QUIET TIME TO UNWORTHY THINGS? HOW CAN I RECLAIM THOSE MOMENTS FOR GOD?

Hidden Miracles

I am greatly encouraged; in all our troubles my joy knows no bounds.
2 CORINTHIANS 7:4

Is THERE A
DREAM I'VE
BEEN WAITING
TO PURSUE?
WHAT IS
HOLDING
ME BACK?

Charles Dickens' book *A Christmas Carol* is one of the best-loved stories of all time. But few know that it grew out of one of the darkest periods in the author's career and changed his life forever.

At age thirty-one, and the peak of his career, Dickens was facing serious financial trouble. News that his other novels were not selling well stunned the young man and resurfaced memories of his childhood poverty. He supported a large extended family, and his wife was expecting their fifth child. What would he do?

After months of depression, Dickens was walking through the black streets of London where "bawdy streetwalkers, pickpockets, footpads, and beggars" roamed. The scene reminded him of a recurring nightmare: a twelve-year-old boy working twelve hours a day, six days a week, to earn the six shillings that would keep him alive. Sitting in that dingy, rat-infested warehouse, the boy saw that the light outside was fading, along with his hopes. His father was in debtors' prison, and the boy felt hopeless, abandoned.

The dream was a true scene from Dickens' childhood. Fortunately, his father inherited some money, paid his debts, and was released from prison.

Suddenly, Dickens knew he must write *A Christmas Carol* for those people he saw who could identify with his own fears. Strangely, with Scrooge's change of heart in the novel, Dickens' own depression faded. The much-loved book helped restore his confidence and paved the way to many more treasured stories.[18]

Miracles often hide in the midst of self-doubt and confusion. Focusing on the joys of Christ renews our hope and restores our faith in what God can accomplish through us.

Reflect upon your present blessings
of which every man has many;
not on your past misfortunes
of which all men have some.

A Dime Too Much

"There is nothing concealed that will not be disclosed, or hidden that will not be made known."

LUKE 12:2

The story is told of a young man who was invited to preach at a church in Nashville. On an impulse he preached on the topic of "Thou shalt not steal."

The next morning he stepped onto a city bus and handed the driver a dollar bill. The driver handed him his change, and he walked to the rear of the bus to sit down. Once seated, he counted his change and noticed there was a dime too much. *The bus company will never miss this dime,* he thought.

Then it hit him; he could not keep money that did not belong to him. He made his way to the front and said to the driver, "You gave me too much change."

"Yes, a dime too much. I gave it to you on purpose," the driver said. "You see, I heard your sermon yesterday, and I watched in my mirror as you counted your change. Had you kept the dime, I would have never again had any confidence in preaching."

Our influence is like a shadow; it may fall even where we think we've never been. There are no time-outs when it comes to keeping the Lord's commandments or being true to our consciences.

Stay on track with what you know is right!

Live to explain thy doctrine by thy life.

Have I BEEN HONEST IN MY DEALINGS WITH OTHERS?

The Way

Who, being in very nature God . . . made himself nothing, taking the very nature of a servant, being made in human likeness.
PHILIPPIANS 2:6-7

What DOES THE GRACE OF GOD REALLY MEAN TO ME? DO I POINT OTHERS TOWARD THE WAY?

One evening, a young man refused to attend church with his family. He was a good guy but could not believe the story of God coming to earth as a man. So he stayed at home and waited for his family to return later.

Shortly after, snow began to fall heavily. A loud thud against his front door startled the young man. He opened the front door to investigate and saw a flock of birds, huddled in the snow. In a desperate search for shelter, they had tried to fly through the front window.

Feeling sorry for the birds, he tried to direct them to a shed in the backyard. He opened the shed doors, but the birds would not come. He scattered breadcrumbs on the snow, making a trail to the shed doorway. Still the birds ignored him. He tried catching them and shooing at them. They only scattered.

Realizing the birds were frightened, he thought, *If only I can think of some way to make them trust me. If I could be a bird—talk with them, speak their language—then I could show them the way.*

Suddenly the church bells began to ring. As he listened, the truth dawned. The young man sank to his knees in the snow.[19]

God sent His Son, Jesus, to earth so that He could relate to us and we to Him. The next time your friends are hurt or lonely, let them know someone truly understands what they're going through. That someone is Jesus.

I never ask the wounded person how he feels; I myself become the wounded person.

The Secret Garden

"Love your enemies, do good to them."

LUKE 6:35

Have

I SOWED
SEEDS OF
GOODNESS OR
SELFISHNESS
IN MY LIFE?
HOW CAN I
CHANGE?

Years ago, some townspeople wanted to share God's love in a practical way. They planted a vegetable garden beside the railroad tracks in a deserted area outside of town. The townspeople hoed, planted, and watered the garden until it produced a great harvest.

After working, they laid down their tools in the garden and went about their business, content to let nature take its course.

Over the next year, they planted nothing else and never picked a vegetable. But the garden grew and grew, yet vegetables seldom rotted in the garden. Weeds were scarce, and the garden always seemed to have that "tended" look.

Was it a miracle? Perhaps. An untold number of homeless men riding the railroads—perhaps hundreds—helped themselves to the crops and often spent many hours looking after the garden.

The homeless men could always count on the blessings of good food—especially tasty because it was the fruit of their hard labors.

All around us are people hungry to know that someone cares. Look for practical ways to share the love of Jesus with anyone who needs Him. You may be surprised by the harvest you reap.

Charity sees the need, not the cause.

Great Expectations

Give thanks in all circumstances, for this
is God's Will for you in Christ Jesus.
1 THESSALONIANS 5:18

DO I FEEL
THAT GOD HAS
LET ME DOWN
IN SOME WAY?
TO RESTORE
MY FAITH AND
TRUST IN
HIM, I CAN . . .

Every year Dear Abby prints a familiar story written by Emily Kingsley titled "Welcome to Holland." Emily, a writer, lecturer, and mother of an adult child with Down's syndrome, knows about expectations. Others have asked her what it's like raising a child with disabilities. In her story, Emily uses a metaphor. She compares the expectation of a child's birth to planning a vacation trip to Italy. She mentions the joy of deciding on tourist spots to visit and the anticipation of all the sights you will see upon your arrival.

She then describes the scenario upon landing in your vacation spot. Surely a mistake has been made, because the stewardess on your plane welcomes you not to Italy, but to Holland. You argue, but nothing changes. You are in Holland, and there you will stay.

Anyone who has ever been to Holland knows that tulips, windmills, and Rembrandts make Holland a beautiful place as well. It's just not what you expected. You had planned on going to Italy.

In her poignant illustration, Emily challenges the reader to focus not on unmet expectations (Italy), but on the beauty of where you are (Holland).

When life doesn't turn out perfectly—the way we planned—we have a choice. Whether it's as minor as a holiday gone wrong or as major as a Prince Charming who turned into an ugly frog, God wants us to celebrate our circumstance.

Good when He gives, supremely good,
Nor less when He denies,
E'en crosses from His sovereign hand
Are blessings in disguise.

Molded by God

The inward man is being renewed day by day.

2 CORINTHIANS 4:16 NKJV

When WAS
THE LAST TIME
I FED MY
SPIRIT WITH
THE WORD?
HOW DID IT
CHANGE MY
OUTLOOK ON
THE DAY?

Clay pots were valuable tools in ancient households. People used large jars to store water and olive oil; jugs to carry water; and small terra-cotta vials to hold perfume. Clay storage jars were filled with grain and other foods. Homemakers used clay pots for cooking. In the evening homes were lit by clay lamps.

A modern potter describes her craft like this: "Both my hands shaped this pot. And the place where it actually forms is a place of tension between the pressure applied from the outside and the pressure of the hand on the inside. That's the way my life has been. Sadness and death and misfortune and the love of friends and all the things that happened to me that I didn't even choose. All of that influenced my life. But, there are things I believe in about myself, my faith in God and the love of some friends that worked on the inside of me. My life, like this pot, is the result of what happened on the outside and what was going on inside of me. Life, like this pot, comes to be in places of tension."

All day long we are beaten up by stress, pulled apart by responsibilities, and pressed by challenges. Without strength on the inside, we would collapse under the external pressure.

Today, feed your spirit with Scripture. Time spent with God will keep you strong and restored *within*. Remember, your inner life gives you the strength you need to become a useful vessel in the household of God.

Renew thyself completely each day;
do it again, and again, and forever again.

The Daily Grind

The joy of the Lord is your strength.

NEHEMIAH 8:10 KJV

Has MY JOY
RESERVOIR
RUN DRY?
WHAT CAN
I DO TO
REPLENISH IT?

Most of us have a daily routine—a series of tasks that demand our time and attention. "Routine," says Jewish theologian Abraham Heschel, "makes us resistant to wonder." When we let our sense of wonder and awe drain away, we lose the sense of our preciousness to God.

Jesus recognized our preoccupation with these duties when He said, "Do not worry about your life . . . ." (Matthew 6:25).

But what do these words mean in the real world of relationships, peer pressure, parental conflict, and stress over schoolwork? The "daily grind" can cause us to lose our sense of God's purpose and presence.

Julian of Norwich, a fourteenth-century English mystic, had a perspective that can help restore joy to joyless days. She said, "Joy is to see God in everything." The psalmist wrote, "The heavens declare the glory of God" (Psalm 19:1 KJV), and the prophet Isaiah wrote, "The whole earth *is* full of his glory" (Isaiah 6:3 KJV). The glory of creation is that it points us to the greater glory of the Creator.

If life's routines are wearing down your enthusiasm, look for God in "everything." Be renewed in your joy of who God is—and who you are to Him—and find His strength and purpose in even your most routine tasks.

People need joy quite as much as clothing.
Some of them need it far more.

Holy Humor

> He who sits in the heavens shall laugh.
>
> PSALM 2:4 NKJV

In WHAT AREAS OF MY LIFE DO I NEED TO "LIGHTEN UP"?

Is laughter theologically correct? We rarely think of a knee-slapping belly laugh when we think of being spiritual. But is that God's perspective?

In Umberto Eco's novel *The Name of the Rose*, a villainous monk named Jorge poisons anyone who comes upon the one book in the monastery library that suggests God laughs. Jorge fears that if the monks think God laughs, God will become too familiar to them, too common, and they will lose their awe of Him. Jorge probably never considered the idea that laughter is one of the things that sets us apart as made in God's image!

In her book *Spiritual Fitness*, Doris Donnelly states that humor has two elements: an acceptance of life's incongruities and the ability not to take ourselves too seriously. The Christian faith is filled with incongruities—the meek inherit the earth, the simple teach wisdom, death leads to life, a virgin gives birth, a king is born in a stable. And many of life's incongruities are humorous.

Humor also helps us let go of an exaggerated sense of importance to face the truth about ourselves. Anxiety over our own efforts can obscure what God is doing in our lives. "Lighten up" can be good spiritual advice!

How can we renew our sense of humor?

- Be on the lookout for humor. Almost every situation contains some element of humor.
- Spend time with people who have a sense of humor—their perspective will be contagious.
- Practice laughing. Take a five- to ten-minute laugh break every day.

Laughter is an inexpensive way
to improve your health.

Knowledge Bank

I consider everything a loss compared to the
surpassing greatness of knowing Christ Jesus my Lord.
PHILIPPIANS 3:8

HOW CAN I
GET TO KNOW
GOD BETTER
TODAY?

It's tempting to become a know-it-all. Knowing how to do something, how to fix something, or how to find something gives us a good feeling. We have all experienced the rewards associated with learning new skills and developing them to the best of our ability. We enjoy having others turn to us for answers. Much of our self-esteem is derived from what we know and what we can do.

But there must be a balance. We must face the hard fact that we can never know everything there is to know about anything. We can never achieve perfection of skill to the point where we never make mistakes. In fact, the more we know about something, the more we realize how much we *don't* know. The more proficient our skills, the more we are aware that accidents happen, some days are "off" days, and everyone has a slump now and then.

Some people become obsessed with their own perfection and potential, spending all their available time reading, studying, practicing, and taking courses.

A wiser approach to life, however, is to spend more time knowing God. The more you know Him, the easier it is to trust Him; hear His voice; and show His love to your family, friends, neighbors, and classmates. You will learn the things you need to know in order to do His will. Nothing is as satisfying or meaningful as knowing God and serving others.

Instead of trying to become a bank of information, become a channel of blessing!

Teach me, my God and King,
in all things thee to see; and what
I do in anything, to do it as for thee!

Treasure Hunt

"Friend, go up higher."

LUKE 14:10 KJV

Have I BEEN SETTLING FOR LESS THAN GOD'S BEST IN MY LIFE?

An ancient legend of a swan and a crane tells us about God's goodness—which may be different from what we believe to be good.

A beautiful swan came to rest by the banks of a pond where a crane was wading, seeking snails. For a few minutes the crane looked at the swan and then asked, "Where do you come from?"

The swan replied, "I come from heaven!"

"And where is heaven?" asked the crane.

"Heaven!" said the swan, "Have you never heard of heaven?" And the beautiful swan went on to describe the splendor of the eternal city. She told the crane about the streets of gold and the walls made of precious stones. She told about the river of life, which sparkled like crystal. In eloquent language, the swan described the hosts of saints and angels who lived in the world beyond.

The crane didn't appear the least bit interested in this wonderful place. Eventually he asked the swan, "Are there any snails there?"

"Snails? No, of course not!" replied the swan.

"Then you can have your heaven," said the crane, as he continued his search along the muddy banks of the pond. "What I want are snails."

How many of us turn our backs on the good God has for us in order to search for "snails"? Seek out the good that God has for you today. Ask Him to give you a desire for *His* good, instead of what *you* consider to be good.

Our love for God is tested by the question
of whether we seek Him or His gifts.

Sincere Hearts

Let us draw near to God with a sincere heart in full assurance of faith, having our hearts sprinkled to cleanse us from a guilty conscience.
HEBREWS 10:22

What SINS DO I NEED TO CONFESS BEFORE I LIE DOWN TO SLEEP TONIGHT?

The Internal Revenue Service once received an envelope containing one hundred $100 bills—no name, no address, no note—just money. Someone was feeling guilty. On another day, the IRS received a large box containing a stack of hand-made quilts and a note suggested that the agency sell the quilts to settle the sender's tax bill; the quilts, of course, were returned. Another woman wrote to the IRS and said she felt guilty about cheating on her taxes; enclosed was a check. "If I still can't sleep," she said, "I'll send more."

One of the best examples of a man who listened to his conscience was David. He made many mistakes, but he always admitted it when he did wrong. He was a man who couldn't sleep until he made peace with his Maker.

"For I know my transgressions, and my sin is always before me," he said. "Against you, you only, have I sinned and done what is evil in your sight, so that you are proved right when you speak and justified when you judge" (Psalm 51:3-4).

Confessing our sins brings release from guilt, peace of mind, and restful sleep. As you retire for the night, check your heart. If you find any uncon-fessed sin, ask the Lord for forgiveness, and He will give it. He is faithful and just to forgive you from your sins, and He will cleanse you from all unrighteousness (1 John 1:9 KJV).

A fault confessed is a new
virtue added to a man.

Never Forgotten

"Even the very hairs of your head are all numbered."

MATTHEW 10:30 AMP

Do you ever wonder if God has lost your address? Do you ever think perhaps He has lost track of you or even forgotten you altogether? God's Word answers those thoughts with a resounding, "Not so!"

Jesus taught His followers, "Are not two little sparrows sold for a penny? And yet not one of them will fall to the ground without your Father's leave [consent] *and* notice. . . . Fear not, then; you are of more value than many sparrows" (Matthew 10:29,31 AMP).

The psalmist David also recognized God's intimate knowledge of us. Read these words from Psalm 139 and be encouraged. The Lord not only knows *you,* but He knows precisely what you are facing today. Even if you are not aware of His presence, you can rest assured He is by your side:

O Lord, you have examined my heart and know everything about me. You know when I sit or stand. When far away you know my every thought. You chart the path ahead of me, and tell me where to stop and rest. Every moment, you know where I am. You know what I am going to say before I even say it. You both precede and follow me, and place your hand of blessing on my head . . . I can *never* be lost to your Spirit! I can *never* get away from my God! . . . I can't even count how many times a day your thoughts turn towards me. And when I waken in the morning, you are still thinking of me! (Psalm 139:1-7,17-18 TLB).

Before God created the universe, he already had you in mind.

God IS THINKING OF YOU RIGHT NOW; ARE YOU THINKING OF HIM?

Excess Baggage

Let us lay aside every weight, and
the sin which so easily ensnares us.
HEBREWS 12:1 NKJV

What THINGS
ARE SLOWING
ME DOWN
TODAY? ARE
THEY PHYSICAL
OR SPIRITUAL
NECESSITIES?
HOW WILL MY
LIFE CHANGE
FOR THE
BETTER IF I
THROW THEM
OVERBOARD?

In Jules Verne's novel *The Mysterious Island,* he writes of five men who escape a Civil War prison camp by hijacking a hot-air balloon. As they rise into the air, they realize the wind is carrying them over the ocean. Watching their homeland disappear on the horizon, they wonder how much longer the balloon will stay aloft.

As the hours pass and the surface of the ocean draws closer, the men decide they must cast some of the weight overboard because they have no way to heat the air in the balloon. Out go their shoes, overcoats, and weapons, and the uncomfortable aviators feel their balloon rise.

However, it isn't long before they find themselves dangerously close to the waves again, so they toss their food overboard. Unfortunately, this too is only a temporary solution, and the craft again threatens to lower the men into the sea. One man has an idea: they can tie the ropes that hold the passenger car and sit on them. Then they can cut away the basket beneath them. As they do this, the balloon rises again.

Not a minute too soon, they spot land. The five jump into the water and swim to the island. They are alive because they were able to discern the difference between what was really needed and what was not. The "necessities" they once thought they couldn't live without were the very weights that almost cost them their lives.

If you eliminate the excess "baggage" from your life, you will have more time for the things that really matter.

It's not enough to be busy . . . the question is:
What are we busy about?

The Price of Peace

Let your yea be yea; and your nay, nay;
lest ye fall into condemnation.

JAMES 5:12 KJV

In his book *Up from Slavery*, Booker T. Washington describes an ex-slave from Virginia who made a contract with his master two or three years before the Emancipation Proclamation. The contract stated that he could "buy" his freedom by paying so much for his body per year. He was allowed to work where and for whom he pleased.

Knowing he could earn better wages in Ohio, the man went there. When the Civil War ended, the man still owed his master $300. Though the Emancipation Proclamation freed him from this obligation, he walked most of the way back to Virginia and paid the full amount, with interest.

"In talking to me about this, the man told me that he knew that he did not have to pay his debt, but that he had given his word to his master, and his word he had never broken," Washington writes. "He felt that he could not enjoy his freedom till he had fulfilled his promise."

Although born into slavery, the man Washington describes obviously knew his worth. More important, he knew that as a child of God, his word should be trustworthy. He knew he would sleep peacefully if he kept his word to others.

Be aware of all the times you make promises to people, and make sure you follow through. Not only will you sleep more peacefully, but your friends, family, and neighbors will have a new respect for you as well.

Self-respect is the noblest garment with which a man may clothe himself.

Have I MADE PROMISES I HAVE NOT KEPT? HOW CAN I MAKE THINGS RIGHT WITH THOSE WHOM I'VE WRONGED?

Weeds

> "While you are pulling the weeds,
> you may root up the wheat with them.
> Let both grow together until the harvest."
> MATTHEW 13:30

What "WEEDS" MIGHT GOD BE USING IN MY LIFE RIGHT NOW?

One year a potato farmer encountered some problems due to hot weather. Because potatoes are a very temperamental crop and must be in the ground a certain period of time, the farmer was concerned that the planting be done according to schedule.

The weather broke, however, and he planted the potatoes only five days late. As the cultivation program began, everything looked good except for two plots where weeds began to grow out of control two weeks before the harvest. It was too late to destroy the weeds. The farmer had to let them keep growing.

Another more severe problem emerged when a truck strike interfered with the targeted harvest date. The farmer knew that leaving his potatoes too long in the Arizona summer heat would destroy the crop. In the meantime, the "carpet weeds" flourished and provided an almost blanket-like protection over the potatoes, while taller weeds gave additional shade. Later, as the harvesters examined the fields, they discovered that wherever the weeds had grown up, there was no spoilage of potatoes. In weed-free areas, the potatoes were ruined because of the heat. The weeds saved his crops from spoilage.

God often uses seemingly adverse circumstances to shield and shade us from "spoilage" in our lives. The very weeds we chafe about—petty irritations, things that don't go our way, annoying people—are often the means He uses to enhance our growth and develop a harvest of godly character in us.

Strength and growth come only through continuous effort and struggle.

A Day Like No Other

He is not here, for He has risen, just as He said.
MATTHEW 28:6 NASB

What WOULD
MY LIFE BE LIKE
WITHOUT
JESUS?

Along the road called the Via Dolorosa in Jerusalem are shops with vendors touting their wares. Two centuries ago, when Jesus was on His way to Calvary, He trudged that same path, notably called The Way of Suffering.

Was that day like all others? Was everything business as usual? Farmers bringing in fruit and vegetables for selling; skinned animal meat hanging in stalls, ready for the butcher. Noise and shouting all around; bargain hunters negotiating prices. Boys playing loudly in the narrow streets; Roman soldiers striding past black-robed Hebrews, hurrying home for the Sabbath. "Just another crucifixion," a woman groans while buying a trinket. Were people too busy to even look up when Jesus made that lonely walk along the rugged cobblestones?

Amid the noise and congestion and pressing crowds, one may long for the solitude and peace of the garden where Jesus was buried after the Crucifixion. A holy hush rests in that sacred place. From the Via Dolorosa to the garden tomb to living within our hearts, Christ comes to us in victory over death, sin, and the obstacles of every-day life. Nothing about His life, death, and resur-rection is "business as usual."

Because He is risen, the world is changed forever. We are changed forever.

Our Lord has written the promise of
the resurrection not in books alone,
but in every leaf in springtime.

Good Seasoning

He went away again a second time and prayed,
saying, "My Father, if this cannot pass away
unless I drink it, Thy will be done."
MATTHEW 26:42 NASB

Do I REFLECT
CHRIST'S LOVE?
WHAT CAN I
DO TO BE A
LIGHT IN THE
DARKNESS
AROUND ME?

The Garden of Gethsemane, located on the Mount of Olives in Israel, contains an olive tree thought to be more than two thousand years old. Perhaps it is the same one Jesus knelt beneath when He agonized in prayer prior to the Crucifixion.

The Israelites were familiar with the procedure of making oil from the olives through a process of pressing that took about three days. Olive oil became a staple used for food and cooking. To this day, virgin olive oil is much favored by gourmet cooks. In biblical times, olive oil was burned in lamps as a source of light. It was used in preservation, anointing, and healing. There is much spiritual significance associated with olive oil.

Perhaps it is no wonder that Christ knelt beneath an olive tree as He chose the path of the Cross. When we follow Him, we reflect His love; we are a good seasoning for the world; and we are lights in the darkness. When we place our trust in Him, we are preserved until He comes again.

Today the Garden of Gethsemane is a favorite spot for visitors from around the globe. For each person, regardless of race or religion or background, the olive tree stands as a constant reminder of God's grace and redeeming love.

The grace of God is infinite and eternal.
As it had no beginning, so it can have
no end, and being an attribute of God,
it is as boundless as infinitude.

Columbines

> The city has no need of the sun nor of the moon to
> give light to it, for the splendor and radiance (glory)
> of God illuminate it, and the Lamb is its lamp.
>
> REVELATION 21:23 AMP

Despite endless cloudy days that spring, the columbines still managed to bloom. Blue, scarlet, and gold bell-shaped flowers with delicate dangling spurs towered over lacy foliage. Their bright colors attracted hummingbirds. Yet, without enough sunlight, they didn't seem as radiant as in previous springs.

It is the same with humans. Although we follow our genetic codes and grow into healthy people physically, we have no radiance without the Son of God. The windows of our souls appear cloudy, and God's love cannot shine through us.

Just as columbines hunger for the sun's warm rays, our souls hunger for the loving presence of Jesus. Unlike the columbines, however, we can find the Son even on cloudy days of despair.

We can take action to find the Son by simply reading or listening to His Word and obeying it. We can meet Him in a flower garden, where each stem and blossom appears like signposts to His presence. We can hear His praises being sung by the rustle of leaves held in the tree's uplifted branches.

Getting to know Him in a personal way refreshes our souls. His love fills our hearts and lifts our spirits. The Scriptures tell us that in heaven, the sun will not be needed because God himself will be our Light. Take a quiet moment with the source of all Light today, and thank Him for His presence in your life.

The glory of God, and, as our only means to
glorifying Him, the salvation of human souls,
is the real business of life.

When I FEEL DOWN, DO I LOOK TO GOD FOR A HEART-LIFT?

Thirsty Souls

"If any man is thirsty, let him come to Me and drink.
He who believes in Me, as the Scripture said, 'From
his innermost being shall flow rivers of living water.'"

JOHN 7:37-38 NASB

Have I
ALLOWED
JESUS TO FILL
MY SPIRIT
WITH HIS
LIVING WATER?

Plants thrive on slow, deep watering that wets the earth to a depth of four to six inches. When dry weather hits, the plants are more likely to survive, even if they receive water only once a week. Also, watering in the evening hours decreases the evaporation factor that steals moisture from the plants. One thing is certain, healthy plants that produce lush foliage and beautiful fruit or flowers demand plenty of water applied to their roots. Plant experts say the occasional sprinkling here and there seems to do more damage than good.

Just as plants get thirsty, we get thirsty too. When the Samaritan woman at the well met Jesus, He explained to her that physical water is temporary, but spiritual water is eternal (John 4:13-14). To bear fruit, we need the Living Water of Christ dwelling within. If we're always in a hurry and just read a Bible verse here and there, our roots remain shallow and can wither in dry seasons. Through spending extended times alone with God in prayer and in reading His Word, we develop inner sustenance for trials that come.

When we let God put His Living Water in our hearts, not only does He satisfy our spiritual thirst, but He also helps us to grow. In return, we can be a nourishing fountain to others.

Wherever the Son of God goes,
the winds of God are blowing,
the streams of living water are flowing,
and the sun of God is smiling.

Life Force

> "Other seeds fell into the good soil and as they grew up and increased, they yielded a crop and produced thirty, sixty, and a hundredfold."
>
> MARK 4:8 NASB

A century ago a German princess lay dying. While on her deathbed, she requested that her grave be covered with a large granite slab and that stone blocks be placed all around the slabs to seal the grave. She also gave orders for the granite and stones to be held together with large fasteners made of iron. At her request, the inscription in the top of the stone read, "The burial place, purchased to all eternity, must never be opened."

Apparently during the burial, a tiny acorn found its way into the grave. Sometime later, a small shoot began to push its way up through a thin crack in the granite slab. The acorn was able to absorb just enough nourishment to grow. After years of growth, the mighty oak tree broke through the aging iron clamps. The iron was no match for the oak, and the clamps burst, exposing the grave that was never to be opened. New life sprang forth from a deathbed and one tiny seedling.

Every day we are given numerous opportunities to take advantage of fresh new starts. New beginnings often come when something else has ended. When we allow sin to die in our hearts, we find new life in Christ. Perhaps it is no accident that the mighty oak, which is one of the tallest and strongest trees in the world, starts from a tiny little seed.

What seems to be the end may really be a new beginning.

Lord, PLANT A SEED IN ME TODAY THAT GROWS INTO A MIGHTY OAK TREE OF FAITH!

Lighted Pathways

Thy Word is a lamp to my feet,
and a light to my path.
PSALM 119:105 NASB

HOW CAN I
LIGHT A
"CANDLE" IN
MY WORLD
TODAY?

In the 1800s, a monk in Belgium named Walter Denham placed a candle on top of each one of his well-worn leather shoes. With the candles lighted, he could overcome the darkness of the cold stone abbey one step at a time.

Even the smallest light in the right location can illuminate a large area. Such is the case in Israel's museum to honor the children who were killed in the Holocaust. Only six candles light the museum. How? Because they are strategically placed in front of various-angled mirrors, magnifying the flames and casting light throughout the rooms.

Perhaps you are in a set of dark circumstances now—either things you cannot control or habits that you cannot break. You may just feel lonely and empty inside. Just as Walter used the candles to light his physical way, you can find your spiritual way.

Do you need light for your soul today? Relying on God for assistance is like reaching for a lamp in the darkness. As morning light dispels the dark night, the Word of God exposes darkness in our hearts and illuminates truth about a Heavenly Father who cares.

Darkness is the absence of light. But since God is Light, then in Him there is no darkness at all.

God is the light in my darkness,
the voice in my silence.

Distinct

We dare not make ourselves of the number, or compare
ourselves with some that commend themselves:
but they measuring themselves by themselves, and
comparing themselves among themselves, are not wise.

2 CORINTHIANS 10:12 KJV

What SPECIAL QUALITIES DO I BRING TO THOSE AROUND ME? DO I TRULY APPRECIATE THE UNIQUENESS IN ME AND OTHERS?

Butchart Gardens is one of the most famous tourist attractions in Victoria, British Columbia. The elaborate display dates back to 1904, when Jenny Butchart decided to transform part of her husband's limestone quarry into a sunken garden. The result is a botanical wonder that is truly a work of art.

Walking through the colorful grounds, it is impossible to choose the most outstanding exhibition. All the plants are healthy and well attended. Each one provides colorful blossoms that are distinct, yet make a significant contribution in the overall scheme and design.

Likewise, part of our spiritual growth is to realize our importance in God's garden, especially when we exercise the talents and abilities He has given us. At times we may feel inferior about our own gifts, and we compare ourselves unfavorably with others. Yet God designs different people just as He created various kinds of flowers. The lily and the rose each have their own features. In fact, every blossom has its own unique characteristics. Tulips, lilacs, and hyacinths are not alike, yet each kind of flower adds a particular fragrance and beauty to any arrangement.

The same is true in life. Take a few moments to make an inventory of your gifts. You possess unique qualities that no other human being has ever held. Then ask the Holy Spirit to guide you. Through His power, you can make a difference in the lives of others as well as your own.

Give what you have. To someone,
it may be better than you dare to think.

APRIL 27

Thou shalt teach them diligently unto thy children, and shalt talk of them when thou sittest in thine house, and when thou walkest by the way, and when thou liest down, and when thou risest up.
DEUTERONOMY 6:7 KJV

When ASKED ABOUT MY OWN "STORY," DOES MY ANSWER INCLUDE JESUS?

The Polynesians are strong believers in teaching the next generation the history of their families. They sit around and "talk story." They speak with excitement as they tell the children about their ancestry. The younger generation sits in rapt attention, soaking up every detail. The history of these families is passed down in story form that anyone can easily understand. The children pay special attention so that when they grow up, they will be able to pass the family history down to yet another generation.

The animated film *The Prince of Egypt* depicts the story of the Israelites' escape from slavery and search for a Promised Land. Modern Jews still tell these same stories as part of their Passover celebration. Traditionally, the youngest child asks why certain foods are eaten and certain traditions are practiced. The answers are told in story form, reflecting on events that occurred thousands of years ago and that have been passed on from generation to generation.

Jesus taught by telling stories that anyone could understand, even the youngest and most uneducated. Now, more than two thousand years later, those parables are still told. Stories about a wayward son, about planting seeds, about searching for a lost coin, and about showing kindness to others are timeless messages about the kingdom of God.

If a picture is worth a thousand words, then a story must be worth a thousand pictures. Take time to tell others the amazing story of your life— what God has done in and through you.

History is a story written by the finger of God.

Time for Change

> It had been planted in good soil by abundant
> water so that it would produce branches,
> bear fruit and become a splendid vine.
>
> EZEKIEL 17:8

Kelly approached her employer and said, "I've had two years of experience on this job, and I'm still making the same hourly wage I made when I started. It's time I got a raise."

Her boss retorted, "You haven't had two years of experience. You've had one experience for two years!"

Many of us feel that our lives could be described in the same way: one experience over and over again—or at best, boringly few experiences. When this is the pattern of our lives, we not only become depressed, but we also have no growth. We need the enrichment of activities and experiences to broaden our lives and stimulate our souls.

Joseph Campbell once said, "I don't believe people are looking for the meaning of life as much as they are looking for the experience of being alive."

How can we enrich our lives? It must be intentional. Don't think that someone else can do it for you. There are multitudes of ways to get started:

- Take up a sport you always wanted to play.

- Treat your best friend to a movie.

- Be spontaneous—do something you've put off for a long time.

- Volunteer to do work that will help the less fortunate.

- Get involved in a place of worship that challenges you.

In experiences such as these, you will find the Source of all the excitement that you can handle.

Experience is the mother of truth;
and by experience we learn wisdom.

Am I IN A RUT, SPIRITU-ALLY OR EMOTIONALLY? WHAT CAN I DO TO STIMULATE NEW GROWTH IN MY LIFE?

Tested by Fire

He has said to me, "My grace is sufficient
for you, for power is perfected in weakness."
2 CORINTHIANS 12:9 NASB

Who MIGHT
BE WATCHING
MY ACTIONS—
AND
MEASURING
THE VALIDITY
OF CHRIST
THROUGH
THEM—TODAY?

The lodgepole pine is a tall, stately tree found in the high Western mountains. Commonly seen in Yellowstone National Park, the hard wood of the tree is valuable for making railroad ties and poles. Its needle-shaped leaves grow in bundles and produce fruit—a woody pine cone—which takes two years to mature.

An interesting feature of the lodgepole is its response to fire. When flames attack the tree, the heat causes the cones to burst. The seeds are then dispersed and natural reforestation occurs. New growth begins, and a fresh forest eventually replaces the charred remains.

During life's trials, the fruit of our lives is also tested. Our spiritual maturity is revealed by how we respond. Do we see God's hand at work, even when our hearts are scorched by pain and sorrow? Have we become intimately acquainted with our Savior so that we know He will somehow use it for good?

When a teenaged boy was near death, friends gathered at the hospital to pray with the parents. Another mother, grieving over the loss of her own son, watched the praying group. She later received Christ as a result of the family's testimony. Both mothers shared a tremendous loss; but they also share a bright hope of one day seeing their sons again in heaven.

After enduring the fires of adversity, we often learn that others have been watching with powerful results. Through trusting Him, our barren souls burst into life and yield fruit for His glory.

It is not our trust that keeps us, but the
God in whom we trust who keeps us.

WorkWise

> Then the Lord God took the man and put him into
> the Garden of Eden to cultivate it and keep it.
>
> GENESIS 2:15 NASB

Thomas Edison, probably the greatest inventor in history, once said, "I never did a day's work in my life. It was all fun."

He changed the lives of millions with his inventions of the electric light and the phonograph. He also helped perfect the motion picture, the telephone, and the electric generator. Edison patented more than eleven hundred inventions in sixty years.

What was the secret of his success? He defined it himself as "1 percent inspiration and 99 percent perspiration." Perhaps Edison's greatest contribution to modern society was his attitude toward work.

Have you ever thought about the fact that God worked? After He completed His creation work in six days, He rested on the seventh. Some people think work was a condemnation upon human beings after Adam's sin. But work was part of Adam's life from the very beginning. God created Adam in His image, and He placed him in the Garden of Eden to cultivate His creation.

Work has its rewards and laziness its consequences. The ant is a good worker. It busily gathers food for the winter without anyone giving a command. In like manner we are to initiate work ourselves and do our best. Paul reminds us not to grow weary of doing good. Work may not always be fun, but it is essential and gives us a sense of accomplishment that nothing else can bring.

It is our best work that God wants,
not the dregs of our exhaustion.
I think He must prefer quality to quantity.

What IS MY
ATTITUDE AS I
WORK—AT
SCHOOL, AT
HOME, AND
ELSEWHERE?

Seasons of Life

Sow with a view to righteousness, reap
in accordance with kindness; Break up your
fallow ground, for it is time to seek the Lord
until He comes to rain righteousness on you.
HOSEA 10:12 NASB

Which
EXPERIENCES
HAVE TAUGHT
ME THE
MOST IN LIFE?

At a dinner party honoring Albert Einstein, a student asked the great scientist, "What do you actually do as a profession?"

Mr. Einstein said, "I devote myself to the study of physics."

The student exclaimed, "You mean you're still studying physics? I finished mine last year."

It's tempting to divide life into seasons and think of each season as an end within itself. Students may think of the high school diploma as the goal and not relate it to what they want to do with their lives. Graduates may get a good job and never consider that other jobs could be in their futures.

How often have you seen an engaged couple spend thousands of dollars and hundreds of hours preparing for the wedding, with little or no preparation for the years of marriage ahead? Or the couple may look forward to the birth of a child, with no plan for proper parenting.

Life is a continuing cycle of seasons. Those who reap the greatest harvests seem to look both backward and forward. They look to the past to glean from their experiences those things that will help solve the challenges of today. They look to the future to decide which seeds they should plant today to help them attain their goals for the future.

God is present in every segment of our lives, coaxing us to learn from both our experiences and our goals, so that we will reach our full potential.

Though God be everywhere present,
yet He is present to you in the deepest
and most central part of the soul.

Life's Calling

> We say with confidence, "The Lord is my helper; I will not be afraid."
>
> HEBREWS 13:6

He was a skinny kid, although he was a junior in high school. And to his younger brother, it was unbelievable how loudly Don wheezed when his asthma struck in full force. About once a month, Bobby would be awakened by the sound of Don gasping for breath. Just as soon as he could suck in air, Don would shake and gasp for the next breath. Sometimes their parents would rush him to the emergency room for treatment.

The doctors said the hot, sticky atmosphere and the smog of downtown triggered the attacks. They advised Don to stay indoors during the summer months when the humidity was highest. The doctors said that if he stayed indoors, he might be spared the worst of his attacks.

The problem was that Don and his church youth group conducted street revival services every Friday evening, and Don was usually the one to preach. He was determined never to miss an opportunity to fulfill his life calling. So, he continued to preach, no matter the weather, and every once in a while he would fight off the asthma attacks. He counted the cost and decided to take the risk.

More than thirty years later, Don is a seasoned missionary in South America. His dedication to sharing the Good News continues to provide inspiration for others. And he still never misses an opportunity to preach. For his brother, Don's Friday-night bravery remains a source of encouragement as he too grows in his faith.

Trustfulness is based on confidence in God, whose ways I do not understand. If I did, there would be no need for trust.

What WOULD I RISK IN ORDER TO FULFILL THE GREAT COMMISSION?

God Whispers

He Will command his angels concerning
you to guard you in all your Ways.
PSALM 91:11

Some OF
THE INNER
PROMPTINGS
I'VE HAD
LATELY . . .

Author Charlie Shedd once told about a time when he felt God's touch. He believes angels have often made themselves known to him by a pressure, a touch, a warning, or an urging. According to Shedd, the Bible often uses "the hand of God" to reveal His presence.

One evening as Charlie drove into his garage at suppertime, he turned off the automobile ignition but found that his fingers just wouldn't let go. "What's going on here?" he asked out loud.

An inner voice seemed to say, *Go see Roy.* From the spot in his heart where he conversed with God, he knew the Holy Spirit was giving a command. Charlie argued, "But it's suppertime." And God's voice seemed to say, *Supper can wait, Charlie. Go.*

Charlie drove to Roy's house less than a mile away, where he found him on the floor, calling for help. He had tripped over a stump, breaking his glasses and cutting his face.

Later, Roy thanked him for coming, then asked, "How did you know I needed you?"

"I think it was an angel, Roy."

"Makes sense. I was lying there on the floor, praying you'd come," the old man said.

How many times have you heard the quiet voice of the Holy Spirit urging you to respond? How many times have you dismissed Him? Pray this day that God will open your heart to His whisperings. If you listen, you will hear Him in the place where you and the Lord hold a dialogue.

The voice of God is a friendly voice.
No one need fear to listen to it unless he
has already made up his mind to resist it.

New Shoes

> "The King will reply, 'I tell you the truth, whatever you did for one of the least of these brothers of mine, you did for me.'"
>
> MATTHEW 25:40

As the Depression continued, the kitchen cabinets remained empty. Money was scarce. Their father had deserted the family, so the oldest brother Jerry hit the road to try to earn some money. The air was bitterly cold and the ground frozen.

As Jerry walked, he saw some men digging a hole beside the road. "Can I help?" he asked.

"Sure," one of the men said and handed him a shovel.

Jerry worked hard. For hours he dug in the bitter cold through frozen dirt while sleet pelted the ground. The men handed him a few coins before quitting. The teenager stopped by the corner market to buy some canned goods for dinner that night.

As he walked out of the store, the sleet turned to rain. He had placed cardboard inside his shoes to replace the worn-out soles, and that worked until the freezing water soaked his socks and feet. He sat down on the ground to adjust the cardboard.

"Son, are those the only shoes you have?" a man in uniform asked.

"Yes, sir," Jerry replied.

"Come with me," the man said, and he took him to a shoe store down the street, where he bought Jerry his first pair of brand-new shoes.

As Jerry's family enjoyed the meal he had earned that day, the love of Jesus—and the memory of a kind man in uniform—brought tears to Jerry's eyes. He thanked God for taking care of them all, even in the worst of times.

Love goes without, that another may have.

God HAS TAKEN CARE OF ME AND THOSE I LOVE. WHEN I MOST NEEDED HIM, HE . . .

Life Storms

> We know that in all things God works for the good of those who love him, who have been called according to his purpose.
> ROMANS 8:28

How CAN
I DRAW
CLOSER TO MY
FAMILY TODAY?

One cold winter day in the 1960s, a major ice storm hit central Georgia. Power outages were rampant throughout the area. Some people owned fireplaces or gas heaters, but others who were less fortunate were forced to seek shelter in the homes of their neighbors.

One particular family didn't have any source of heat except for the gas stove in their kitchen. For days, while they huddled together around the kitchen table, the heat from the oven kept them warm.

They could cook, but some of their hapless neighbors could not. Many nearby residents brought over cans of soup to heat on their stovetop. Hospitality intensified as a bitter cold spell set in.

Sitting around that table in the glow of a single candle, the family laughed and shared stories and events that were important to each of them. They hadn't done that in months! While the television was out of order, they put their lives back into place. As a result of that storm, the family grew closer. Each one of them remembered the light from that candle for years afterwards.

Sometimes we don't realize what's missing in our lives until we stop all our busyness. Spending quality family time together is important to God. But you don't need to wait for an ice storm or some other crisis to draw close to those you love.

God is so good that He only awaits
our desire to overwhelm us
with the gift of himself.

Cherished Things

Godliness with contentment is great gain.
For we brought nothing into the world,
and we can take nothing out of it.
I TIMOTHY 6:6-7

When Ginger lost the sapphire ring that had belonged to her mother, she was devastated. The ring had been passed on to her after her mother died that November. Ginger planned to have the ring sized to fit her smaller hand. For safekeeping, she placed the ring into a plastic bag and soon forgot about it altogether.

As winter turned into spring, a friend planned a garage sale. Ginger decided to donate an old chest of drawers that she no longer needed. Afterwards, she realized that her mother's jewelry had been inside the chest of drawers, and it was now sold.

Fortunately, Ginger's friend had the phone number of the woman who had bought some of the jewelry. Relieved, Ginger called but was shocked when the woman denied having any of the valuable pieces.

Furious, Ginger's anger and resentment began to build. Finally, her best friend said, "Try to remember it was only a worldly possession. I know it's hard, but let it go." Ginger eventually turned the situation over to God and prayed for deliverance from her anger. Two years passed. One day, the woman who had bought the jewelry called and said her own mother had died. Suffering with back pain, the woman had been unable to attend her mother's funeral. She returned the cherished ring to Ginger, and within a short time the woman's back pain disappeared.

In Philippians 4:11, Paul says, "I have learned the secret of being content in any and every situation."

Am I CLINGING TO SOMETHING THAT NEEDS TO BE RELINQUISHED TO GOD?

Peace of heart and mind is better
than material possessions, no matter
how much we cherish them.

Teenage Trauma

Charm is deceptive and beauty is fleeting, but a woman who fears the Lord is to be praised.
PROVERBS 31:30

Have I SHUT MY PARENTS OUT OF MY LIFE? HOW CAN I IMPROVE COMMUNICATION BETWEEN US?

"But, Mom, all the girls are wearing black lipstick," Audrey cried.

"I don't care if they're wearing blue lipstick," her mom said. "You are not going out of this house dressed like a witch!"

Audrey stomped her foot and flounced out of the kitchen, and her mom winced as she heard her slam the bedroom door. First it was mini-skirts and a pierced nose, and now this. She fumed as she slapped mustard on a ham sandwich for Audrey's school lunch. What on earth was she going to do about that girl?

Remember when you wore mini-skirts and white go-go boots? the still, small voice of God reminded her. *Remember pale pink lipstick and bare midriffs?*

Yes, Lord, she argued inside, *but You don't approve of her rebellion, do You?*

God seemed to answer, *I loved you even when you were still in your sins.*

Carol did love her daughter, despite Audrey's outrageous behavior. And she had to admit that she'd done some pretty stupid things herself when she was her daughter's age. Carol sighed. She didn't want to drive her daughter away like her own mother had done to her.

"Audrey," she said, tapping at the door. "Can we talk?"

"Go away!" Audrey sobbed.

"Please?" Gently, Carol opened the door and sat down on the bed beside her daughter. "I love you, you know. That's why I care so much. Talk to me."

Keep the lines of communication open between you and your parents. Someday you'll be glad you did!

God comes to us in theater [in] the way we communicate with each other, whether it be a symphony orchestra, or a wonderful ballet, or a beautiful painting, or a play.

Godly Confidence

A heart at peace gives life to the body.

PROVERBS 14:30

Sam's eyes widened. There, atop the best sledding hill in Connecticut, her eighty-year-old grandmother was preparing for the ride of her life. Poised on the toboggan, she sat upright, her long fur coat wrapped around her legs and her fur cap pinned perfectly into place. A small push with her hand and she was off.

Halfway down the hill, the toboggan toppled to the side, and Sam watched in horror as her grandmother tumbled three times before sliding to a halt. Running full tilt to the rescue, Sam arrived breathless in front of the disheveled lump of fur that was her grandmother.

"Are you all right?" Sam cried. "Nana, are you OK?"

Bright, mischievous eyes met Sam's fearful gaze. With a confident laugh, Nana grabbed hold of Sam's hand. "Again! Let's try it again!"

That afternoon outing—followed by laughter and steaming mugs of hot chocolate around the kitchen table—made for a memorable winter day.

Whether it's an attempt at sledding or risking the exposure of your heart, God offers us the peace that brings comfort in the midst of life's chaos. In fact, it gives Him great pleasure. If we ask, God will give us the confidence to step into life's adventures, knowing that His hand will always be there to catch us.

The circulation of confidence is better than the circulation of money.

In WHAT AREA OF MY LIFE DO I LACK GODLY CONFIDENCE?

Expectations

The LORD has compassion on those who fear him;
for he knows how we are formed.

PSALM 103:13-14

DO I EXPECT
TOO MUCH
FROM OTHERS?
HOW DO I
FEEL WHEN
SOMEONE
PLACES
UNREALISTIC
EXPECTATIONS
ON ME?

"Watch out! Can't you be more careful?"

It seemed like Jackie had been saying those words far too often to six-year-old Katie. This time her sister's love of ketchup had resulted in a large tomato stain on Jackie's favorite pair of khakis, left hanging over the back of a chair near the ironing board. It had been a long day, and Jackie's temper flared as the angry words escaped her lips. But as the words tumbled out, she saw a tear slip out of the corner of Katie's eye.

Jackie felt terrible. She knew Katie had not intentionally squirted ketchup all over the table.

"I'm sorry I yelled at you, Katie," she said. "Will you forgive me?"

Katie nodded a reply, and they locked in a soggy embrace for several seconds.

Later, while finishing her homework, Jackie thought again of the ketchup incident. She thought about how much Katie had changed since she was a baby, when Jackie dressed her up as if she were a baby doll. As Katie matured, Jackie forgot too easily that she was still only six years old. She often expected her to behave as if she were nine or ten.

Thankfully, God isn't like that. Yes, He has expectations for us, but He readily forgives us when we do something wrong. He restores broken relationships and gives us direction for living. Best of all, God remembers how He made us. And in His compassion, He never expects more from us than He knows we can do or be.

Tis expectation makes a blessing dear;
Heaven were not heaven
if we knew what it were.

A Balanced Life

I desire to do your will, O my God;
your law is within my heart.

PSALM 40:8

IS MY LIFE TOO CROWDED WITH ACTIVITIES? WHAT CAN I LET GO IN ORDER TO GAIN A BETTER BALANCE?

Carl tried with all his might to follow God. He attended church faithfully. Several nights a week he volunteered at a mission downtown. On other nights, he attended youth meetings at church. He had a part in every program and every event the church sponsored. Being such a dedicated Christian, all the other kids looked to him for advice. He was the big man on campus at the youth group, and he prided himself on his spiritual maturity.

One night when Carl arrived home from his after-school Bible study, his family was not there. Dinner was nowhere in sight, and he didn't know how he'd get to church later on for his youth leadership meeting. After another hour, his family still had not returned, so he finally called a friend and bummed a ride to the meeting.

When he arrived home later that evening, everybody was preparing for bed. Upset, Carl asked his mom where they had been.

"We were at Keith's sports award banquet, honey. You were supposed to be there too, remember?" she replied.

Carl hung his head. At that moment, he realized he had neglected his own family while seeking to serve others for God. Yet his family had been patient and understanding with him.

Are you working too hard for God and sacrificing the most important gift of all—the love and welfare of your family and friends?

It's interesting—the way in which one has to balance life—because you have to know when to let go and when to pull back. . . .

The Wrong Color

Don't link up with those who will pollute you.
I want you all for myself. I'll be a Father to you;
you'll be sons and daughters to me.
2 CORINTHIANS 6:17-18 THE MESSAGE

Have I STARTED TO HANG OUT WITH THE WRONG CROWD? HOW DO MY FRIENDS' BEHAVIORS AFFECT ME?

Has a red shirt ever ended up in your washing machine with a load of whites? What happens? Pink socks for everyone. The red shirt may not seem to fade much, but it sure leaves its mark on everything around it.

The same thing happens when you spend a lot of time with people who do things that go against God's law of love. You begin to pick up their "hue." Consider using God's name as a curse, for instance. This may not be a habit you've struggled with, but after spending time with people to whom it's second nature, you may not notice it much anymore. It may even seem humorous, at times. The next thing you know, words you never thought you'd say are slipping out of your mouth.

This doesn't mean you should never spend time with people whose values differ from God's. You can't love people without spending time with them. But if their habits begin influencing your own, watch out. You soon may find yourself in hot water.

Good company and good discourse
are the very sinews of virtue.

Captive Thoughts

God wants you to be holy and to stay away from sexual sins.
He wants each of you to learn to control your own body in
a way that is holy and honorable. Don't use your body
for sexual sin like the people who do not know God.

I THESSALONIANS 4:3-5 NCV

It all began with a thought—harmless enough. But that thought led to another. Which became a second look. Which progressed to a minor indiscretion. Which gave birth to a lie. Which led to rationalization. Before Michael knew it, he was having sex with a girl from the fast-food restaurant where he worked nights and weekends. His friends wondered how Mr. Righteous could have gotten involved in something like this.

Turning away from God is like setting up a line of dominoes. A little dishonesty here. A white lie there. A secret habit off in the corner somewhere. One by one, each domino is placed right behind the other. All it takes is a little added pressure for the whole line to come tumbling down.

Other people can't see your every thought, but God knows them intimately. And if it all begins with a thought, it can end there as well. Willpower is useless. (Try *not* thinking of a pink elephant!) God's power is the only answer. Ask Him to help you "take your thoughts captive," as the apostle Paul said. With His Spirit living inside you, all things are possible!

What we think about when we are free
to think about what we will—that is
what we are or will soon become.

Do I ENTERTAIN THOUGHTS THAT CAN ONLY LEAD TO BAD ACTIONS? WHY IS WILLPOWER INFERIOR TO GOD POWER?

Keep Running!

It is God who arms me with strength and makes
my way perfect. He makes my feet like the feet
of a deer; he enables me to stand on the heights.
2 SAMUEL 22:33-34

**Am I
PERSISTENT
WHEN THE
GOING GETS
ROUGH?**

Bob Kempainen was determined to make the 1996 U.S. Men's Olympic marathon team. He was willing to go to any lengths, no matter how gut-wrenching. On a hilly course in Charlotte, North Carolina, he won the trials—but was sick five times in the last two miles.

Kempainen, the American record-holder in the marathon, has experienced stomach troubles since junior high school. But that hasn't kept this medical student from pursuing marathoning.

"To stop was out of the question," he said, when asked about his physical condition. With the goal in sight, he knew there would be plenty of time to rest after the race and five months to prepare for the Olympics.

When God puts a desire in your heart to achieve a specific goal, you can have the confidence that He will give you the strength and the ability to accomplish it. We all face difficulties and challenges on the road to success—and the difference between those who succeed and those who fail is simply persistence.

Life is not a level, smooth path but rather a series of hills and valleys. There are times spent on the mountaintop, and there are times when we feel like we're wandering around in a dark cavern, feeling our way along and trusting God for every step of faith.

Be persistent in your faith—God will lead you, pick you up when you have fallen, give you strength to go on, and ultimately bring you to victory.

**Obstacles are those frightful things you see
when you take your eyes off the goal.**

The Maze Walk

> We have this treasure in earthen vessels,
> that the excellence of the power
> may be of God and not of us.
>
> 2 CORINTHIANS 4:7 NKJV

Ihara Saikuku, the author of *The Millionaire's Gospel*, had this to say about the challenges we all face in the pursuit of personal success: "To be born thus empty into this modern age, this mixture of good and ill, and yet to steer through life on an honest course to the splendors of success—this is a feat reserved for paragons of our kind, a task beyond the nature of the normal man."

Interestingly, Saikuku wrote this more than three hundred years ago! He lived from 1642 to 1693. What was true about human nature three hundred years ago is still true today.

Each one of us is born into what may be likened to a maze—with many options for false starts, unproductive detours, and dead ends. The person who makes wise choices is most likely to make it through the maze of life successfully.

The analogy of a maze holds true for each day also. In any given day, we face numerous opportunities to make wrong turns or give in to temptation instead of taking that big leap of faith to continue in God's plan for our lives.

The Scriptures would agree with Saikuku that steering an honest course is "beyond the nature of the normal man." However, this ability to make good moral choices is regarded by Scripture as evidence of the Holy Spirit at work in a person's life. It is the Spirit who helps us choose good and refuse evil.

Whenever you are faced with a decision today, ask the Holy Spirit to guide you. Ask Him to show you the way through today's maze!

HOW CAN I KNOW WHETHER A DECISION IS RIGHT OR WRONG? DOES GOD GIVE ME CLUES IN HIS WORD?

Before us a future all unknown, a path untrod;
beside us a friend well loved and known—
That friend is God.

Faulty Assumptions

The pride of thine heart hath deceived thee,
thou that dwellest in the clefts of the rock,
whose habitation is high; that saith in his heart,
Who shall bring me down to the ground?
OBADIAH 1:3 KJV

Have I BEEN
TOO QUICK TO
ASSUME THE
WORST ABOUT
SOMEBODY?
WHAT OTHER
SCENARIOS
MIGHT
ACCOUNT
FOR THEIR
BEHAVIOR?

A teenaged traveler at an airport went into a lounge and bought a small package of cookies to eat while reading a magazine. Gradually, she became aware of a rustling noise. Looking from behind her paper, she was shocked to see a neatly dressed man helping himself to her cookies. Not wanting to make a scene, she leaned over and took a cookie herself.

A minute or two passed, and then she heard more rustling. He was helping himself to another cookie! By this time, they had come to the end of the package. She was angry but didn't dare allow herself to say anything.

Still fuming later when her flight was announced, the girl opened her purse to get her ticket. To her shock and embarrassment, there was her pack of unopened cookies!

It's so easy to make assumptions about what is happening around us. We expect things to be a certain way based on past experience, what we know, or what we have been told about a situation. Assumptions are not always wrong, but they are never to be trusted. Too many times they lead to embarrassment and even destruction.

The Bible tells us that assumption is based on human reasoning and the driving force behind it is pride. As Obadiah 1:3 says, it is pride—thinking we know everything—which allows us to be deceived.

Avoid prideful assumptions by walking in God's love. See other people and situations through His eyes. After all, your vision is limited, but He knows exactly what's going on!

Pride is at the bottom of all great mistakes.

The Voice of Wisdom

My conscience is clear, but that does not make me innocent. It is the Lord who judges me.

1 CORINTHIANS 4:4

Do I REGARD MY CON-SCIENCE AS A FRIEND OR AN UNWANTED NUISANCE?

Author Rolf Zettersten writes about his good friend, Edwin, who bought a new car. The car had lots of extra features—including a recording of a soft female voice, which reminded him if he failed to fasten his seat belt or was running low on fuel.

On one of his many road trips, the voice informed him he needed to stop and fill his tank. "Your fuel level is low," the voice cooed. Edwin nodded his head knowingly and thanked her with a smile. He decided, however, that he had enough gas to take him at least another fifty miles, so he kept on driving.

The problem was, in only a few minutes the voice spoke the warning again—and again and again and again until Edwin was ready to scream. Although he knew, logically, that the recording was simply repeating itself, it really seemed as though the voice spoke more and more insistently each time.

Finally, he'd had all he could take. He pulled to the side of the road and, after a quick search under the dashboard for the appropriate wires, gave them a good yank. *So much for that "extra feature,"* he thought.

He was still feeling very smug for having had the last say when his car ran out of gas! Somewhere inside the dashboard, he was almost certain he could hear the laughter of a woman's voice!

God has given us a built-in warning voice. It's called the conscience. Sometimes we may think it's a nuisance, overly insistent, or just plain wrong. However, most of us will learn sooner or later that it is telling us exactly what we need to know. Follow it today, and see if you don't experience more peace about every decision you make.

I will place within them as a guide
My Umpire Conscience, whom if
they will hear, Light after light well
used they shall attain, And to
the end persisting, safe arrive.

Take a Breather

The Lord God formed man of the dust of the ground,
and breathed into his nostrils the breath of life.

GENESIS 2:7 NKJV

The AREAS OF
MY LIFE IN
WHICH I NEED
A BREATHER
ARE . . .

The fast-paced, relentless duties of life often cause us to declare with a sigh, "I need a breather." We may be voicing more truth than we realize! Medical researchers have discovered that for virtually every person who *works*—whether at physically demanding manual labor or intellectually demanding white-collar labor—performance level improves when a person breathes properly.

Good breathing is defined as regular, deep, and slow. The opposite—uneven, shallow, and rapid—is a sure sign to most physicians that something is seriously wrong. Good breathing is essential for good health. It supplies oxygen to the bloodstream, which is vital for the functioning of all bodily organs, especially the heart and brain.

The Scriptures tell us that God breathes His life into us both physically and spiritually. Jesus breathed upon His disciples to impart the Holy Spirit to them. (See John 20:22.) The early church experienced the Holy Spirit as a rushing, mighty wind—a manifestation of the breath of God. (See Acts 2:1-2.)

Today in our personal lives, an awareness of the Spirit of God working in us is often experienced as a fresh breeze, one that cleanses and revives us in every part of our being. The word *inspiration* literally means to have the things of the Spirit put *into us*.

We do well to take a periodic "breather" in the Lord's presence. When we do, we find our spirits are refreshed and renewed at a level deeper than the superficiality of our daily routine.

Rest is the sweet sauce of labor.

Who's Watching?

That ye would walk worthy of God, who hath
called you unto his kingdom and glory.

1 THESSALONIANS 2:12 KJV

Roy had been a kidnapper for twelve years, but while in prison he invited Jesus Christ into his life. Several years later he was paroled, and just before he went out, he was handed a two-page letter written by another prisoner, which said:

"You know perfectly well that when I came into the jail, I despised preachers, the Bible, and anything that smacked of Christianity. I went to the Bible class and the preaching service because there wasn't anything else interesting to do. Then they told me you were saved, and I said, 'There's another fellow taking the Gospel road to get parole.' But, Roy, I've been watching you for two-and-a-half years. You didn't know it, but I watched you when you were in the yard exercising, when you were working in the shop, when you played, while we were all together at meals, on the way to our cells, and all over, and now I'm a Christian, too, because I watched you. The Saviour [sic] who saved you has saved me. You never made a slip."

Roy says, "When I got that letter and read it through, I broke out in a cold sweat. Think of what it would have meant if I had slipped, even once."

Who might be secretly watching you? A class-mate, a sibling, a boss, or a family member who needs to know Jesus? You are His representative to those people.

A good example is the best sermon.

When OTHER
PEOPLE WATCH
ME, WHAT DO
THEY SEE?
HOW MIGHT
I WANT TO
CHANGE?

Anchored Hope

He will not fear evil tidings;
His heart is steadfast, trusting in the Lord.

PSALM 112:7 NASB

Did I LEAVE
HOME
WITHOUT MY
"ANCHOR"—
MY HOPE IN
JESUS—TODAY?

No one knows for sure when ships were first used for water transportation. The earliest evidence of sailing vessels dates from Egypt about the third millennium B.C. Since then, ships have changed considerably.

Today's passenger and cargo ships have no oars, sails, or masts. Modern vessels have all the conveniences of a great luxury hotel—gourmet cuisine, an array of entertainment, recreation, even swimming pools! One thing, however, has remained remarkably the same—the anchor. Except for the differing sizes, the anchor on Paul's ship of the first century and the anchor on the *Queen Elizabeth II* of the twentieth century are not much different.

The same could be said of human life. Technology has brought staggering changes in virtually every arena of our lives. However, people are still people. We experience the same struggles, temptations, joys, hopes, and sorrows of our ancestors—and our souls still need an anchor.

When Paul and his companions were shipwrecked on the coast of Malta, they dropped four anchors, which kept the ship from being dashed against the rocks. The writer of Hebrews tells us we have an anchor—our hope in Jesus Christ. Just as no experienced sailor would go out to sea without an anchor, we must never go anywhere without Jesus!

Hope is like the sun, which,
as we journey toward it, casts the
shadow of our burden behind us.

Heart Gifts

Inasmuch as ye have done it unto one of the least
of these my brethren, ye have done it unto me.
MATTHEW 25:40 KJV

HOW CAN I
MAKE EACH
DAY OF THE
YEAR SPECIAL
FOR SOMEONE?

Twenty large toy boxes lined the front of the auditorium. The lids were open, with the names of children visible on the inside of each. As families arrived, parents came forward with their children and placed gifts in the appropriate toy box. It wasn't long until every single toy box was filled to the brim.

The highlight of the service that morning was not the sermon; it was the choir from the children's home—the very same children for whom the toy boxes were filled. They sang with transparent gratitude to God. This was their Christmas, and the small church in Austin, Texas, was their family.

Later that evening, Heather looked up at her father and asked, "Dad, do those kids really not have a mom or dad?"

"Yes, that's true," he replied.

"Well, then I feel good that we gave them presents, but won't they be sad without a mom and dad?"

"Sweetheart, I am sure that there are days in their lives when they are very sad. But I also know that they are very special to Jesus. And because of people like you and your brother, they know that they are loved."

What is a true gift? One for which
nothing is expected in return.

Sowing Peace

"Blessed are the peacemakers,
for they shall be called sons of God."
MATTHEW 5:9 RSV

What KIND OF SEEDS AM I SOWING IN MY LIFE? WILL I REAP A GOOD HARVEST BECAUSE OF MY ACTIONS?

The entire European continent felt the blows of hatred delivered by the evil tyrant Adolf Hitler. Millions of people died as a result of his platform of hate; millions more were scarred for life.

Heinz was an eleven-year-old Jewish boy who lived with his family in the Bavarian village of Furth during the 1930s. When Hitler's henchmen came tearing through the village, Heinz's father lost his job as a schoolteacher. Recreational activities were forbidden, and Furth's streets became battlegrounds.

Neighborhoods were terrorized by the Hitler youth looking to make trouble. Heinz always kept alert to stay clear of them. When he saw them coming, he sought cover to get out of their way.

One day, Heinz couldn't avoid a face-to-face encounter with a Hitler bully. A brutal beating seemed inevitable, but Heinz walked away from the fray without a scratch. This time he used his persuasive abilities and language skills to convince his enemy that a fight was not necessary. This would not be the last time this young Jewish boy would use his peacemaking skills in Hitler-occupied Europe.

Eventually Heinz and his family escaped to safety in America, where Heinz would make his mark. He became known as a mediator and peacemaker among world leaders and nations. The young boy who grew up as Heinz anglicized his name when he came to America. We know him as Henry Kissinger.

Today, put your talents to use as a peacemaker and work together with those of different opinions. When you sow seeds of peace, you are doing God's work on earth, and you will reap a harvest of goodness.

First keep the peace within yourself,
then you can also bring peace to others.

Legacies

Good will come to him who is generous and lends
freely, who conducts his affairs with justice.

PSALM 112:5

Marian Wright Edelman, attorney and found-
ing president of the Children's Defense Fund, often
speaks of how Martin Luther King had a profound
impact on her life. All Americans have been
affected by Dr. King's life in some way, and most
have heard his famous comment, "I have a
dream." But it was not his public persona that had
an impact upon her; it was his willingness to admit
his fears.

She writes, "I remember him as someone able to
admit how often he was afraid and unsure about his
next step. . . . It was his human vulnerability and his
ability to rise above it that I most remember."

She should know about rising above fear and
uncertainty because her life was not an easy one,
and one wonders just how often she drew strength
from the self-honesty and candor of Dr. King.

Ms. Edelman grew up during the days of segre-
gation, one of five children, the daughter of a
Baptist minister. She graduated from Spelman
College and Yale University Law School and was
the first black woman to pass the bar in the state
of Mississippi. She is a prolific writer and has
devoted her life to serving as an activist for disad-
vantaged Americans, especially children.

Hers is an incredible testimony to the belief in
helping others to help themselves. She never
doubted that she could make a difference. We have
the same opportunity. Will we respond as well as
she? Will we help change the world?

Charity is helping a man to help himself.

How CAN
I MAKE A
DIFFERENCE IN
THE PLACES I
GO EVERY DAY?

Instruction Manual

Pay attention and listen to the sayings of the wise.
PROVERBS 22:17

When I MESS UP, IT'S TIME TO REREAD GOD'S "INSTRUCTION MANUAL" FOR LIFE.

Angrily, the young man flung his wrench across the driveway and rolled away from the car. He had been trying for hours to change the brake pads on his small foreign car. It didn't help matters that he was at best a mediocre mechanic. Finally, in exasperation he stormed into the house and informed his father that something was seriously wrong with his car.

"I don't know if anyone can fix it!" he shouted.

His father called his friend, a master mechanic. After he explained the situation, father and son ventured to the nearest library where they found a manual for the car. They made copies of the pages giving directions on how to change the brake pads. Next, they stopped at a foreign-car auto-parts store and purchased a small but vital tool necessary for this particular job. Finally, they proceeded home to the car, and within thirty minutes the repair job was complete.

What made the difference? Three things: first, the young man contacted his father and then a master mechanic. The first instruction God gives us is to call upon Him. Second, they found the right set of instructions and carefully followed them. Sometimes, we insist on trying to do things without consulting the instructions. Finally, they secured the proper tool to do the job. God will always give us the right tool if we will go and secure it.

Whether we are talking about brake pads or critical life decisions, it is amazing how well things work out when we follow instructions.

A single conversation across the table with a wise man is worth a month's study of books.

The Gift of Flight

As each one has received a gift, minister it to one another, as good stewards of the manifold grace of God.

1 PETER 4:10 NKJV

They call their flights "missions." On any given day, the volunteers of AirLifeLine can be called into action to provide needy patients with transportation to hospitals for lifesaving surgeries and medical treatments. Without their assistance, many of the recipients, financially devastated by catastrophic illness, could not afford airfare to reach their medical facilities as quickly as needed.

You might not recognize these angels immediately. With members in all fifty states, AirLifeLine representatives come from every possible profession and walk of life. But they share an enthusiasm for flying and a desire to give something to their communities. These weekend pilots are happy to donate their time, skills, and use of their aircraft to help those in need.

Their passengers are every bit as varied. The case could be a child in need of a kidney transplant or a cancer patient flying to a faraway research center for experimental treatment.

"Every mission I fly is heartwarming. I just thank the good Lord that I can afford to fly an airplane. You get so much back yourself from doing this."

What could be more rewarding than doing something you love and helping others at the same time? The Lord's gifts to us are bountiful, but they are multiplied when we take a talent He has given us and spread it around.

A generous action is its own reward.

What DO I FIND REWARDING IN LIFE? ARE THEY WORTHY ACTIVITIES?

Ripple Effect

O God, thou art my God; early will I seek thee.

PSALM 63:1 KJV

What

PERSONAL
DISCIPLINES
WILL HELP
ME STRUCTURE
A DAILY
QUIET TIME
WITH GOD?

Early in the morning a lake is usually very still—no animals, no people, no noise, no boats, no cars. All is quiet. This is the best time to skip rocks. By taking a small, flat pebble and throwing it at the right angle, you can skip it across the water, leaving circles of ripples every time it makes contact with the lake. The ripples form small and very defined circles at first, then spread out and break apart until they vanish. If several people skip rocks at the same time, the ripples cross over one another and blend together to make miniwaves across the lake. The impact can be pretty amazing.

For most of us, mornings are filled with so many things that need our attention that we find it difficult to spend time alone with God. However, the Lord set a marvelous example for us by rising early to listen to God. If we don't make time for this quiet morning time with God, we often find we don't have time during the day. Then we end up going to bed with regret or guilt. *Maybe tomorrow,* we think. But many times, tomorrow never comes.

When we spend time alone with God at the beginning of each day, we become acquainted with Him and start becoming like Him. Throughout our days, the ripple effect of our time with God in the early morning will impact the lives of those with whom we have contact.

So here hath been dawning another blue day;
think wilt thou let it slip useless away?

Using Your Talent for God

[He has sent me] to bestow on them a crown of beauty instead of ashes, the oil of gladness instead of mourning, and a garment of praise instead of a spirit of despair.

ISAIAH 61:3

Since seventh grade, Sharon had found it difficult to write the kind of poetry she had once loved. And she knew exactly why; she still remembered the December day that her teacher gave the class an assignment to write a poem.

Her poem, so different from those of her classmates, was about the birth of Christ. She rewrote the poem until it shone as though it were the star of Bethlehem itself.

"This is wonderful," the teacher said the next day. "Did you do this all by yourself?"

Beaming, Sharon said she did. Then the teacher read the poem to the entire class. She was beside herself with joy that day.

Several days later, however, the teacher took her aside and accused her of copying the poem from a book. It would be years before Sharon would even attempt to write another poem. Then one day, with Christmas again approaching, she wrote several Christmas poems. This time, instead of facing rejection, she discovered that other people not only liked her poetry but also recognized it as her creation.

Are you neglecting your talents because someone criticized you in the past? Don't let your gifts become ashes; turn them into a crown of beauty for God. Bless others with your talent! No matter what your talent is, use it for His glory.

Doubt is the hammer that breaks the windows clouded with human fancies and lets in the pure light.

HOW CAN I GLORIFY GOD WITH THE TALENTS HE HAS GIVEN ME?

Breaking the Ice

You are to judge your neighbor fairly.

LEVITICUS 19:15 NASB

Do I NEED TO
LOOK "TWICE"
AT SOMEONE
TODAY?

Carissa couldn't believe it—her mother was going to make her go caroling with people she hardly even knew! They had just recently moved into this new neighborhood, and Carissa did not like the looks of the people who lived around her. The elderly man next door only grumped at her whenever she said hello; the weird couple behind her house kept a toilet on their front porch.

But still, Carissa knew her mother was having a hard time adjusting too. As the neighbors caroled from house to house, Peggy tagged along for her mother's sake, listening to conversations. What she heard surprised her. The "impatient" neighbor lady took care of a handicapped son who required round-the-clock supervision. The "grumpy" neighbor had a speech impediment that made his words come out in grunts and growls. The "weird" man with the toilet used his unusual porch decoration as a unique conversation starter to tell others about God's love. The more Peggy heard, the more she realized that her first impressions of her neighbors had been wrong.

Later, as the neighbors gathered around steaming mugs of cocoa, Carissa decided to break the ice and make some "second" impressions. She smiled at the "impatient" neighbor and said, "Hi, I'm Carissa. We just moved in across the street. I heard you could use some help—would you like me to read to your son sometime?"

Don't judge anyone harshly until you
yourself have been through his experiences.

God's Instructions

> Let the Word of Christ dwell in you richly as you
> teach and admonish one another with all wisdom.
>
> COLOSSIANS 3:16

Sarah's worn and tattered journal sat on a desk in her bedroom. In it she had written her deepest thoughts and feelings, not realizing that she was creating a priceless record of her journey toward maturity.

HOW CAN I APPLY BIBLICAL WISDOM TO A PROBLEM IN MY LIFE TODAY?

Lying next to her journal was the Bible she had received in sixth grade. Like the journal, its pages were worn. It held clippings of memorable events that had taken place in her life and the lives of her friends throughout middle school and high school. Ink spots dotted the pages of her favorite Scripture passages. After so many years of use, certain verses were difficult to read.

"Learning to understand the Bible and using it as a guideline for life is the most important part of living," her mother had said on the day she gave Sarah the blank journal and her first "adult" Bible. "This is God's instruction book designed especially for us. Everything that you will ever need to know about life is written on these pages."

Sarah learned for herself that a used Bible is the most valuable tool for living. She sought God's guidance through His Word on a regular basis. It provided her with security and hope and helped her to live a life pleasing to Him.

That tattered Bible explained a lot about Sarah's life. All the instructions were there; she only needed to follow them in order to find the strength, wisdom, and courage that characterized her life.

Wisdom is oftentimes nearer when
we stoop than when we soar.

Our Unchanging God

The steps of a good man are ordered by the Lord.
PSALM 37:23 NKJV

HOW CAN I BEST EXPRESS MY GRATITUDE TO GOD FOR THE "SURE THINGS" IN MY LIFE?

In his book, *The Chance World,* Henry Drummond describes a place in which nothing is predictable. The sun may rise, or it may not. The moon might rise instead of the sun. If you jump up in the "chance world," you don't know if you will ever come down again—even if you jumped up and came down yesterday. Gravity and other natural laws change from hour to hour.

In the final analysis, *The Chance World* is a frightening world. While most people enjoy a certain amount of spontaneity in their lives, they enjoy life more when it is lived against a backdrop of predictability, surety, and trustworthiness.

The Scriptures promise us that the Lord does not change. He is the same yesterday, today, and forever (Hebrews 13:8). Furthermore, His natural laws do not change unless He authorizes their change for the good of His people. His commandments do not change. His promises to us are sure promises. We can know with certainty that "The steps of a good man are ordered by the Lord."

The Lord may have some surprises for you today. They are a part of His ongoing creation in your life. But His surprises are always custom-designed for you on the rock-solid foundation of His love. It is always His desire that you experience the highest and best in your life. You can count on Him!

All but God is changing day by day.

The Morning Sacrifice

Their duty was . . . to stand every morning
to thank and praise the Lord.

1 CHRONICLES 23:28, 30 NKJV

The Levites were never given the option of skipping morning devotions. They were required to perform certain rituals, like trimming the wicks on the oil lamps, burning incense, and making a "peace" offering. Once a week, the priest replaced the bread that was on constant display before the Lord.

The priest performed these functions in silent worship, wearing a highly symbolic vestment. As he worked, the only sound was that made by the bells on the hem of his garment.

This ancient ritual may seem strange and even meaningless to us today, but there's a great deal we can learn from it. The lamps symbolize our need for light—the ability to see with spiritual eyes. The incense represents our need to dwell in an atmosphere infused with God's holy presence. The peace offerings are a sign of our need for peace with God and with others. And the bread demonstrates our need for daily provision, which only the Lord can provide.

This ritualistic ceremony clearly communicated its wordless message: "We need You. Without You, we have no life, no wholeness, no meaning."

We may not have a ritual to follow in our morning devotional times, but we must come before the Lord with the same spirit of dependency and obedience. The day ahead of us is not ours. Our lives belong to God.

HOW CAN I MAKE MY MORNING DEVOTIONS MORE MEANINGFUL?

Everything we need, He will supply. The day
is His, even as we are His. For anything
worth having, one must pay the price; and
the price is always work, patience, love,
self-sacrifice, no paper currency, no
promises to pay, but the gold of real service.

The Blessings of Morning

God called the light Day, and
the darkness He called Night.

GENESIS 1:5 NKJV

What ARE
THE BLESSINGS
I CAN THANK
GOD FOR EACH
MORNING?

God promised the children of Israel they would see the glory of the Lord in the morning (Exodus 16:7). This promise came to them when they were hungry and in need of bread to eat. God supplied manna every morning until they reached the Promised Land. Like the children of Israel, we too can see the glory of the Lord when we seek Him in His Word. Each morning He provides the nourishment we need for the day.

Another blessing of morning time is that it often brings an end to suffering and sadness (Psalm 30:5) by bringing us a new opportunity to seek God for a fresh perspective on the problems and needs in our lives. When we give every minute and every circumstance of each day to the Lord, we can expect to see His light dawning throughout our day.

There are many examples in Scripture about people who rose early to meet God or to be about doing God's will; among them were Abraham, Moses, Joshua, Gideon, Job, and even Jesus. The Gospels tell us that Jesus went at dawn to teach the people who gathered in the temple courts.

The most glorious event of Christianity—the Resurrection—occurred in the early morning. Each morning we can celebrate Jesus' Resurrection as we watch the light of the day dispel the darkness of night.

Make it the first morning business of your life
to understand some part of the Bible clearly,
and make it your daily business to obey
it in all that you do understand.

Light of the World

The path of the just is like the shining sun,
That shines ever brighter unto the perfect day.

PROVERBS 4:18 NKJV

How CAN I
LET THE LIGHT
OF GOD SHINE
THROUGH MY
LIFE TODAY?

Once upon a time a Cave lived under the ground, as caves have the habit of doing. It had spent its lifetime in darkness. One day it heard a voice calling to it, "Come up into the light; come and see the sunshine."

But the Cave retorted, "I don't know what you mean. There isn't anything but darkness." Finally the Cave was convinced to venture forth. He was amazed to see light everywhere and not a speck of darkness anywhere. He felt oddly warm and happy.

Turnabout was fair play and so, looking up to the Sun, the Cave said, "Come with me and see the darkness."

The Sun asked, "What is darkness?"

The Cave replied, "Come and see!"

One day the Sun accepted the invitation. As it entered the Cave it said, "Now show me your darkness." But there was no darkness!

The apostle John opens his Gospel account by describing Jesus as the Word and as the Light—"the true light that gives light to every man" (John 1:9). It is John who also records Jesus proclaiming, "I am the light of the world. Whoever follows me will never walk in darkness, but will have the light of life" (John 8:12).

As this day begins, remember that you take the Light of the World with you wherever you go; and regardless of what may happen during your day, His light cannot be put out.

Light is above us, and color around us; but
if we have not light and color in our eyes,
we shall not perceive them outside us.

Called to Be Faithful

"The last will be first, and the first will be last."
MATTHEW 20:16

HOW DOES
GOD WANT ME
TO USE THE
SKILLS I
POSSESS TODAY
TO FURTHER
HIS KINGDOM
ON EARTH?

In the J. M. Barrie play, *The Admirable Crichton*, an earl, his family, and several friends are shipwrecked on a desert island. These nobles were highly regarded at home, but they could not build an outdoor fire, clean fish, or cook food—the very skills they needed to survive. The knowledge the nobility had acquired over the years was useless in their current situation. Had it not been for their resourceful butler, Crichton, they would have starved to death. He was the only one who possessed the basic skills to sustain life.

In a great turnabout, Crichton became the group's chief executive officer. He taught the earl and his family and friends the skills they needed and organized their efforts to ensure their survival until their rescue.

It is always good to remind ourselves of our "relative" place in society. If we are on top, we need to remember we can soon be at the bottom. If we perceive ourselves to be at the bottom, we need to know that in God's eyes, we are among "the first."

We may not achieve the fame and recognition from people that we would like to have in this life, but God doesn't call us to be well known or admired. He calls us to be faithful to Him in whatever situation we find ourselves. When we are, we can see more clearly when He promotes us and gives us favor with others.

He who knows himself best
esteems himself least.

Only the Best

Therefore God exalted him to the highest place and
gave him the name that is above every name.
PHILIPPIANS 2:9

When God sprinkled the stars across the universe, He knew exactly where He wanted to place each and every one. He took control of the gravitation of earth, the tilt of its axis, and the orbit of the moon. Knowing exactly how much heat the world would need, He provided the sun and all of its glory.

God even thought of little things when He formed the universe. He knew that His children would enjoy snow sometimes and warm weather at other times. He knew that the joy of nature would bring peace and contentment to hearts and souls everywhere. God also thought of the fact that without a mate, His children could become lonely. He wanted only the best for His creation, so He planned out everything carefully.

He wanted to be sure that when the nights seemed too long and the days too short, His children could continue to experience peace, so He provided many wonderful gifts along the way. The gift of salvation is the most wonderful present that could ever be offered or received. He provided the sacrifice in the form of a man—a perfect man, no less. His name was Jesus, the Name above all names. He lived, died, and lives again, and that enables us to live forever.

Because He lives, beauty can be found in the darkness, just as it can be found during the daylight hours. Looking at the stars and seeing the glow of the moon can bring joy to the soul of man. Sleepless nights can become blessings if God's children use that time to seek His face.

The power of God can be magnificent in the quietness of the night. His presence can be felt in an uplifting way through prayer and worship. He is worthy of our praise, even when the night seems long.

I felt CLOSE
TO GOD
WHEN . . .

✚

O for a thousand tongues to sing
my great Redeemer's praise!

The Tarnished Cup

Stop being mean, bad-tempered and angry. Quarreling, harsh words,
and dislike of others should have no place in your lives. Instead,
be kind to each other, tenderhearted, forgiving one another,
just as God has forgiven you because you belong to Christ.
EPHESIANS 4:31-32 TLB

Do I NEED
TO FORGIVE
MYSELF?
WHO ELSE?

After hours of searching through dusty cartons in the basement, brushing aside spider webs and dust bunnies, Kelly found the box that contained the baby cup that had been her grandmother's. It was wrapped in yellowed newspaper from many years earlier, as evidenced by the dates on the paper. Kelly removed the wrapping and discovered that the cup was now blackened by tarnish. Frustrated and disappointed, she stuffed the cup back into the carton.

That night Kelly was unable to sleep. After an hour of tossing and turning, it finally occurred to her that she was uneasy because her neglect and lack of concern had allowed the cup to deteriorate. She got up quickly and retrieved the cup from the basement. Finding some silver polish, she gently cleaned the cup until the beautiful silver again was revealed. With much work and love, she restored the cup to its original beauty.

Often our relationships with family and friends tarnish and deteriorate under layers of hurt feelings, anger, and misunderstanding. Sometimes the deterioration begins with a comment made in the heat of the moment, or it may begin under the strain of other stresses. If the air isn't cleared immediately, the relationship tarnishes.

When we put work and love into our relationships, they can be restored. Then we rediscover the beauty that lies underneath the tarnish and realize that it has been there all along.

If you're lying awake tonight, unable to sleep because you've been hurt by a loved one or you've said hurtful words or retaliated in kind, remember the teachings of Jesus and ask forgiveness for yourself and your loved one.[20]

If men would consider not so much
wherein they differ, as wherein they agree,
there would be far less uncharitableness
and angry feeling in the world.

Use That Powerful Engine!

> It is God who arms me with strength
> and makes my way perfect.
>
> PSALM 18:32

What a pleasure it is to drive a car with a powerful engine on a level highway. Picture a sunny day when there's no traffic and you're not in a hurry to get anywhere. You sing along with your favorite music tape and enjoy driving solely for driving's sake.

We are more likely to find ourselves in a much less powerful vehicle, however, climbing a series of steep hills . . . in the rain . . . with lots of traffic behind us and in front of us . . .and late for an appointment.

But is it possible to ride the rougher road and have the same peace and tranquility inside as when we drive the level highway? The Bible says it is.

The difference is simply the powerful engine, which makes the hills seem less steep and rush hour less tedious. It's a lot easier to keep moving steadily through traffic when you have a continuous hum from the motor, instead of lurching, dying, starting . . . lurching, dying, starting . . . in your own strength.

God is our powerful engine. He makes the difficult highway become manageable.

Perhaps your day started out smoothly, but by now you've left the easy stretch of road and come to the rolling hills. Now more than ever is the time to remind yourself that your Father in heaven loves you and wants to help you.

With God's strength, you can stay alert and focused, maintaining an even pace and an even temperament regardless of the challenge. He will help you work through any problems that arise without compromising your integrity. He may even show you some shortcuts—and the gas mileage is great!

All you have to do is ask God to strengthen you and get back on the road. Before you know it, you will be on the mountaintop with a clear view!

I need GOD'S STRENGTH TO . . .

When a man has no strength, if he leans on God, he becomes powerful.

Putting the Pieces Together

[Look] away [from all that will distract] to Jesus, Who
is the Leader and the Source of our faith
[giving the first incentive for our belief] and is also its
Finisher [bringing it to maturity and perfection].

HEBREWS 12:2 AMP

How CAN I
BE MORE
AWARE OF
THOSE THINGS
THAT ARE
"FITTING
TOGETHER"
IN MY LIFE?

If you have ever worked a complicated jigsaw puzzle, you know three things about them. First, they take time. Many large and complex puzzles take several days, even weeks, to complete. The fun is in the process; the satisfaction in the accomplishment. Second, the best way to start a puzzle is usually to begin by fitting together the border pieces. Third, complicated puzzles are a lot more fun to put together when others help you.

Consider the day ahead of you to be like a piece in the jigsaw puzzle of your life. Its shape is likely to be just as jagged, its colors just as unidentifiable. You aren't likely to see the big picture of your life by observing only one day. Even so, you can trust that there is a plan and purpose. All the pieces will come together according to God's design and timetable.

On some days, we find the "border" pieces of our life's puzzle—truths that become part of our framework. On other days, we find interior pieces that fit together, so we understand more about ourselves and about God's work in our lives. And on all days, we can know the joy of sharing our lives with others and inviting them to be part of the process of discovering who we are.

The main thing to remember is to enjoy the process. Live today to the fullest, knowing that one day you'll see the full picture.

Faith is the daring of the soul
to go farther than it can see.

Transforming Power

In the day of trouble he will keep me safe in
his dwelling; he will hide me in the shelter of
his tabernacle and set me high upon a rock.

PSALM 27:5

If you've ever been seriously injured, you probably needed to go through a battery of medical tests. Most of these tests are no fun, and some are downright scary. Take magnetic resonance imaging for one. An MRI test can bring out the claustrophobia in anyone; so common is the problem that health care workers are specifically trained to handle the myriad of negative reactions patients may have to the narrow MRI "tunnel."

One woman found herself on the verge of panic during her first experience in an MRI tunnel. She decided to start praying for other people to take her mind off the dread she felt. She began praying alphabetically. She prayed for Albert's sore knee, Amy's decision about work, and Andrew's upcoming final exams. She moved on to *B* and continued through the alphabet. By the time she reached the letter *D*, she was totally oblivious to her environment.

Thirty minutes later, she was only halfway through the alphabet, and the test was done. The following day, she was able to complete her alphabetical prayers for others as she waited in the doctor's office for the test results.

Many of the experiences we must go through in life are not at all pleasant. What matters, of course, is how we choose to handle those experiences. When you find yourself in an unpleasant situation, turn it over to God. He has the ability to transform it into a powerful occasion for good.

What UNPLEASANT CIRCUM-STANCE AM I FACING THAT I CAN TRUST GOD TO TRANSFORM?

Faith is the capacity to trust God while not
being able to make sense out of everything.

100 Percent

Whatever you do, do all to the glory of God.
1 CORINTHIANS 10:31 RSV

What TASKS
NOW SEEM
SIGNIFICANT?

"To love what you do and feel that it matters—how could anything be more fun?" asks Katharine Graham. That's what we all desire, isn't it?

No matter what work we do, our attitude toward our work is vital to our basic sense of self-worth. The ideal for everyone is to love the work they do and feel that it has significance. While no job is enjoyable or pleasant all the time, it is possible to derive satisfaction from what we bring to a job—the attitude with which we perform our tasks.

For example, Brother Lawrence, the 17th-century Carmelite, found joy in his job washing dishes at the monastery. In the monotony of his routine work, he found the opportunity to focus on God and feel His presence.

Modern-day entrepreneurs Ben Cohen and Jerry Greenfield make and sell ice cream with a purpose. The bottom line of Ben & Jerry's Homemade, Inc. is "How much money is left over at the end of the year?" and "How have we improved life in the community?"

"Leftover money" goes to fund Ben & Jerry's Foundation, which distributes funds to worthy nonprofit causes. These are charities that help needy children, preserve the Amazonian rain forest, provide safe shelter for emotionally or psychologically distressed people, and fund a business staffed by unemployed homeless people. By helping others with their profits, Ben and Jerry put more *meaning* into their ice cream business.

The Scriptures teach that all service ranks the same with God, because it is not *what* you do that matters, but the *spirit* in which you do it. A street sweeper who does his work to serve God and bless the people who travel on the streets is as pleasing to Him as the priest or pastor who teaches and nurtures their congregations.

If you feel your work is insignificant, ask God to open your eyes! When you do all for Him and serve others, no task is unimportant!

✠

Every gift which is given, even though it be small, is great if given with affection.

Escape Valve

Be merciful (sympathetic, tender, responsive, and compassionate) even as your Father is [all these].

LUKE 6:36 AMP

Have you just about had enough of that bully at school or the bossy girl who sits behind you in class? Are you tired of the attitude of that person you can't seem to avoid?

We all encounter people—sometimes on a frequent basis—whom we just don't like. And to make matters worse, even those we do like can have a bad day!

Eleanor Roosevelt gave advice for that situation:

A mature person is one who does not think only in absolutes, who is able to be objective even when deeply stirred emotionally, who has learned that there is both good and bad in all people and in all things, and who walks humbly and deals charitably with the circumstances of life, knowing that in this world no one is all knowing and therefore all of us need both love and charity.

Certainly we would all like to attain such a level of maturity! But how? Jesus taught His followers in Luke 6:37 AMP that there were three specific things they needed to do to get along with other people:

- *Judge not—neither pronouncing judgment nor subjecting to censure—and you will not be judged.* Don't speak ill of anyone, it only adds fuel to hard feelings. Instead, speak a word of encouragement to them.

- *Do not condemn and pronounce guilty, and you will not be condemned and pronounced guilty.* Don't "write off" someone as hopeless or without merit; don't snub them. That only creates more tension.

- *Acquit and forgive and release (give up resentment, let it drop), and you will be acquitted and forgiven and released.* Say to the Lord, "This person is Your child, and therefore Yours to discipline. Help them, and help me."

Refuse to let another person put you in a pressure cooker today. Release the "steam" you feel in acts of kindness and prayer.

I need TO RELEASE STEAM ABOUT . . .

✠

Anger is quieted by a gentle word
just as fire is quenched by water.

A Lifestyle of Giving

"God so loved the world, that He gave."
JOHN 3:16 NASB

What COULD
I GIVE UP THAT
WOULD BE A
BLESSING TO
SOMEONE
ELSE?

The word "lifestyle" has been popular for several decades. In simplest terms, this word denotes how much money we have to spend and where we spend it. Some people gravitate toward a simpler life, while others would love to emulate the lifestyles of the rich and famous.

The two paths—one toward a materially leaner life and the other toward a materially fatter life—are like opposite lanes on a highway. We are going either in one direction or the other. We are seeking to discard and downsize or to acquire and add.

The Scriptures call us to neither a poor nor a rich lifestyle, but rather to a lifestyle of generosity—a life without greed or hoarding, a life of giving freely, of placing everything we have at God's disposal. Our lifestyle is not about how much we earn, what we own, or where we travel and reside. It's how we relate to other people and how willing we are to share all we have with them.

Look at all that you have, all of your possessions, including your clothes, your CDs—everything. Ask yourself, "Would I be willing to loan, give, or share these with other people?" Then ask the even tougher question, "Do I actually share, loan, or give what I have to others on a regular basis?"

Giving brings pleasure to the giver.

Living Examples

> "[The mustard seed] indeed is the least of all seeds: but when it is grown, it is the greatest among herbs, and becometh a tree, so that the birds of the air come and lodge in the branches thereof."
>
> MATTHEW 13:32 KJV

In the mid-1800s a humble minister lived and died in a small village in Leicestershire, England. He lived there his entire life and never traveled far from home. He never attended college and had no formal degrees, but he was a faithful village minister.

In his congregation was a young cobbler to whom he gave special attention, teaching him the Word of God. This young man was William Carey, later hailed as one of the greatest missionaries of modern times.

The village minister also had a son—a boy whom he taught faithfully. The boy's character and talents were profoundly impacted by his father's life. That son grew up to be one of the greatest public orators of his day: Robert Hall. Admired for his godly character, he preached powerful sermons that influenced the decisions of statesmen.

It seems the village pastor accomplished little in his life. No spectacular revivals, great miracles, or major church growth occurred because of him. Yet his faithful witness had much to do with giving India William Carey and England Robert Hall.

When you think you are having no impact in the world by talking to your friends about God or taking a stand for righteousness when all those around you cave in to peer pressure, remember the little country preacher who influenced two nations for the Lord.

Am I LIVING IN SUCH A WAY THAT OTHERS WILL WANT TO FOLLOW JESUS TOO?

We never know what ripples of healing we set in motion by simply smiling on one another.

The Importance of Everyday Talk

JUNE 12

Let your conversation be always full of grace.
COLOSSIANS 4:6

I need TO
TALK TO
GOD MORE
ABOUT . . .

The banquet hall is festively adorned with beautiful flowers and ribbons. Across the front of the room a large banner reads, "A Golden Congratulations for a Golden Couple." It is their fiftieth wedding anniversary, and family and friends have gathered from far and near to pay tribute to them. The four children each take a turn at describing their fondest memories and greatest lessons learned from their parents. Then the cake is cut, pictures are taken, and everyone enjoys visiting with one another.

Too soon, the afternoon draws to a conclusion. Friends say good-bye; family members repack mementos in the cars and everyone leaves. Later that evening, one of the grandchildren asks, "What is the secret, Grandma, to being happily married for fifty years?" Without hesitation, her grandmother replies, "We were always able to talk about everything."

Recent research supports her conclusion. A study of couples happily married for more than twenty-five years found only one thing they all had in common—each couple "chitchatted" with each other daily. Perhaps, since they already know how to converse with one another, they are more able to talk out their differences when tough times come. The same most likely holds true for our relationship with God. If we commune with Him regularly, then we will automatically turn to Him first when crisis comes.

Have you had a quiet time talking with God today?

A daily chat with God is
meaningful conversation.

Unorthodox Style

Ye are a chosen generation, a royal priesthood, an holy nation, a peculiar people; that ye should shew forth the praises of him who hath called you out of darkness into his marvellous light.

1 PETER 2:9 KJV

Jean-Claude Killy, the French ski champion, did more than train hard. The goal in ski racing is to ski down a prescribed mountain course faster than anyone else. Killy began experimenting to see if he could pare any seconds off his time. He found that if he skied with his legs apart, he had better balance. He also found that if he sat back on his skis when executing a turn, instead of leaning forward as was customary, he had better control, which also resulted in faster times. Rather than regarding his ski poles as an accessory for balance, Killy tried using them to propel him forward.

Killy's style was unorthodox. But after he won most of the major ski events in 1966 and 1967, including three gold medals at the Winter Olympics, skiers around the world took notice. Today, the Killy style is the norm among downhill and slalom racers.

As Christians we are not called to conform to the world's standards but to God's standards. Our lifestyle should challenge people to come to Jesus Christ and live according to His higher ways and purposes. The Christian "style" may seem odd to the unbeliever, but in the end, it is the style that will prevail!

Don't be afraid to be a little "unusual" today in the eyes of those who observe you. Your example may help win them over to a championship lifestyle.

The world is a net; the more we stir in it, the more we are entangled.

HOW HAVE I BEEN TEMPTED TO CONFORM TO THE WAYS OF THE WORLD?

Keep Going

He [Jesus] stedfastly set his face to go to Jerusalem.

LUKE 9:51 KJV

HOW HAVE I ALLOWED MYSELF TO BECOME SIDETRACKED LATELY?

The Saturday of the dogsled derby dawned as a bright, clear, cold winter morning. The contestants were all children—ranging from teenagers with several dogs and big sleds to one little guy who appeared to be no more than five years old. His one dog pulled a small sled.

The racers took off in a flurry, and the youngest contestant with his little dog was quickly outdistanced. In fact, the larger and more experienced racers disappeared so quickly down the course that the young boy was hardly in the race at all. Although he was in last place, he stayed in the competition, enjoying every minute of it.

Halfway around the course, the second-place team began to overtake the lead team. The dogs came too close, and soon the two teams were in a fight. Then, as each sled reached the fighting, snarling animals, they joined in the fracas.

None of the drivers seemed able to steer their teams clear of the growling brawl, and soon all of the dogs and racers became one big seething mass of kids, sleds, and dogs—except the one little fellow and his dog. He managed to stay the course and finish the race alone.[21]

Each day holds the potential for something to sidetrack us from our intended purpose. No matter how great the distraction, we can finish the course if we stay focused and keep going!

If your determination is fixed,
I do not counsel you to despair.
Great works are performed not
by strength, but perseverance.

Healing through Helpfulness

Pray for each other so that you may be healed.

JAMES 5:16

David was an eight-year-old with a speech impediment that made him hesitant to read aloud or speak up in class. His mother also had a problem; she was afflicted with multiple sclerosis. One winter day she and David were out walking, and her cane slipped on an icy patch, causing her to fall. David wished he could do something to help her.

Some time later, David's teacher assigned her students to come up with an invention. David ended up inventing a cane with a retractable point at the bottom that would grip the ice. Much like a ballpoint pen, the point could be popped out of sight by releasing a button, so the cane could be used inside or when the sidewalks were not icy.

David's invention earned him first prize in a national contest. As the winner, he was required to make public appearances and explain his project to others. The more he talked about the cane, the less noticeable his speech impediment became.[22]

Other people may not need you to invent something for them. They may simply need a word of encouragement or prayer for a particular need. You will find, as you extend the effort, time, and energy to help someone else, that something inside you will be softened, healed, renewed, or strengthened. An outward expression toward others always does something inwardly that enables, empowers, and enhances the character of Christ Jesus in us.

If you pray for another,
you will be helped yourself.

I can HELP SOMEONE TODAY IF I . . .

Delayed Reaction

Do not withhold good from those to whom it is due,
when it is in the power of your hand to do so. Do
not say to your neighbor, "Go, and come back, and
tomorrow I will give it," when you have it with you.
PROVERBS 3:27-28 NKJV

What TASKS

HAVE I BEEN

PUTTING OFF?

Morning is a great time to make a list of things to do and plan the day. It's also the best time to tackle those tasks that are the most difficult or that we like least. If we procrastinate as the day wears on, rationalization sets in, and sometimes even the tasks we had considered to be the most important are left undone.

As part of your morning prayer time, ask the Lord to help you overcome any tendency to procrastinate and help you prioritize your projects for the day according to His plans and purposes.

Often we ask the Lord, "What do You want me to do?" but then fail to ask Him one of the key follow-up questions, "When do You want me to do this?" When we have a sense of God's timing, and in some cases His urgency about a matter, the conviction to get the job done right away begins to grow within us.

God's "omnipresence" means He is always with you. And God, of course, is always "timely"; He's with you in the "now" moments of your life. He is concerned with how you use every moment of your time. He wants to be such an important part of your day that He is ready to help you manage your time more efficiently. And when you do, you'll have more time for the important things, like serving God and others.

Nothing is so fatiguing as the eternal
hanging on of an uncompleted task.

Little Opportunities

> Let us behave decently, as in the daytime . . .
> clothe yourselves with the Lord Jesus Christ.
>
> ROMANS 13:13-14

What IS THE CUMULATIVE EFFECT I'M HAVING ON OTHERS? AM I SHOWING THEM THE LOVE OF JESUS?

High above the tour group in a factory, a five-hundred-pound steel bar was suspended by a chain. Nearby, a cork hung from a silk thread. The tour guide announced that the cork would soon set the steel bar in motion. Taking the cork in her hand, she pulled it to one side and released it. The cork swung gently against the steel bar.

For ten minutes the cork, with pendulum-like regularity, struck the bar. Finally, the bar vibrated slightly. By the time the tour group passed through the room an hour later, the great bar was swinging like the pendulum of a clock.

Many of us feel we are not exerting any influence on others. Not so! We simply can't see the cumulative effect we're having on those around us. Tap by loving tap, in God's time, even the quietest Christian can make a huge difference in the lives of others.

One modern-day philosopher has estimated that the average person encounters at least twenty different people in the course of a day, with a minimum of eye contact and exchange of a few words or a gesture of some sort. That's at least twenty opportunities for a cork to "tap" the lives of other people.

As you go about your day, remember that even a smile can warm a stranger's heart and draw him to Jesus.

The entire ocean is affected by a pebble.

All That Really Matters

Don't store up treasures on earth!
MATTHEW 6:19 CEV

DO I SECRETLY
WANT IT ALL?
DO I TRULY
UNDERSTAND
WHAT REALLY
MATTERS?

Jason's parents had it all: a mansion, two luxury cars, a vacation house on the lake, a prolific investment portfolio, and the respect of all who knew them. Success was sweet, and money made their world go round. But then, the bottom dropped out of their lives. A business partner embezzled nearly half a million dollars from them, and the Couple Who Had It All started down the road to becoming the Couple Who Lost It All. In the midst of their problems, the police came to their door late one night to tell them Jason had been killed in a car accident.

This couple discovered something vitally important in the course of putting their lives back together. A neighbor invited them to church, and thinking that they had nothing to lose by going, they started attending, eventually becoming regular members. To their amazement, they found they were enjoying Bible study, making lots of genuine friends, and feeling accepted for who they were—not for what they had in the way of material possessions. The two surviving children also found a place where they could belong.[23]

Most of us will not have to lose it all in order to find it all. In fact, our Heavenly Father wants us to live abundantly. Keeping our priorities straight, remembering to put God first and others ahead of ourselves, is the key to having all that really matters.

Building one's life on a foundation
of gold is just like building a house
on foundations of sand.

Lord of the Details

This is the confidence we have in approaching God:
that if we ask anything according to his will, he hears
us. And if we know that he hears us—whatever we
ask—we know that we have what we asked of him.

1 JOHN 5:14-15

What "LITTLE THINGS" CAN I TRUST GOD FOR MORE OFTEN?

The tension was thick as Cathy and her mother searched for a parking spot near the ferry landing; it looked for all the world as if they would miss the ferry from Seattle to their home on Bainbridge Island. "I told you we needed to get away from your office sooner," Cathy chided. "You just can't count on finding a parking place within walking distance of the ferry when the waterfront is full of summer tourists and conventioneers!"

"God knew about that last-minute customer I had, and He knows we have to make this ferry in order to get home in time to fix dinner and make it to the church meeting," Elaine assured her. Then she prayed aloud, "Lord, we'll circle this block one more time. Please have someone back out, or we're not going to make it."

"Mom, there it is!" Cathy shouted, as they rounded the last corner. "Those people just got in their car. I have to admit—sometimes you have a lot more faith than I do. Who would think God would be interested in whether or not we find a parking place?"

"But that's the exciting part of it," Elaine explained. "God is interested in every part of our lives—even schedules and parking places. Now, let's run for it!"[24]

The Lord knows all the circumstances of your day—and your tomorrow. Trust Him to be the "Lord of the details."

Anything large enough for a wish to light
upon is large enough to hang a prayer on.

Only You

I will praise thee; for I am fearfully and
wonderfully made; marvellous are thy works;
and that my soul knoweth right well.
PSALM 139:14 KJV

How CAN I
LEARN TO
APPRECIATE
WHO I AM AND
BECOME THE
PERSON GOD
INTENDED ME
TO BE?

When you stop to think about all the intricate details involved in the normal functioning of your body—just one creation among countless species and organisms on the planet—one word is likely to come to your mind: awesome. Think about it: No one but you has ever had or ever will have your exact fingerprints, handprints, footprints, or voiceprint. And no one but you has ever had or ever will have your genetic code—the exact positioning of the many genes that define your physical characteristics.

Furthermore, nobody else has your exact history in time and space. Nobody else has gone where you've gone, done what you've done, said what you've said, or created what you have created. You are truly a one-of-a-kind masterpiece.

The Lord knows precisely how you were made and why you were made. When something in your life goes amiss, He knows how to fix it. When you err or stray from His commandments, He knows how to bring you back and work even the worst tragedies and mistakes for your good when you repent.

You have been uniquely fashioned for a specific purpose on the earth. He has a "design" for your life. It is His own imprint, His own mark. Make a resolution to be true to what the Lord has made you to be and to become.

Man is heaven's masterpiece.

A Room with a View

> O Lord, I pray, open his eyes that he may see.
>
> 2 KINGS 6:17 NASB

How CAN I BRING BEAUTY AND PEACE TO MY HOME? MY SCHOOL?

A story from England called "The Wonderful Window" tells about a London clerk who worked in drab and depressing circumstances. His office building was in a run-down part of the city and had not been maintained.

But that ordinary clerk was not about to let his outlook on life be determined by the dreariness of his surroundings. So one day he bought a beautiful, multi-colored Oriental window painted with an inspiring scene.

The clerk took his window to his workplace and had it installed high up on the wall in his office. When the dispirited clerk looked through his window, he did not see the familiar slum scenes. Instead he saw a fair city with beautiful castles and towers, green parks, and lovely homes on wide tree-lined streets. A knight rode on horseback through the city, watching over the people with pride.

Somehow as he worked long hours at tedious accounting, trying to make everything balance, the clerk felt he was working for the knight on the banner. This feeling produced a sense of honor and dignity. He had found a noble purpose helping the knight keep the city happy, beautiful, prosperous, and strong.

You don't have to let your circumstances or surroundings discourage you. God has sent you to the place where you are to do noble work for Him. You are His worker, bringing His beauty to everyone around you.

It is our best work that God wants,
not the dregs of our exhaustion.
I think He must prefer quality to quantity.

A Humbling Truce

I say unto you, Love your enemies.
MATTHEW 5:44 KJV

Who HAVE I
RESISTED
LATELY? I CAN
BE MORE
LOVING
TOWARD
THEM BY . . .

Aaron and Abbey had dated for nearly a year when Aaron bought Abbey a "present" she never wanted: a great big Chow puppy with paws the size of baseballs. Abbey reminded Aaron that she and dogs did not get along; Aaron insisted she would get used to him.

Determined to make sure he understood his place as her enemy, Abbey silently launched a campaign against Pup—who retaliated by stealing towels, tearing up shoes and furniture, and carrying off whatever Abbey was using the minute she turned away.

Then one day, Pup began to greet Abbey joyously each time she came home, nudging her hand and licking her fingers in a friendly "hello." Whenever she had to feed him, he sat for a moment and gazed at her adoringly before he began eating. To top it off, he began to accompany her on her early morning walks, staying close at her side to ward off other dogs as she walked down their deserted road.

Little by little, Pup loved Abbey into a humbling truce. Today, Abbey says that Pup's persistence has taught her a lot about loving her enemies. She says Pup is winning—but don't tell Aaron.

Maybe there is someone you know—perhaps even someone in your own family—who needs an expression of your love, rather than your resistance. Humble yourself, and determine to call a truce. Most of all, love that person unconditionally.

We should conduct ourselves
toward our enemy as if he
were one day to be our friend.

Changing Seasons

> The grass withers and the flowers fall,
> but the Word of our God stands forever.
>
> ISAIAH 40:8

Marie enjoyed washing dishes on Saturday mornings. It gave her an opportunity to slow down, think, and observe the changing of the seasons as she gazed out the kitchen window that faced the garden.

Over the past year Marie had watched a sparrow preparing her nest and then bringing food to her babies in the springtime. A hummingbird made regular stops after he discovered the window feeder during the summer. In autumn, squirrels scampered around in the crisp, fallen leaves in search of an acorn. And that winter, Marie saw a deer standing majestically in her yard.

As the cycle of seasons began again, Marie watched flowers pop up through the soil when the weather got warmer. Their brilliantly colored blossoms always brought her happiness. In the summer, the green grass filled her heart with peace and tranquility. She knew she would again see leaves gradually transformed to shades of gold after a few weeks back in school and then again winter would follow.

Life is like the changing seasons. Marie often reflected on her mother's comments about the seasons. Her mother spent days filled with fun and joy as Marie played with frogs and tadpoles as a young child. Her teen and young adult years—the summer of her life—were marked by enthusiasm as she tried to find herself in the fast lane of life. Even as a teen, Marie too had fond memories of her season in life. She began to realize that whatever season she's in right now is the best season of her entire life.

There's nothing wrong with looking back at the previous seasons of our lives. But God has a purpose for allowing us to be in the season we're in right now. So enjoy where you're at on the way to where you're going!

My SUMMERS ARE SPECIAL BECAUSE . . .

Make the season you're in right now
the best season of your life.

Obedience and Trust

Abide in Me, and I in you.

JOHN 15:4 NASB

As I SPEND
TIME WITH
GOD, I CAN
TRUST HIM
MORE
WITH . . .

While on safari, a missionary family stopped for lunch. The children were playing under a tree a distance away from their parents and the other adults on the team. Suddenly the father of one child jumped up and yelled to his son, "Drop down!" and the son did so instantly. Others in the group were shocked to learn that a poisonous snake was slithering down the tree ready to strike the child. It would have meant certain death if the snake had bitten him. Only the father of the child saw the snake.

Amazement was expressed over the instant response of the child to his father's command. The father explained the abiding love he and his son enjoyed had developed from the trust they had in each other. The boy did not question when his dad gave the command; he trusted him and responded accordingly. The missionary father also expected his son to respond to his command.

The peaceful rest that both of them were able to enjoy later that day was evidence of the abiding rest that God has for each of us as we learn to trust Him. Are you abiding in Christ?

God wants to live in us and He wants us to live in Him. Abiding comes more easily for some than others. It is not always easy to know what God has planned for us, but we can be assured that whatever it is, He is ready to equip us with what we need to endure and hold on to that place for as long as He wants us there. Abiding starts with trust and ends with complete rest.

All my requests are lost in one,
"Father, thy will be done!"

Staying Rooted

Just as you received Christ Jesus as Lord,
continue to live in him, rooted and built up
in him, strengthened in the faith as you were
taught, and overflowing with thankfulness.

COLOSSIANS 2:6-7

What DO I
NEED FROM
THE LORD
TODAY?

A tree is nothing without its roots; young roots absorb water and minerals from the soil, while older roots take these materials and send them into the stem. The roots also store food, which provides needed energy when the weather changes and it's time for new growth.

The God who cares enough about trees to set up an intricate feeding system for them gives each of us the food, water, and air we require to survive. He gives us family and friends, opportunities, and provision to accomplish His plan for our lives. We can't see God with our physical eyes, but like the finely developed web of roots beneath the ground, we know He's there, working on our behalf. That is His nature as Jehovah Jireh—the God who provides.

Have you ever been hungry? Jesus is the Bread of Life; He promises that whoever comes to Him will never go hungry (John 6:35 KJV). Have you ever been thirsty? As Jesus told the Samaritan woman at the well, "Whoever drinks the water I give him will never thirst" (John 4:14). Do you ever find yourself gasping for breath? Job knew whom to thank for the air we all breathe. "In his hand is the life of every creature and the breath of all mankind" (Job 12:10).

Stay rooted in the Lord and watch Him provide for your every need!

He that so much for you did do,
Will do yet more.

Just Like a Diamond

He knoweth the way that I take: when
he hath tried me, I shall come forth as gold.
JOB 23:10 KJV

How CAN I
ALLOW THE
HOLY SPIRIT
TO SPARKLE
WITHIN ME?

Taking some time alone is a wonderful way to regroup, rethink, and refresh. Solitude is especially important when we are a bit frayed from the day's activities, but we still have hours of activity ahead of us. We can't always take a break, but without this break, the remaining tasks may threaten to take us under.

Drawing on the refreshing power of the Holy Spirit will help get us to the end of a stressful day. We can gain renewed patience, a fresh sense of humor, and a new surge of creativity and insight by enlisting the aid of the Spirit's ministry within us.

When you feel as if you're going under at the end of the day, you can learn a valuable lesson from the "underwater" test used by jewelry experts. Jewelers claim that one of the surest ways to determine the authenticity of a diamond is to place it underwater. A genuine diamond will continue to sparkle, while an imitation stone will not.

The power of the Holy Spirit can continue to sparkle within you, refreshing and renewing you in spite of the day's harassments. The authenticity of your faith will continue to shine through, and others will be able to see that there is something genuinely different about your life.

Ask the Holy Spirit to impart His power and presence to you today, in this very hour. Pray for Him to help you in the ways you need Him most—to shine like a diamond underwater!

Breathe on me, breath of God; Fill me with
life anew, That I may love what thou dost
love, And do what thou wouldst do.

Take a Bite Out of Your Problem

*I can do all things through Christ
who strengthens me.*

PHILIPPIANS 4:13 NKJV

Have you ever had a difficulty that gives you "2:00 A.M. wake-up calls"? It could be a project at school, a committee you've suddenly ended up chairing, or simply trying to figure out how to get everything done with only two hands. Whatever the issue, it ruins your sleep and saps your energy for the upcoming day.

The developer of a popular series of business training films describes the phenomenon of discovering your problem-solving skills are going nowhere:

You start thinking, *I'm uncomfortable. I'm anxious. I can't do this. I should never have started to try. I'm not creative. I was never creative in school. I'm a complete failure. I'm going to be fired, and that means my spouse will leave me and—in other words, you start enjoying a real, good, old-fashioned panic attack.*[25]

Problems can feel ten times as large in the middle of the night. But in reality—and by daylight—solutions might not be as distant as they seem.

Inventor Charles Kettering had a unique problem-solving method. He would divide each problem into the smallest possible pieces, then research the pieces to determine which ones had already been solved. He often found that what looked like a huge problem was already 98 percent solved by others. Then he tackled what was left.

In bite-sized pieces, problems become more manageable. Remember that, with God, all things are possible. He can give us peace in our darkest nights, and bring wisdom with the morning.

Small pieces solve a bigger puzzle.

One THING I COULD BREAK INTO SMALLER PIECES AND SOLVE IN BITES IS . . .

The Upward Pull

I will never leave you nor forsake you.

HEBREWS 13:5 NRSV

I can

REFOCUS ON

HIS UPWARD

PULL IF I . . .

A speedboat driver once described a harrowing racing accident in which his boat veered slightly, striking a wave at a perilous angle. The combined force of the boat's speed and the size and angle of the wave sent the boat flying into the air in a dangerous spin. The driver was thrown out of his seat and propelled deep into the water—so deep, he had no idea which direction was "up." He had to remain calm and wait for the buoyancy of his life vest to begin pulling him toward the surface to know where the surface was. Then he swam quickly in that direction.

Life can put us in a tailspin at times, making us wonder which way is up? We can lose our sense of direction and the focus that keeps us on course. How do we recover our bearings?

The answer may be as simple as that discovered by the speedboat driver: Stay calm and let the "upward pull" bring you to the surface. The upward pull in our lives is that which looks beyond our finite selves to the greater reality of God.

Our Heavenly Father never loses sight of us and never leaves us. As long as we remain aware of His presence and are sensitive to His "upward pull," we will always know which way is up!

Behind the dim unknown standeth
God within the shadow,
keeping watch above his own.

The Best Gift

> Today in the city of David there has been born
> for you a Savior, Who is Christ the Lord.
>
> LUKE 2:11 NASB

I give MORE OF MYSELF TO JESUS IF I . . .

How would you feel if a party was given in your honor, and the people attending gave presents to one another but not to you?

That's the question the youth pastor addressed at the group's weekend retreat. As the students settled into their seats, the youth pastor said, "We like to visit with one another, but from this point on, let's talk only about Jesus. He is our guest of honor this weekend."

As the students listened intently, the youth pastor began to talk to them about Jesus. The focal point of his talk was a wooden cross. The students discussed everything from Jesus' humble birth to His death on the cross and His glorious resurrection.

Then the youth pastor announced, "Every party has gifts. Now it's time for us to give our gifts to Jesus." He passed around a basket filled with tiny decorated boxes. At the appointed time, each student opened a box in an attitude of prayer and read aloud a Scripture, along with the companion "gift" to place on an altar. These included such things as the student's heart, faith, future, hopes, plans, and dreams.

During the touching, intimate moment, several students moved to a kneeling position and then wept softly. That day became special, because they chose to give Jesus the most meaningful gift of all: themselves.

He who knows God reverences him.

Sky-High

"My thoughts are not your thoughts, neither
are your ways my ways," declares the Lord.
ISAIAH 55:8

What DO I
SEE WHEN I
VIEW MY LIFE
FROM "ABOVE
THE CLOUDS"
TODAY?

Denise rested her flushed face against the cool window of the airplane, which was preparing to taxi onto the runway. This trip, unlike many others, brought no pleasure to her heart as the plane began to move. This trip to visit her father in a distant state was a somber one.

Her father was sick; her mom was frustrated and angry at being forced to raise kids alone; her brother was starting to hang around the wrong crowd—kids even Denise feared and disliked. Why was all this taking place now? *Why, Lord?* she prayed. She had always lived a life worthy of blessing and reward—or so she had thought.

As the plane slowly rose into the air, Denise surveyed the land below her. Dark and dreary under a rainy sky, the entire landscape seemed to fit her mood. Slowly, the plane began to break through the clouds, and Denise could no longer see the land below. They seemed to be lost in a gray mist until they climbed on top of the clouds. What a difference! The dark, menacing clouds were transformed into soft white blankets. The blue sky and sunshine were bright and unwavering on the other side.

Does life seem dark and dreary from your perspective? Are you living beneath the dark clouds of depression or sadness? It's hard to see the light in the midst of the storm. But remember, just beyond the cloud cover is an amazing sight. Today, allow God to show you life from His perspective.

**The brightest light is just above
the storm clouds.**

A Friend in Need

*For where your treasure is,
there your heart will be also.*
MATTHEW 6:21

Surrounded by stacks of money, Theresa could not believe how much they had made at the youth group car wash on Saturday. As the youth group treasurer, she was responsible to count the money—and figure out ways of raising more cash for future outreach events. All the other kids had left after the youth meeting, but Theresa had promised Jack and Shannon, their leaders, that she'd stay to complete the car wash numbers and create a plan for the next event. She was getting tired.

Yawning, Theresa picked up her Coke and walked down the hall to the church's fellowship hall. One of the other girls in the group, a shy girl named Angela, sat at a table reading her Bible.

"What are you doing here?" Theresa asked, surprised.

"Oh, hi, Theresa," Angela said. "I thought I'd hang around tonight so you wouldn't be here alone. I called my dad and told him to pick me up by 8:30."

"You don't have to stay," Theresa said.

"I know, but I just wanted to. Is there anything I can help you do?"

"Wow! Thanks," Theresa said. "It just so happens there is."

Angela smiled and closed her Bible. "That's what friends are for."

My friend looks me in the face
and sees me, that is all.

I was
A FAITHFUL
FRIEND
WHEN . . .

Seeds of Love

A new command I give you: Love one another.
As I have loved you, so you must love one another.
JOHN 13:34

I can

WARM OUR
RELATIONSHIP
THAT HAS
BECOME LIKE
HARD SOIL
IF I . . .

As Jennifer eased the sliced green tomatoes into the frying pan, the aroma brought back vivid memories of her mother marrying the man from Alabama. Jennifer was a teenager from the city, and she couldn't stand this man from the "sticks." To her, he was nothing but a country bumpkin.

Early one spring morning, everything changed. She was sitting on the backyard swing, watching as he turned the soil with a shovel on a sunny spot behind the house. Each day, he did something different: he'd break up dirt clods, toss rocks out, and add compost, finally raking the soil smooth. Curious, Jennifer walked across the garden, feeling the coolness of the newly worked earth between her toes.

"Here," said her stepfather, "take these." He poured some seeds into her open hand.

"What are they?" she asked, feeling her resentment dissipate in the cool morning.

"Squash," he said. "Later, I'll plant pole beans and tomatoes."

She watched that day as he planted the seeds, covering them with dirt and patting it down. Following his example, she soon completed a row of little mounds. Later that summer, she enjoyed looking under the leaves of the squash plants and plucking the golden vegetables. She also liked the taste of a young cucumber, but most of all she loved the green tomatoes her stepfather taught her to fry. What her stepfather had done that day was to crumble the wall between them, much like he'd broken up the soil.

Are you sowing seeds of love? Break up the hard ground of resentment and allow God to cause love to grow in your heart.

Seeds of love grow without boundaries.

At the Crossroads

*The shepherds went back, glorifying and
praising God for all that they had heard
and seen, just as had been told them.*

LUKE 2:20 NASB

While on vacation, Kenda's family rented a car to drive on the back roads of beautiful British Columbia. He parents sat in the front; and she and her sisters, Kaylyn and Kyleigh, sat in the back.

Her father was driving along when they saw a dirt road angling to the right with the correct highway number posted. Her mother said, "Surely that isn't the main road. Maybe the sign was turned. Look, the road straight ahead is paved and lined with utility poles too."

After a lighthearted discussion, the family took a vote and decided to stay on what appeared to be the main highway. After a few miles, the girls' father drove up a little hill, and then suddenly all they could see was water, a few small buildings, and a campground sign. The road came to a dead end right there, at a lovely lake and campsite. The family began laughing as Dad wheeled the car around and headed back to the turn they had passed, the one that led to a dirt road. Eventually, the humble highway meandered through the most magnificent scenery of all.

We could easily stay on the broad, paved road and mindlessly travel to the dead end. Or we could change our thinking and our plans, turn down the narrow road to the Cross, and worship the King. Which will you choose?

The crossroads are down here:
which way to pull the rein?
The left brings you but loss,
the right nothing but gain.

How HAVE I HANDLED THE DECISIONS I'VE HAD TO MAKE AT THE CROSSROADS OF MY LIFE?

Say That Again

So shall My Word be that goes forth from
My mouth; it shall not return to Me void,
but it shall accomplish what I please, and it
shall prosper in the thing for which I sent it.
ISAIAH 55:11 NKJV

I can LISTEN
TO GOD'S
VOICE BETTER
WHEN I . . .

In 1954, Sylvia Wright wrote a column for *The Atlantic* in which she coined the term "mondegreen," her code word for misheard lyrics. She recounted how, upon hearing the Scottish folk song, "The Bonny Earl of Morray:"

> *Ye highlands, and ye lowlands,*
> *Oh! whair hae ye been?*
> *They hae slaine the Earl of Murray,*
> *And layd him on the green.*

that she misheard the last line as "and Lady Mondegreen." It saddened her immensely that both the Earl and the Lady had died. Of course, she was later chagrined to learn that those were not the lyrics at all. But they made so much sense at the time.

Since then, mondegreen collectors have been on the lookout for newer and more comical misunderstandings. For example:

In "America the Beautiful," one young patriot heard, "Oh beautiful, for spacious skies. . ." as "Oh beautiful, for spaceship guys. . . . "

Another considered *Away in a Manger* a little unsettling as he sang, "the cattle are blowing the baby away. . . "

Then there was the Mickey Mouse Club fan who, when the cast sang, "Forever hold your banners high. . ." thought they were encouraging her to "Forever hold your Pampers high!"[26]

It's no wonder that, with all our earthly static and clamor, we sometimes think we're singing the right words when we're not. But if we begin each day in quiet conversation with God, His Word comes through loud and clear. There can be no misunderstanding of God's lyrics.

Earth changes, but thy soul
and God stand sure.

Heeding God's Warnings

> There is . . . a time to plant and a time to uproot.
>
> ECCLESIASTES 3:1-2

After months of searching, a lawyer and his family found a house they loved, one with a shady backyard. The contract went well—until the inspector finished his examination of the foundation. The problem? A tree growing too close to the house.

The lawyer's wife grew angry as the inspector described the problems the tree could cause. "The reason we wanted this house was because of the trees, especially that one!" she said. "We'll take our chances!"

So they moved in. They planted an expensive garden underneath the tree and enjoyed the shade all year long. One day, the lawyer noticed large cracks on the inside walls, and a jagged line followed the two-inch split in the outside brick wall—only a few feet from the tree roots.

The disgusted lawyer listed the house for sale immediately, but no one would buy the home. Finally, two years later, a real estate agent found a buyer, but there was one condition to the sale: the owners had to repair the house.

By this time, the foundation needed a complete restoration. The cost? Just over ten thousand dollars. Eager to move out, the lawyer paid the money and sold the house at a substantial loss.

Like the lawyer's shade tree, little problems in life often appear harmless. If we ignore God's warnings, those problems will eventually grow large enough to erode our spiritual foundation. We can avoid needless costly mistakes by heeding God's words.

One's first step in wisdom is to question everything. And one's last is to come to terms with everything.

What ARE THE LITTLE PROBLEMS IN MY LIFE THAT COULD BECOME BIG PROBLEMS IF I IGNORE THEM?

Never Alone

Where can I go from your Spirit?
Where can I flee from your presence?
PSALM 139:7

HOW HAVE I
TRIED TO RUN
FROM GOD'S
PRESENCE
LATELY?

"How did you know I was here?" Patty rested her head against the steel post of the bridge and swung her legs gently over the water below.

"Where else would you be?" her father asked. He stood behind her, respecting her need for space. "This is where you always come when your heart hurts. After all these years, you don't think I know that?" Patty beckoned him to sit beside her. He sat there, quietly supporting and loving her, knowing she needed to be alone but not alone, separate but still loved.

Our Heavenly Father knows us even more intimately than our own parents do. When we try to run and hide from God's presence, He is always there—not as an intruder or an accusing presence, but as a loving companion. He is a friend who holds us even when we're afraid to look Him in the eye. His love knows no hiding place. There is nothing to run from if we belong to Him. Often He won't speak a word when we try to escape Him. He just waits, acknowledging our choices and loving us just the same.

Have you run away from your Father? He is there if you want to talk to Him. He knows your heart, and He wants to be with you. Even in the moments of aloneness, God is your silent companion.

Though God be everywhere present,
yet He is present to you in the deepest
and most central part of the soul.

Locks of Love

Do not forget to do good and to share with others,
for with such sacrifices God is pleased.

HEBREWS 13:16

Rebecca Borkovec could easily play a child's version of the wife in the beloved Christmas story "The Gift of the Magi." When she was eight years old, Rebecca heard about the Locks of Love organization and decided to let her hair grow for charity.

For the next two and a half years, Rebecca let her hair grow. The long, beautiful locks would one day make a wonderful Christmas present for a child who had lost her hair during chemotherapy. Rebecca's mother encouraged her, took time to braid her hair, and kept fixing it in creative ways. And Rebecca often reminded her mother that they needed to get her hair trimmed so it would look even nicer for another child, one she would never meet.

On February 9, 2000, Rebecca settled into a chair at Barbara's hair salon and signaled Barbara to start cutting. Was Rebecca sad to see her locks fall? She just sat there smiling. Why? "Because I was going to help people," she said.

But Rebecca didn't stop there. "I'm going to do it again," she promised, "so I can help them again. It will probably take about three years."

Many people give to charities, but often they give only if they experience some kind of benefit, such as a tax write-off. Rebecca's gift brought her no tangible returns—only the sheer joy of knowing she gave a headful of love to someone in need.

True charity is the desire to be useful to others without thought of recompense.

The LAST TIME I GAVE SOMETHING SIMPLY OUT OF THE JOY OF GIVING WAS WHEN I . . .

A Welcome Sight

Good news from far away is
like cold water to the thirsty.
PROVERBS 25:25 TLB

What ARE
SOME OTHER
WAYS I CAN
CONNECT
WITH PEOPLE
THROUGHOUT
THE YEAR?

Does your family get a lot of Christmas letters? They come every December—if the sender is well prepared. Some don't arrive until late January—if the sender was too harried before Christmas. But no matter when they arrive, holiday letters serve as reminders that your family has friends and other relatives who find it difficult to stay in touch throughout the year.

What do you and your family do with those letters? Many families read them aloud at dinnertime throughout the Christmas season. Some put them aside and read them later on, when the rush of the season has slowed down.

Christmas letters can serve a purpose far greater than that of simply sharing news; they can prompt you to pray for the people who send them. Why not make that suggestion to your own family? Instead of reading them only at Christmas, put them aside for a few weeks and begin selecting them at random to read after dinner. Then pray together as a family for the sender. You could even start a new tradition by writing back and enclosing a family letter of your own—say, on the Fourth of July or another holiday.

In this age of electronic communication, a letter in a mailbox is a welcome and rare sight. But that small gesture can serve to remind the recipient that someone out there is thinking about them, praying for them, and loving them.

Life is the flower of which
love is the honey.

Calculated Risk

> Therefore, prepare your minds for action, keep sober in spirit, fix your hope completely on the grace to be brought to you at the revelation of Jesus Christ.
>
> 1 PETER 1:13 NASB

Trying something new can be frightening and may even be dangerous. That's why it's much smarter to take a calculated risk than a reckless plunge.

A calculated risk is what Charles Lindbergh took when he decided to fly across the Atlantic, alone, in a single-engine plane. Was Lindbergh afraid? No. He was an experienced pilot and mechanic who spent months overseeing the construction of his plane. He participated in the planning of every detail of his historic flight. The end result was a safe trip, one that he finished ahead of schedule with fuel to spare.

Likewise, heroic spiritual moments are nearly always grounded in advance preparation. Moses grew up in Pharaoh's court, unknowingly being prepared for the day he would demand that Pharaoh let his people leave Egypt. Daniel was a man of prayer years before the king issued a decree banning prayer. The violation landed Daniel in the lions' den, where his prayers of protection were answered. David spent years in preparation for the day when he would assume the throne. Those years were spent wisely as he learned to trust God, and God alone, to preserve him, protect him, and help him rule an empire.

You may not see clearly what God's purpose is for your life, but you can trust in the fact that He is preparing you for it. He will not waste a moment of your life. He is grooming you for future greatness!

Every experience God gives us, every person He puts in our lives, is the perfect preparation for the future that only He can see.

HOW CAN I PREPARE MYSELF TODAY FOR WHAT MAY COME MY WAY IN THE FUTURE?

A Wild Ride

Preserve me, O God, for in You I put my trust.
PSALM 16:1 NKJV

What
"WILD RIDE"
THREATENS
TO CAUSE ME
TO FALL?

Nervous at the prospect of her first horseback ride, a little girl cried out, "What do I do? I don't know how to ride a horse! I haven't done this before!" Her grandfather reassured her. "Don't worry about the horse or about how to ride it," he said. "Just hold on to me, darlin', just hold on to me."

That's great advice for us as well. On our difficult and scary days, we need to "just hold on" to the Lord. And one of the best ways we can do that is through constant communication with Him—a continual flow of prayer and praise. Even a "thought" prayer turns our will and focus toward the Lord and puts our trust in Him. When we lose touch with the Lord, though, we are in danger of "falling" into panic and the frustration, frenzy, and failure that can come with it.

The Lord knows the end from the beginning of each day, and He knows how long the current upheaval in your life will last. Above all, He knows how to bring you safely through each "wild ride," keeping you in His divine peace all the way.

Always remember that you don't ride the beasts of this life alone. The Lord is with you, and He has the reins firmly in His grasp. Just hold on!

Whatever God calls us to do, He also makes possible for us to accomplish.

Hearing with the Heart

Thine heart was tender.

2 KINGS 22:19 KJV

"We've wasted my whole Saturday," moaned John as his father gently woke him.

The plaintive, anguished tone of his voice created an instant reaction in his father and flash of anger surged upward. It had been a very long day of painting and hanging wallpaper in Mom's new office and Dad was tired. John had worked hard earlier in the day, but as the novelty wore off he became bored and eventually fell asleep on a couch in an adjacent office. Now his Dad, Richard, was waking him so that they could head home.

Before Richard could voice the quick retort that formed in his mind, something caused him to pause. In a flash, he saw the Saturday spent working in Mom's new office from a teen's point of view.

With newfound compassion he responded to his son, "John, I know that Saturday is just about the most important day of the week when you're this age. I appreciate so much your willingness to give up your Saturday to help us get Mom's office decorated. It has been a very long day and I bet that you're tired too. But, I would like to show you how much I appreciate your support by taking you and a few of your friends to the movies next Friday night. What do ya say?"

In response to Dad's caring attitude, John's anguish and despair turned to pride and he quietly said, "You're welcome, Dad. I would like that."

Sometimes, when we listen with our heart and not our ears, love wins and relationships flourish. For as Johann Wolfgang Von Goethe says, "Correction does much, but encouragement does more."

One THING THAT CAN HELP ME TO RESPOND WITH COMPASSION INSTEAD OF ANGER IS . . .

Compassion brings us to a stop, and for a moment we rise above ourselves.

Believe in Me

And the Lord make you to increase and abound in love one toward another, and toward all men.

I THESSALONIANS 3:12 KJV

I am
ENCOURAGED TO SUCCEED WHEN . . .

Cynthia was amazed and grateful for what she was seeing. She watched as Ms. Nelson, a fifth grade teacher at the private school, quietly greeted each child and their parents at the door of her classroom. Cynthia was so excited to assist Ms. Nelson as a senior student aid. Ms. Nelson spoke with pride to each parent of the work of his or her child. She took time to mention the child by name and to point out something on that child's work that was particularly noteworthy. As a result, both the parent and the child glowed with satisfaction.

This was not a special event—it was the morning of a normal school day, and Ms. Nelson made it a habit to be at the door every morning.

As Cynthia stepped into the classroom, she was struck by the impact of Ms. Nelson's genuine comments and actions. Cynthia couldn't help but think of a gardener fussing over the flowers and plants of the garden—eager to provide the right nourishment and attention so that each plant grows strong and healthy.

Later that afternoon, Cynthia asked one of the fifth-grade boys how he liked being in Ms. Nelson's class. He responded, "I like it a lot. She is a really neat teacher because you always know that she believes in you. Even when you don't get everything right, she still believes in you."

What a gift—the ability to believe in others and communicate it to them daily, just as our Lord loves and believes in us without fail. We can all learn to pass this gift on to those we care about.

Correction does much, but encouragement does more. Encouragement after censure is as the sun after a shower.

The Celebrity Garden

I am a rose of Sharon. . . . Like a lily among thorns is my darling among the maidens.
SONG OF SONGS 2:1-2

Erica's mother, Sherry, had finally cleared a spot in her backyard for a rose garden—her dream for many years. Erica helped her mother select from her magnitude of options. "Just like a Christmas wish list," her mother said. "Which ones should I pick? A white John F. Kennedy, a large, pink Peggy Lee, a red Mr. Lincoln, the delicate Queen Elizabeth rose?"

Sherry closed her eyes as if in deep thought. Suddenly, she cried with excitement, "I'll plant my own celebrity garden."

Erica went with her mother the next day to her local nursery and bought a dozen roses—all colors and sizes. Erica noticed each day as she returned from school how much effort her mother put into carefully planting each rose all that week. Finally, her task was done and Sherry decided to throw a party and invite all her friends to help her celebrate her celebrity rose garden.

Erica was shocked when she stood with her mother's friends as Sherry unveiled the celebrity names she had placed on each rose. One by one, they read their own names beside the flowers. The celebrities in Sherry's garden were none other than her friends. Erica even spotted one with her own name on it. But in the middle of the fragrant bouquet, one rose still remained a mystery.

Finally, Sherry unveiled the label which read, "Rose of Sharon." "This One is the love of my life," she said, "and everything else centers around Him."

A thousand "celebrities" cry out for our time and attention. Relationships, like a healthy garden, need ample doses of love and affirmation. When Christ is at the center of our affection, all other loves will fall in place.

The dearest friend on earth is a mere shadow compared with Jesus Christ.

In THE GARDEN OF MY LIFE, MY CELEBRITIES ARE . . .

Send in the Clowns

Whatever you do, work at it with all your heart,
as working for the Lord, not for men.
COLOSSIANS 3:23

The LAST
TIME I HAD A
REALLY GOOD
LAUGH WAS
WHEN . . .

When the circus came to town, posters went up on the grocery store bulletin boards; billboards announced the performance dates, and television commercials urged listeners to "come one; come all!" Lion tamers, wire walkers, and trapeze artists were part of the three-ring extravaganza. But the most anticipated performers were the clowns. With their crazy antics and outlandish costumes, they livened up each performance.

Clowns work hard at their profession. In fact, in order to travel with the Ringling Brothers Circus, clowns must successfully complete clown college—an intense course of study that covers everything from makeup to pratfalls, costuming to making balloon animals, juggling to sleight of hand. Only after clowns have mastered all of these skills can they take their place in the circus ring.

As Kyle bent over his math homework, he sensed a connection to this group of performers in the circus. Though he didn't wear a clown costume or clown makeup, he worked hard at juggling—balancing his time among home, family, school, sports, friends, and church. He wasn't skilled at card tricks or sleight of hand, but he could work "magic," transforming everyday occurrences into fits of laughter seven days a week. The outgoing and spontaneous personality and gift of favor God had given him made it easy for him to make friends.

God's Word says that we are to work at whatever we do with all our hearts, remembering that whatever we do is for the Lord. Whether we're clowns or students, minstrels or friends, we should enjoy the gifts God has given us. And when we do, we might just provide our friends and families with some laughter along the way!

The sound of laughter is a
picture of happiness.

The God of Tomorrow

> For I am the Lord—I do not change.
>
> MALACHI 3:6 TLB

When the microwave buzzed, Rebecca slid her chair away from her laptop computer and retrieved the hot water for her tea. She had been writing a science research paper on new technologies and how they would impact our lives in the next century. The whole topic was unsettling. The more research she did on the Internet, the more disturbed she became about cloning, supercomputers, and spy satellites. Where would it all end?

Suddenly, she had an urge to hear the comforting whistle of a teakettle and the crackling of a real fire instead of the hiss of a gas log. The world was moving too fast, and at times like these, she wanted to crawl up in her grandpa's lap and smell his sweet cherry pipe.

"Grandpa," she remembered asking one time, "did you have spaceships when you were little?"

He chuckled. "No, honey, when I was a little boy, we rode in a horse-drawn wagon to town. Airplanes had just really gotten off the ground."

"But you had trains."

"Yep, I guess I always liked trains the best."

The sound of a train whistle still reminded her of Grandpa and how he looked in his navy-blue conductor's uniform. Sometimes he would let her carry around his big silver watch. "All aboard!" she'd call, and Grandpa would pretend to be a passenger.

She knew what Grandpa had to say about life today. He'd tell her not to worry. "Honey," he'd say, "I've been in some pretty tight places in my day: train wrecks, labor strikes, and world wars. I reckon if God pulled us through all of that, He can see us the rest of the way home."

She "reckoned" He would. The God of her grandpa's era would be the same God in the twenty-first century. And *that* was a comforting thought.

I am GLAD GOD DOESN'T CHANGE BECAUSE . . .

God is and that not in time but in eternity, motionless, timeless, changeless eternity, that has no before or after; and being One, he fills eternity with one now and so really is.

Wrong Bus

Wait for the Lord; be strong and
take heart and wait for the Lord.
PSALM 27:14

When I
REALIZE I NEED
TO BE MORE
PATIENT, I
SHOULD . . .

Lizzy and Karen had broken free of the evangelism conference and wanted to explore Seattle before the evening session. They'd been waiting for the bus for twenty minutes and found themselves impatient and eager. There was so much to see.

Moments later, a bus pulled up. "It's not the one they said we should take, but it's headed in the same direction," Lizzy said. "Let's go!" They climbed on board—two Midwestern girls, heading for the sights. As the bus made its way through the dark and scary underbelly of the city, the girls huddled together in a small corner of the bus. The driver seemed amused by their predicament.

Lizzy and Karen ended up staying on the bus for the whole route. Arriving back at the hotel, they were slightly shaken and had lost only a little time. They waited . . . and waited . . . and waited for the right bus.

Is there a "bus" you're tempted to climb aboard because you're tired of waiting? A relationship, a job, a direction you're thinking of taking that may not be God's best for you? There is much to be gained by waiting in the lobby for the right bus. God will not abandon you in your search. He is there, ready and waiting with His answer, reminding you of His sovereign will and His ability to take you where you need to go. Wait on Him. It's much safer and a whole lot wiser.

All comes at the proper time to him
who knows how to wait.

Playful Joy

[There is] a time to weep and a time to laugh.

ECCLESIASTES 3:4

Grandma Lu watched her grandson, a bit perplexed by his actions. Benjamin, in all his six-year-old glory, was spinning. Not for any apparent reason, he was simply spinning, around and around and around. His little arms were stretched out on either side of his body, and his head was thrown back as a deep belly laugh escaped from his rosy lips. It didn't seem that he was doing much . . . hardly anything amusing or interesting.

Grandma Lu paused.

Was there something fun about spinning? She glanced around the lobby of the hotel where she sat. There were only a few people nearby, and they were buried deep in magazines and newspapers. She stood up and set her purse on the seat, blushing even as she walked toward her spinning grandson. She wasn't sure if there was any special technique, so she watched him for a moment before spreading out her own arms. She began slowly at first, careful not to bump into anything, worried she might slip and fall. Then she threw caution to the wind and began to speed up. She threw her head back and laughed, and felt the momentum of her own body carry her in circles. What fun!

A few minutes later, she slowed to a stop. Benjamin stood before her, his mouth open, his eyes wide. He began to laugh, and she laughed with him. They made quite a pair in that hotel lobby—disheveled, flushed, spinning grandmother and grandson. But people smiled, because their joy was real.

Laughter is God's gift of healing for a saddened heart. It gives lightness to the spirit and gets the blood flowing. Find a way to laugh today; rent a funny movie or read the comics. Do things you wouldn't normally think of doing and allow yourself to enjoy them. There is a time to laugh. Take that time today and revel in the abandonment of playful joy.

Several THINGS I THINK ARE REALLY FUN TO DO ARE . . .

✠

Joy is the most infallible sign of the presence of God.

Future Father

> And whoever welcomes a little child
> like this in my name welcomes me.
> MATTHEW 18:5

Who DO I
KNOW THAT
I CAN OFFER A
FEW WORDS OF
ENCOURAGE-
MENT TO
TODAY?

Max, the oldest of six, surveyed the crowd before him. The noise seemed too much, almost overwhelming as everyone tried to speak at once. It was Sunday dinner and all the family was gathered around the large table. Steaming platters of food were being handed from person to person as plates were piled higher and higher with delectable treats.

Down near the end of the table Max noticed Daniel, a friend of his little brother, Nate. Daniel was only eight years old and looked flustered and nervous as people passed food around and over him. Max watched as one of the other children noticed and attended to him. "Would you like some of these potatoes, Daniel?"

The small boy nodded and smiled a simple grin of appreciation. The others seemed to take notice of him then and began asking him questions about school and friends. Daniel had a difficult home life and often spent evenings with Max's family. Max noticed how his brothers and sisters focused on his hopes and dreams and seemed genuinely interested in Daniel. "What do you want to be when you grow up?" asked one of the children.

Daniel hesitated and looked around at the family. "I want to be a dad. With lots of kids, like this family."

The room got quiet as everyone mulled over what he had said. Finally, Max smiled broadly and patted Daniel on the back. "Sounds great, Daniel! You'll make a great father!" he said, winking, "as long as you have a better group than this one to work with!"

The room exploded as all the kids laughed and began shouting over each other, yelling their defense. Max looked at his mother and then watched Daniel in the rising commotion. He was sitting quietly with a smile on his face. Finally he grabbed his fork and seemed to nod to himself as he ate his first big bite. He seemed . . . triumphant.

Just a few small words of encouragement, a pair of listening ears, an afternoon in the midst of your family, can make a difference in the life of a child.

The deepest principle in human nature
is the craving to be appreciated.

Eat Your Breakfast!

"I have food you don't know about." Then Jesus explained: "My nourishment comes from doing the will of God, who sent me, and from finishing his work."

JOHN 4:32, 34 NLT

Breakfast is the most important meal of the day. Don't leave home without breakfast. A good breakfast will stay with you the entire day.

These phrases and others like them have become well known in our culture, but they aren't just Mom's advice anymore! Scientists and doctors have spent millions of dollars to discover what moms have known all along.

However, even more important than a naturally nutritious breakfast is a spiritually nutritious breakfast. Proverbs 31:15 says the virtuous woman rises early to get spiritual food for her household. David said in Psalm 63:1: *"O God, You are my God; Early will I seek You."*

Jesus once said to His disciples, "I have food to eat of which you do not know," then He explained, "My food is to do the will of Him who sent Me, and to finish His work" (John 4:32, 34 NKJV). Jesus was saying that He was motivated and energized by walking in obedience to the Father and doing His will. His life flowed from the "inside out." The same must be true for those of us who seek to follow in His footsteps.

When we spend the first part of our day in the Word of God, prayer, meditation, and praise and worship, we acquire an inner strength and energy that adds vitality to our entire day. This "food for the soul" is truly food that the world does not know about, that prepares us to do the Lord's will. Regardless of where our day may take us or the situations we may encounter, we have a renewed mind to think the thoughts of God, to feel His heartbeat, and to say and do what Jesus would say and do.

After having breakfast with God, you will be prepared to face whatever the day may bring—and end the day with less stress and frustration. God promises that if we seek His kingdom first, all other things will be added to us (Matthew 6:33). When you make your relationship with the Lord your top priority, you are setting yourself up for blessings all day!

I need
TO TELL GOD
ABOUT . . .

✠

God reveals himself unfailingly
to the thoughtful seeker.

Your Personal Sanctuary

Jesus . . . withdrew again to a mountain by himself.
JOHN 6:15

For MY
PERSONAL
SANCTUARY IN
MY DAILY LIFE
I NEED TO . . .

A sanctuary is a place of refuge and protection—a place where you can leave the world behind. Travelers in the Middle Ages found shrines, bearing a cross and the image of a saint, along the roadways. People stopped at these "sanctuaries" for rest and prayer, regaining strength to continue their journey.

Our contemporary world doesn't have wayside shrines for rest stops. But our minds and hearts still get weary. We have to devise our own wayside stops, not on actual roads, but in the road of daily life.

No matter how inspiring a weekend worship service may be, we usually need something to keep us going until the next service. We need stopping places during the week, intimate sanctuaries where we can let God refresh our soul with His presence.

Reading Scripture, especially a favorite passage or Psalm, can become a sanctuary, as can reading a devotional book, such as the one you are reading now. A trusted Christian friend with whom you can be yourself is a type of sanctuary. Your own communion service during the week gives you a chance to take part in the nourishment of the Lord's Supper. Going to a park or sitting in your own backyard and reading gives you a chance to rest while enjoying God's creation. Singing praise songs out loud helps to restore your joy.

You need to be refreshed and strengthened to continue your journey; establishing your own personal sanctuary can help keep you going.

What sweet delight a quiet life affords.

Too Good to Miss

> As we have therefore opportunity, let us do
> good unto all men, especially unto them
> who are of the household of faith.
>
> GALATIANS 6:10 KJV

A fellow approached a cab driver in New York and said he wanted to go to London. "Drive me down to the pier; we'll put the taxi on a freighter to Liverpool; and you'll drive me to London, where I'll pay you whatever is on the meter," he said. The driver agreed. When they arrived in London, the passenger paid the total on the meter, plus a thousand dollar tip.

Soon after, an Englishman hailed the cab driver and said, "I want you to drive me to New York." The cab driver couldn't believe his good luck. When the passenger began to say, "First, we take a boat . . . " the driver cut him off. "That I know. But where to in New York?" The passenger said, "Riverside Drive and 104th Street." The driver responded, "Sorry, I don't go to the West Side." Do you think the driver was a bit shortsighted?

Jesus was well schooled in the Scriptures, and He often followed the traditions of His heritage. He also had a daily routine of praying and ministering to the needs of the people. However, He didn't allow traditions or personal preferences to stand in the way of carrying out God's will for the day.

Look for God-given opportunities to serve Him by serving others. Don't allow your daily routines, personal biases, or shortsightedness to cause you to miss what the Lord wants to do in you and through you today.

A good deed is never lost; he who shows
courtesy reaps friendship, and he who plants
kindness gathers love.

Today I
MIGHT BE
MISSING . . .

Simple Pleasures

> I will give you a new heart and put a new
> spirit within you; I will take the heart of stone
> out of your flesh and give you a heart of flesh.
> EZEKIEL 36:26 NKJV

What SIMPLE
PLEASURES
AM I
OVERLOOKING
TODAY?

In 1994, Jim Gleason underwent a life-saving heart transplant at age fifty-one. After he survived one of the most extreme surgeries imaginable, many asked how it felt to live with a new heart. His analogy was "like being born again, but with fifty years of memories and experiences built in."

He tells of coming home just ten days after his transplant. He wanted to go for a short walk around the yard. Accompanied by his daughter, he gazed in wonder at the green grass—so brilliant after weeks of drab hospital room walls. He recalls: "I stopped walking. 'Look at that!' I exclaimed to Mary. I was pointing to our small maple tree, so vibrant with the colors of that crisp, clear fall day. Then I spied a grasshopper and, like a young child, exclaimed in glee, 'Look at that! A grasshopper!'

"Her response, in disbelief at my reaction, was an almost sarcastic, 'Well, if that's exciting, look here—a ladybug!'"

After four years with his new heart, Jim still cherishes life's simple pleasures. And when is the danger of losing that gift the greatest? "As friends and family wish you would return to being 'normal,'" he reflects. "I struggle to never become 'normal' in that sense again."[26]

With God's help, we, too, can walk in newness of life—no surgery required. Give thanks that we don't have to be "normal."

Think not on what you lack as
much as on what you have.

A Perfect Combination

"You are the salt of the earth. But if the salt loses
it saltiness, how can it be made salty again?
It is no longer good for anything, except
to be thrown out and trampled by men."

MATTHEW 5:13

Sodium is an extremely active element that always links itself to another element. Chlorine is a poisonous gas. When combined, chlorine stabilizes sodium, and sodium neutralizes the poison of the chlorine. The result, sodium chloride, is common table salt, a highly stable substance used through the centuries to preserve meat, enhance flavor, and, prior to modern medicine, help clean and heal wounds.

For a Christian, love and truth can be like sodium and chlorine. Both are essential elements in a believer's life, but pursuing one without the other can be unmanageable and even dangerous. Love without truth is flighty, sometimes blind, and often willing to combine with strange or perverse doctrines. It is highly unstable, tossed to and fro on a sea of emotions.

On the other hand, truth by itself can be offensive, sometimes even poisonous. Spoken without love, it can turn people away from God. It can wound, even kill, a person's longing for the nurturing presence of the Heavenly Father.

When truth and love are combined in an individual, however, we have what Jesus called "the salt of the earth." We are able to heal those with spiritual wounds, preserve and encourage the best in one another, and bring out the personal zest and unique gifts of each person.

Today as you deal with others, seek to let your words and actions be grounded in truth and delivered with love.

I can KNOW
MY WORDS
AND ACTIONS
COME FROM
LOVE IN MY
HEART IF I . . .

Love looks not with the eyes,
but with the heart.

Darkness into Light

You are my lamp, O Lord;
the Lord turns my darkness into light.

2 SAMUEL 22:29

I brighten
THE LIVES

OF THOSE

AROUND ME

IF I . . .

One night, a pastor received a call from one of the wives in his church's couples group. Her husband's plane had gone down, and she didn't know if he was alive. The pastor immediately called the other group members, who rallied around her. They sat and prayed with her until word came that her husband was dead. Then various women took turns baby-sitting and staying with her during those first difficult nights.

Group members opened their homes to out-of-town relatives who came for the funeral. The men kept her car running and did yard work. And when she decided she would have to sell her house and find a smaller place to live, they helped her locate an apartment, pack, unpack, and settle into her new home.

For many people, this experience would seem like a night without end, a shadow on their lives that would never be erased. But because her friends let their lights shine into her darkness, they reminded her of the God who understood her pain and promised to see her through it.

"You are the light of the world," Jesus said. "A city on a hill cannot be hidden" (Matthew 5:14). In a world that seems to grow darker day by day, let the Lord turn your darkness into light. Then you can brighten the lives of those around you by being one of God's "night lights."

I don't have to light all of the world,
but I do have to light my part.

Erosion

We are his workmanship.

EPHESIANS 2:10 RSV

We see it as we walk along an ocean shore, where steep cliffs meet with the rise and fall of the tides. The splashing of sand- and rock-laden waves have cut away at the towering sea cliffs. Day after day, night after night, the continual lapping of the ocean water silently undercuts the stone walls. Then in one sudden blow the entire structure can shift and fall thundering into the sea. On a daily basis, the wear and tear of water on sea cliffs is imperceptible, yet we know that every wave hitting the rock is washing away some of its hard surface.

We see the same shaping influence in another aspect of nature—trees that grow at the timberline in a harsh, remote setting. The extra resins that flow in the trees, as a result of the severe winds and snow-storms at the timberline, produce a grain of wood that has a rare and desirable texture. Such wood is sought by violin makers because it produces instruments of the finest quality and resonance.

Each of us is exposed to the wear and tear of life. In God's hands, however, those stresses and changes become His tools for shaping our life for His purpose. As our lives are yielded to and shaped by Him, He creates within us the ability to resonate His presence.

Commit your life to the Lord again today. Trust Him to take all that happens to you—both good and bad—and make you stronger and wiser, using you in His great plan.

God works in moments.

My AWARENESS THAT GOD IS WORKING BEHIND THE SCENES CHANGES MY ATTITUDE TOWARD HARD TIMES BY . . .

First Place

"Seek first His kingdom and His righteousness;
and all these things shall be added to you."
MATTHEW 6:33 NASB

What GOALS
WOULD I
PLACE AT
THE TOP OF
MY LIST? WHY
ARE THESE
IMPORTANT
TO ME?

Our society is inundated with the idea of being first. We want to be first in every line to get the best seat. Winning first place carries the most weight, the largest award, and the most recognition. Rarely are we able to recall the second runner-up in any event. No doubt about it, first is the crème de la crème. Or is it?

There is nothing wrong with obtaining first-place status. As a matter of fact, the Bible encourages us to set high goals and reach for them with perseverance. Each of us knows people we admire because of the goals they have set and reached through committed determination. But what about those who do their very best and never get the top grade, never win the trophy? What do they do with God's promises?

God has a plan for each of us. The stakes are often very high. The game plan may be interrupted many times in life. We will doubt, be discouraged, and face what seem to be impossibilities. However, God promises us that if we seek Him first, we have whatever we need—all of His blessings and all of His promises.

Some never make it to the finish line in athletic competitions, yet their labor is rewarded because they did their best. So it is with us if we "run the race of faith" with our eyes on Jesus.

The great thing in the World is not
so much Where We stand, as in
What direction We are moving.

Giving Thought

You care for the land and water it; you enrich
it abundantly. The streams of God are
filled with water to provide the people
with grain, for so you have ordained it.
PSALM 65:9

One of America's most popular contemporary painters, Andrew Wyeth, portrays life in rural Pennsylvania and Maine so meticulously that it sometimes appears surreal. A story told by his brother Nat gives a great deal of insight into the source of Wyeth's intensity:

"Andy did a picture of Lafayette's quarters near Chadds Ford, Pennsylvania, with a sycamore tree behind the building. When I first saw the painting, he wasn't finished with it. He showed me a lot of drawings of the trunk and the sycamore's gnarled roots, and I said, 'Where's all that in the picture?'

"'It's not in the picture, Nat,' he said. 'For me to get what I want in the part of the tree that's showing, I've got to know thoroughly how it is anchored in back of the house.'"

The act of thinking things through can't be underestimated in life. Do you stop and think before signing up for a difficult new course at school? How about the decision to break up with a boyfriend or girlfriend? It's been said that anything worth doing is worth doing right.

Wall Street legend Bernard Baruch emphasized this need, stating, "Whatever failures I have known, whatever errors I have committed, whatever follies I have witnessed in private and public life have been the consequence of action without thought."

Ask God for His advice as you plan your daily activities. When you have an important task to think through, stop and pray, "Lord, what is Your will?" He will be glad to help.

Four steps to achievement: Plan purposefully,
prepare prayerfully, proceed positively,
pursue persistently.

When
I ASK GOD
BEFORE I ACT,
I FIND . . .

Quiet, Please

The seed whose fruit is righteousness is sown in peace by those who make peace.

JAMES 3:18 NASB

Right NOW IS A GOOD TIME TO BE STILL AND LISTEN. WHAT IS THE LORD SAYING TO ME?

The role of quiet places played a very important role in the Bible, especially in the area of faith. Christ was alone during much of His life on earth. He would often retreat from the multitudes for quiet reflection. Moses went alone to the mountain to speak with God. While there, he received the Ten Commandments, one of the cornerstones of our faith. Daniel risked death three times a day when he ceased from his labors to pray.

The Holy Spirit often speaks to us when we are alone. Quiet places produce peace and contentment. Noise breeds confusion. Order is often regained in silence.

Our culture has become so noisy with technology, industry, entertainment, and transportation that we seldom find time and place for quiet. Yet we may yearn for times when we can think, be quiet, and listen to God. Finding time—actually, *making* time—for stillness is often quite a challenge.

If righteousness is sown in peace, then the quiet times when we just sit, listen, and wait for the Lord to speak must produce what is essential for spiritual growth. Seeking quiet time for reflection helps us commune with God. As a result, His righteousness wears off on us, and we begin to pick up some of His characteristics.

The Lord has time to spend with us and is ready to grow His Spirit within us. It is up to us to make the appointment.

The best remedy for those who are afraid, lonely or unhappy is to go outside, somewhere where they can be quiet, alone with the heavens, nature and God.

Blessed to Give

> A generous man will himself be blessed,
> for he shares his food with the poor.
>
> PROVERBS 22:9

A farmer whose barns were full of corn always prayed that the poor be supplied, but when anyone in need asked for corn he said he had none to spare. One day after hearing his father pray for the needy, his little son said, "Father, I wish I had your corn."

"What would you do with it?" asked the father.

"I would answer your prayer," the boy replied.

Another child must have felt the same way. Supported by the community on Make a Difference Day, twelve-year-old Jessica Burris; her seventeen-year-old brother, Jeffrey; and eleven-year-old friend Corey Woodward collected forty-five hundred pairs of socks and hundreds of other clothes, shoes, blankets, books, and toiletries for people seeking help at free medical clinics.

Others make a difference as well. Twelve men from the United Men of Hollandale in a Mississippi Delta farming area decided to help answer some prayers. In this area, 92 percent of people live in poverty. Most jobs and stores are fifteen to twenty miles away, and there is no public transportation. These men serviced eighteen cars for free for single and elderly women who were short on money.

We are blessed, not so we can tear down our barns and build bigger barns to hold our goods, but so we can bless others with the abundance of our hearts and lives. We are blessed so that we can give.

Life is made up, not of great sacrifices or duties, but of little things, in which smiles and kindness and small obligations win and preserve the heart.

Someone
RECENTLY
BLESSED ME
WHEN . . .

The Worry Tree

"Do not worry about tomorrow,
for tomorrow will worry about itself.
Each day has enough trouble of its own."
MATTHEW 6:34

What

WORRIES CAN
I GIVE TO
GOD TODAY?

At the end of each day, a certain man stopped at an old tree in his front yard before entering his home. As he passed the tree, he reached out to touch the trunk and branches.

He did this so he could mentally "hang his troubles" on the branches—and not take them inside to his wife and children. He left his troubles there, assuming that if the problems were important, they would still be hanging on the tree when he came out the next morning. But many mornings he found they had disappeared.

Author David Mackenzie describes another practical method for casting your cares on God:

> We took a paper bag, wrote "God" on it, and taped it up high on the back of our kitchen door. As I prayed about matters . . . I would write down each concern on a piece of paper. Then those pieces of paper would go in the bag. The rule was that if you start worrying about a matter of prayer that you've turned over to God, you have to climb up on a chair and fish it out of the bag. I don't want to admit how much time I spent sifting through those scraps of paper.

Using God as your "Worry Tree" takes practice, but it's a skill worth developing. Your effort will be rewarded with the peace of knowing God is with you, ready to handle your heavy load—if you will only let Him.

Worry is like a rocking chair.
It gives you something to do
but doesn't get you anywhere.

The Bulldog Way

Let us not be weary in well doing: for in
due season we shall reap, if we faint not.
GALATIANS 6:9 KJV

Are you in the midst of a frustrating struggle?
Before you throw in the towel, remember this story
about the bulldog.

A man once owned two very fine bird dogs,
and he had spent many hours training them. One
day he looked out his window just in time to see
an ugly little bulldog digging his way under the
fence into his bird dogs' yard. As the dog wriggled
under the fence, the man realized it was too late to
stop him.

He thought to himself how uneven the fight
would be. The poor little bulldog was surely no
match for his animals. Snipping, barking, growling—tails and ears flying—the battle raged. When
the little dog had had enough, he trotted back to
the hole under the fence and shimmied out.

Amazed that none of the dogs looked any the
worse for the fight, he didn't give the incident
another thought until the next day, when he saw the
little bulldog coming down the sidewalk toward the
hole in the fence. To his amazement, a repeat performance of the previous day's battle began. And
once again, the little bulldog picked his moment to
end the fight, left the bird dogs barking and
snarling, and casually slid back under the fence.

Day after day for over a week the unwelcome
visitor returned to harass his bigger canine counterparts. Then the man was obliged to leave for a
week on business. When he returned, he asked his
wife about the ongoing battle.

"Battle?" she replied, "Why, there hasn't been
a battle in four days."

"He finally gave up?" asked the bird dog owner.

"Not exactly," she said. "That ugly little dog
still comes around every day . . . he even shimmied
under the fence until a day or so ago. But now all
he has to do is *walk* past the hole and those bird
dogs tuck their tails and head for their doghouse
whining all the way."

When I
WANT TO
GIVE UP, I . . .

✙

He that perseveres makes every
difficulty an advancement and
every contest a victory.

The People Factor

Greater love hath no man than this,
that a man lay down his life for his friends.
JOHN 15:13 KJV

Things THAT

MOTIVATE

ME ARE . . .

Wanted: someone willing to risk his life to rescue 200 Jewish artists and intellectuals from the Nazis. Faint of heart need not apply.

Would you jump at the chance to take on this job? Varian Fry did. A high-school Latin teacher from Connecticut, he went to Marseilles, France, in August 1941, intending to stay only three weeks. He stayed fourteen months.

Forging passports and smuggling people over the mountains into Spain, Fry and a handful of American and French volunteers managed to save almost 4,000 people from the Nazi scourge. Among them were the 200 well-recognized Jewish artists and intellectuals he originally intended to rescue.

Did Fry have a difficult time motivating himself each day to face the task in front of him? Probably not. He had little doubt what he was doing had divine purpose and tremendous significance.

Most of us will never find ourselves in Fry's position, and often we wonder if what we do throughout our day has any significance at all. But in many cases, it takes more strength to do the trivial tasks than the monumental ones.

If the job we do is difficult, we must ask God to show us how to make the task less strenuous. If the job is dull, we need to ask God to reveal ways to make it more interesting. If we think our work is unimportant, we need to remember that being in God's will and doing a good job for Him will not only bring blessing to others, but blessing to us now and for eternity.

Often it is the *people* factor that keeps us motivated. God gives us purpose and makes our lives meaningful, but He is always working to bless us so we can turn around and bless other people.

The tasks you face today are significant as you work to meet a need or to see growth in others. You will see God's love moving through your life to others in everything you do for them—from putting a bandage on a child's skinned knee to inventing a machine which helps people with asthma breathe.

All service ranks the same with God.

Love Your Enemies

> How good and pleasant it is when
> brothers live together in unity!
>
> PSALM 133:1

With the Cold War over, Americans and Russians seem to be looking at each other in a new way. Imagine being an American soldier stationed in Bosnia-Herzegovina, working alongside your Russian counterparts. How do you work together after decades of mistrust?

American and Russian officers who were asked this question agreed that when it comes right down to it, people are people, and soldiers are soldiers. When there's a goal to reach, one finds a way to communicate. The mission is kept in focus, ground rules are established, language barriers are overcome, mutual interests are discovered, and before long, friendships develop!

The early Christian believers certainly thought they had an enemy in Saul of Tarsus, and the feeling was mutual. Saul was extremely active in persecuting Christians in Jerusalem and was determined to deal the same harsh blows to believers in Damascus. But then Jesus appeared to him and his life was dramatically changed.

Believers in Damascus were suspicious of Saul when he arrived and declared he was also a believer in Jesus Christ. But as they witnessed his manner of living, God dramatically changed their hearts. In the end, the apostle *Paul* became an ardent friend of believers everywhere.

Have you secretly been at "war" with a classmate or teacher? Beginning today make a concerted effort to find common ground with that person. Smile when your instincts tell you to grimace. Stay focused on your goals and stick to the ground rules when working or volunteering together. Talk to them. Seek out hobbies, concerns, or family interests you hold in common. Start treating the person as you would a friend, not an enemy. After all, it's when your enemy is no longer your enemy that the fun begins!

The Bible says to love your enemies and pray for those who despitefully use you, and in doing so you heap coals upon their heads (Romans 12:20). The coals are blessings! When you sow blessings, you reap blessings!

One PERSON I COULD IMPROVE MY RELATIONSHIP WITH IS . . .

✠

Two enemies are two potential friends
who don't know each other.

Leaving a Legacy

My heart is steadfast, O God; I will sing
and make music with all my soul.
PSALM 108:1

I can LEAVE
AN IMPACT
ON PEOPLE
WITH . . .

William Congreve said, "Music alone with sudden charms can bind the wand'ring sense, and calm the troubled mind." Walter Turnbull, founder of the Boys Choir of Harlem, would add that music can also change the life of a child.

The success of Turnbull's work is well documented. An astounding ninety-eight percent of his choir members finish high school and go on to college. More important, they benefit from Turnbull's teachings. A healthy dose of old-fashioned values is mixed in with the music he teaches—the kind of values Turnbull learned as a child in rural Mississippi.

He believes America's sense of community is slipping away, and he hopes to impress upon his choir members the importance of nurturing one another to excel. For twenty-six years, Turnbull has demonstrated this principle to his students by taking them around the world—to Europe, Japan, Canada, and the Caribbean. With a current roster of 450 boys and girls, eight to eighteen years old, that's no small feat. But numbers and age do not matter to Turnbull. Character does. His satisfaction comes from knowing that his choir members are learning to be better people.

Most of us would love to leave the kind of legacy Walter Turnbull is leaving to the world. What we need to recognize is that Turnbull didn't create his 450-member choir in a day. He started where he was with a small group of neighborhood kids in a church basement. He didn't have money for choir robes or music. But he did have a desire to introduce those children to the joy of music.

Do what you can, where you are, with the people God has placed in your path right now. Today. Regardless of how you help others, you *will* put a song in their hearts.

Nothing great was ever done
without much enduring.

The Big Picture

I go to prepare a place for you.
And if I go and prepare a place for you,
I will come again and receive you to Myself;
that where I am, there you may be also.

JOHN 14:2-3 NKJV

During World War II, parachutes were constructed by the thousands in factories across the United States. From the workers' point of view, the job was tedious. It required stitching endless lengths of colorless fabric, crouched over a sewing machine eight to ten hours a day. The result of a day's work was a formless, massive heap of cloth that had no *visible* resemblance to a parachute.

To keep the workers motivated and concerned with quality, the management in one factory held a meeting with its workers each morning. The workers were told approximately how many parachutes had been strapped onto the backs of pilots, copilots, and other "flying" personnel the previous day. They knew just how many men had jumped to safety from disabled planes. The managers encouraged their workers to see the "big picture" of their job.

As a second means of motivation, the workers were asked to form a mental picture of a husband, brother, or son who might be the one saved by the parachute they were sewing.

The level of quality in that factory was one of the highest on record![27]

Don't let the tedium of each day's chores and responsibilities wear you down so you see only the "stitching" in front of you. Keep your eyes on the big picture. Focus on *why* you do what you do and who will benefit from your work, including those you don't know and may never meet. You may not have all the answers to the question, "Why am I here?" but you can rest assured, the Lord does!

Ultimately, the Bible tells us we will be in heaven for eternity—and that is the biggest picture of all! God is preparing us for heaven, just as He is preparing heaven for us. He is creating us to be the people He wants to live with forever.

Whatever mundane tasks or trivial pursuits you undertake today, see them in the light of eternity. They will take on a whole new meaning!

The MOST BORING TASK I HAVE IS LESS MUNDANE BECAUSE . . .

✞

It is our best work that God wants,
not the dregs of our exhaustion.
I think he must prefer quality to quantity.

What Are You Doing Today?

Praise the Lord, all you Gentiles! Laud Him, all you peoples! For His merciful kindness is great toward us, and the truth of the Lord endures forever.

PSALM 117:1-2 NKJV

What I DO IS

IMPORTANT

BECAUSE . . .

In the Middle Ages a man was sent to a building site in France to see how the workers felt about their labor. He approached the first worker and asked, "What are you doing?"

The worker snapped at him, "Are you blind? I'm cutting these impossible boulders with primitive tools and putting them together the way the boss tells me. I'm sweating under this hot sun. My back is breaking. I'm bored. I make next to nothing!"

The man quickly backed away and found a second worker, to whom he asked the same question, "What are you doing?"

The second worker replied, "I'm shaping these boulders into useable forms. Then they are put together according to the architect's plans. I earn five francs a week and that supports my wife and family. It's a job. Could be worse."

A little encouraged but not overwhelmed by this response, the man went to yet a third worker. "What are you doing?" he asked.

"Why, can't you see?" the worker said as he lifted his arm to the sky. "I'm building a cathedral!"[28]

How do you see *your* work today? Do you see it as drudgery without reward or purpose? Do you see it as "just a job" or "just schoolwork"? Or, do you see your work as part of God's master design, not only for you but for others? Do you see yourself as a partner with Him in establishing *His* kingdom on the earth?

How we regard our work may not affect whether a task gets done or not. It will, however, have an impact on the quality of our work and our productivity. The real impact of how we *feel* about a job lies in this: the more positive we feel about our work, the greater the satisfaction we have at day's end, and the less damaging stress we internalize. Those who see value in their jobs enjoy a greater sense of purpose.

Any job can be done with grace, dignity, style, and purpose . . . you only have to choose to see it that way!

✠

If your daily life seems poor, do not blame it; blame yourself. Tell yourself that you are not poet enough to call forth its riches.

Quality Time

Thou wilt shew me the path of life:
in thy presence is fulness of joy.

PSALM 16:11 KJV

Busy—so busy! The sun has long since set and there is still so much to do. Work, family, church, and much more seem to demand hours God never put in the day. Still, we Christians think all these accomplishments will please our Heavenly Father. After all, faith without works is dead, right?

When we finally fall into bed at night, can we say we've actually spent any time with the Father we're trying so hard to please?

In his book, *Unto the Hills,* Billy Graham tells a story about a little girl and her father who were great friends and enjoyed spending time together. They went for walks and shared a passion for watching birds, enjoying the changing seasons, and meeting people who crossed their path.

One day, the father noticed a change in his daughter. If he went for a walk, she excused herself from going. Knowing she was growing up, he rationalized that she must be expected to lose interest in her daddy as she made other friends. Nevertheless, her absence grieved him deeply.

Because of his daughter's absences, he was not in a particularly happy mood on his birthday. Then she presented him with a pair of exquisitely worked slippers, which she had handmade for him while he was out of the house walking.

At last he understood and said, "My darling, I like these slippers very much, but next time buy the slippers and let me have you all the days. I would rather have my child than anything she can make for me."[29]

Is it possible our Heavenly Father sometimes feels lonely for the company of His children? Are we so busy doing good that we forget—or are too weary—to spend some quiet time with Him as our day draws to a close?

Take a walk with your Heavenly Father as the sun sets. Spend some quality time talking to Him about anything and everything. You will be blessed and so will He!

When I
SPEND TIME
WITH GOD, I
LIKE TO . . .

We are not forced to take wings to find Him, but have only to seek solitude and to look within ourselves. You need not be overwhelmed with confusion before so kind a Guest, but with utter humility, talk to him as to your Father; ask for what you want as from a father.

Final Meditation

This book of the law shall not depart out of thy mouth; but thou shalt meditate therein day and night, that thou mayest observe to do according to all that is written therein: for then thou shalt make thy way prosperous, and then thou shalt have good success.

JOSHUA 1:8 KJV

Before I GO
TO SLEEP I LIKE
TO THINK
ABOUT . . .

One of the translations for the word "meditate" in Hebrew, the language in which the Old Testament was written, is the verb "to mutter"—to voice under one's breath, to continually repeat something. When we are taught to meditate upon the Lord and His Word day and night, we are to repeat God's Word to ourselves continually. When we do this, God's Word becomes foremost in our thinking. It becomes our mind-set, our worldview, our perspective on life.

The Scriptures promise that when we think and speak in accordance with God's law, we will act accordingly. Thus we will enjoy success and prosperity!

In the opinion of Henry Ward Beecher, a great preacher from the 1800s, "A few moments with God at that calm and tranquil season, are of more value than much fine gold."

The psalmist proclaimed, "My mouth shall praise thee with joyful lips: when I remember thee upon my bed, and meditate on thee in the night watches" (Psalm 63:5-6 KJV).

Have your last conscious thoughts before sleeping been about God's Word? Turn off the late show, close the novel, put away the work, and rest in the Lord, recalling His Word. You'll find it easier to do this if you choose a passage of Scripture on which to meditate in the morning and then meditate upon it all day—muttering phrases and verses to yourself in the odd moments of your schedule. Then, just before you fall asleep, remind yourself one final time of God's truth.

Those who do this report a more restful night. A peaceful mind focused on God's Word seems to produce peaceful sleep and deep relaxation for the body. In this day and age, with nearly a billion dollars spent each year on sleep aids, we have the greatest sleep aid of all—the Word of God!

Meditation is the soul's chewing.

His Promise of Peace

> Be still, and know that I am God.
>
> PSALM 46:10 KJV

A woman who grew up on a large farm in Pennsylvania fondly remembers some special times with her father. Because the growing and harvest seasons were pretty much over from November through March, she recalls thinking that her father set aside that time each year just to be with her.

"During the winter months," she says, "Dad didn't have to work as hard and long as he did the rest of the year. In fact, it seemed like there were some times when he didn't work at all as far as I could tell.

"During those long winter months, he had a habit of sitting by the fire. He never refused my bid to climb up on his lap and he rewarded my effort by holding me close for hours at a time. Often, he would read to me, or invite me to read a story to him. Sometimes I would fall asleep as we talked about all the things that are important to dads and little girls. Other times, we didn't talk at all. We just gazed at the fire and enjoyed the warmth of our closeness. Oh, how I treasured those intimate moments.

"As I grew, I thought it odd that other kids dreaded the 'indoor' days of winter. For me they meant the incredible pleasure of having my father very nearly all to myself."[30]

Just as winter is God's season of rest for the earth, we sometimes experience "winter" in our spiritual lives. The world may seem a cold place. Like children who dread "indoor days," we can feel stifled and penned in by these spiritual winters.

If you are going through a dry, wintry time, why not snuggle close to the Heavenly Father tonight and listen to His gentle voice? The love and comfort He wants to give you will surely warm your heart!

I feel CLOSEST TO GOD WHEN . . .

A great many people are trying to make peace, but that has already been done. God has not left it for us to do; all we have to do is to enter into it.

Fragments

One day Jesus was praying in a certain place. When he finished, one of his disciples said to him, Lord teach us to pray.

LUKE 11:1

I can
INCLUDE GOD
IN MY LIFE
MORE BY
SHARING . . .

Margaret Brownley tells of her son's first letters from camp: "When my oldest son went away to summer camp for the first time, I was a nervous wreck. Although he was nine years old, he hadn't as much as spent a night away from home, let alone an entire week. I packed his suitcase with special care, making sure he had enough socks and underwear to see him through the week. I also packed stationery and stamps so he could write home.

"I received the first letter from him three days after he left for camp. I quickly tore open the envelope and stared at the childish scrawl, which read: *Camp is fun, but the food is yucky!* The next letter offered little more: *Jerry wet the bed. Who's Jerry?* I wondered. The third and final letter had this interesting piece of news: *The nurse said it's not broken.*

"Fragments. Bits of information that barely skim the surface. A preview of coming attractions that never materialize. It made me think of my own sparse messages to God. 'Dear Lord,' I plead when a son is late coming home, 'keep him safe.' Or, 'Give me strength,' I pray when faced with a difficult neighbor or the challenge of a checkbook run amuck. 'Let me have wisdom,' is another favorite prayer of mine, usually murmured in haste while waiting my turn at a parent/teacher conference or dealing with a difficult employee. 'Thank-you, God,' I say before each meal or when my brood is tucked in safely for the night.

"Fragments. Bits and pieces. Are my messages to God as unsatisfactory to Him as my son's letters were to me? With a guilty start, I realized that it had been a long time since I'd had a meaningful chat with the Lord.

"When my son came home, he told me all about his adventures. It was good to have him home and safe. 'Thank-you, God,' I murmured, and then caught myself. It was time I sent God more than just a hasty note from 'camp.'"[31]

✛

A single grateful thought raised to heaven is the most perfect prayer.

Building for Eternity

> We fix our eyes not on what is seen,
> but on what is unseen. For what is seen
> is temporary, but what is unseen is eternal.
> 2 CORINTHIANS 4:18

Eternity is a difficult concept for us to grasp. In human terms, it seems a matter of time—or more accurately, timelessness. But eternity is more than a measure of time. Things said to be "eternal" have a quality of permanence. The benefits of eternal things are not found solely in the hereafter; they provide an incredible sense of satisfaction in this life as well.

The late Lorado Taft, one of America's great artists, often said that a real work of art must have in it "a hint of eternity." The writer of Ecclesiastes says that God has set eternity in the hearts of people. (See Ecclesiastes 3:11.) When we do a good piece of work, whether it is part of our vocation or not, we may find in it a hint of eternity, the abiding value that outlasts silver or gold.

Ascending to the top of one of the magnificent stairways in the Library of Congress, one reads this inscription on the wall: "Too low they build who build beneath the stars."

In building your life, build with God for eternity. In building the Church, build to the glory of Jesus Christ for the salvation of souls.

Ask the Lord to show you how to make your life and effort count for eternity. Pray for an awareness of eternity as you face every decision and task each day.

If we build to please ourselves, we are building on the sand; if we build for the love of God, we are building on the rock.

Am I BUILDING FOR ETERNITY OR MERELY FOR TODAY?

Finishing Well

As he had begun, so he would also complete this grace in you.

2 CORINTHIANS 8:6 NKJV

When I DO THE THINGS GOD SETS BEFORE ME . . .

Putting the finish on a piece of furniture is the final step in its construction. The bulk of the work that gives the chest, table, or chair its *function* happens much earlier in the process. But it is the finish—the staining and varnishing—that gives a piece of furniture its *beauty*. The finish brings out the grain and luster of the wood, the smoothness of the craftsmanship, and the shine that speaks of completion.

As Jesus exhaled His last breath on the Cross, He declared, "It is finished" (John 19:30). This was a triumphant statement that marked the completion of His earthly mission to satisfy and fulfill God's law for all people. The Cross became the beacon that shines brightly into sinful hearts and says, "You can be free." It also became the prelude for a "new beginning" at His resurrection—offering new life for all.

We are each called to end our lives well, but our finish is not simply at our death. It is also in our bringing closure to each day in such a way that we allow for our resurrection the following morning. It is saying with thankfulness and humility, "I've done what the Lord put before me to do today, to the best of my ability. And now, I give my all to Him anew so that He might recreate me and use me again tomorrow."

The God who began a good work in you will finish it day by day, and ultimately bring it to completion. (See Philippians 1:6.)

Know the value of time; snatch, seize, and enjoy every moment of it. No idleness, no laziness, no procrastination. Never put off till tomorrow what you can do today.

Ships in the Night

God hath given thee all them that sail with thee.

ACTS 27:24 KJV

As Rebecca's one-year-old son, Dylan, played in the bathtub with his favorite toy—a little sailor—she silently asked God how they should spend the rest of the day. Every day seemed to be the same, a combination of errands and housework.

Dylan grabbed the sailor and plopped him in his boat, splashing water in Rebecca's face. Somehow, the splashing water reminded her that Navy ships had recently docked in their port city. "There are men in those ships!" she shouted.

Rebecca's family always enjoyed visiting the Navy vessels, but this time she sensed God directing them to minister to the six hundred servicemen who had been at sea for the last five months. But how? Rebecca grabbed a towel and her dripping-wet baby and took off to go shopping for the newly arrived sailors.

As night drew near, her family climbed aboard a guided missile destroyer carrying gifts. The sailors, eager to see what was inside the green and gold boxes, greeted them. After the command duty officer was summoned on deck to receive their gifts, the officer offered to take Rebecca's family on a private tour.

To their surprise, when they visited the wardroom, they saw that one of the boxes had already been placed at the head of the captain's table. Trying not to notice, Rebecca quickly looked away, staring at a portrait. In the reflection of the glass, she watched an officer take something out of the box. She sensed the Lord whispering to her, *I want them all, so I start at the top.*

Lightly touching the rails, Rebecca's family prayed for each man who would hold that rail during the stormy seas of life. As the sailors lowered the American flag and illuminated the friendship lights, Rebecca's family bid them farewell.

Tonight, ask the Lord how He wants you to spend your tomorrow. Be available for Him. In doing so, you may touch many lives and make new friends.

Something
THAT
HAPPENED
RECENTLY
REMINDS ME
TO PRAY
ABOUT . . .

✠

You never know till you try to reach them how accessible men are; but you must approach each man by the right door.

An Open Door

I run in the path of your commands,
for you have set my heart free.
PSALM 119:32

When I GET
STILL BEFORE
GOD I . . .

One warm summer afternoon, a woman was attending the baptism of her grandniece in a great old stone church in the English countryside. The massive doors of the church were flung wide to allow the warm sunshine into the chilly stone structure.

As she sat enjoying the ritual, a small bird flew in through the open doors. Full of fear, it flew backward and forward near the ceiling, vainly looking for a way out into the sunshine. Seeing the light coming through the dark stained glass windows, it flew to one, then the next, and finally back toward the ceiling. It continued flying about in this way for several minutes, quickly exhausting its strength in frenzied panic. The woman watched the bird with concern and frustration. How foolish he was not to fly back out the same door through which he had entered!

Nearly ready to fall to the floor, the bird made a final lunge for one of the large rafters. Realizing he was in no immediate danger, he hopped a little on the beam, turned around, and suddenly saw the open door. Without hesitation he flew out into the sunshine, loudly singing a joyful song as he went.

The bird had captivated the woman's imagination. Suddenly she realized that she was like the bird. She had flitted about, trying to live a "good" life of noble works without recognizing that the door of salvation had been open to her all the time. She suddenly understood that to avoid flying into places that offered no hope of eternal life, she need only stop flapping and be still in the Lord's presence. From that vantage point, she could better see the door of grace that He had prepared for her.

During your time with God today, let your spirit fly up to a high place and sit with the Lord. He will show you how to fly out of your current problems.

God gives the shoulder
according to the burden.

Thirst-Quenchers

> Whosoever will, let him take the water of life freely.
>
> REVELATION 22:17 KJV

Water is essential to the survival of plants, animals, and people. The life processes of an organism depend on its cells having moisture. A tree, for example, may be 80 percent sap, which is primarily water. Sap contains minerals, carbohydrates, vitamins, and proteins, which circulate through the tree's vascular system to feed all parts of the tree.

The amount of the water supply in an area determines whether it is a desert or a forest. It determines whether a tree is shriveled and stunted or towering and majestic. Water comes to trees through dew, clouds, mists, fog, summer rains, and winter snows. Trees also take in water through their roots, which tap into springs, streams, or rivers.

A tree does not hoard moisture for itself, but after the water travels through the framework of the tree, it is given off into the surrounding air. The moisture, along with the oxygen expelled into the air, gives the forest a fresh fragrance.

The spiritual lesson we learn from nature is that it is nearly impossible to be a blessing to others when we are grossly undernourished ourselves. Like the tree, we must be well-watered with God's Word and His Spirit to bring a sweet fragrance to those around us.

If you are feeling empty and dry this afternoon, go to the watering hole of God's Word and take a long, refreshing drink. Feel His truth permeate every cell of your being and rejuvenate love, peace, and joy in your heart. It won't be long until you're looking for ways to help someone else!

Take rest; a field that has rested
gives a bountiful crop.

The MOST RECENT THING I LEARNED FROM GOD'S WORD WAS . . .

Without Worry

Don't worry about anything; instead, pray about everything. Tell God what you need, and thank him for all he has done.
PHILIPPIANS 4:6 NLT

The WORRIES
I NEED TO
GIVE TO
GOD ARE . . .

Many people lose sleep by worrying. They lie awake in bed, wondering if they made a right decision the day before—if they did the wrong thing—and what they should do tomorrow.

Here's a creative way one woman handled worry. With so many things to worry about, she decided to set aside one day each week to worry. As worrying situations occurred, she wrote them down and put them in her worry box. Then, on Worry Wednesday, she read through each worry. To her amazement, most of the things she was disturbed about had already been taken care of in some way. Thus, she learned there was seldom a justifiable reason to worry. As the psalmist wrote in Psalm 127:2 NKJV, "It is vain for you to rise up early, to sit up late, to eat the bread of sorrows; for so He gives His beloved sleep."

American poet Ellen M. Huntington Gates described God's perfect rest for those with weary hearts in her poem "Sleep Sweet."

Sleep sweet within this quiet room,
O thou, whoe'er thou art,
And let no mournful yesterdays
Disturb thy peaceful heart.
Nor let tomorrow mar thy rest
With dreams of coming ill:
Thy Maker is thy changeless friend,
His love surrounds thee still.
Forget thyself and all the world,
Put out each garish light:
The stars are shining overhead
Sleep sweet! Good night! Good night![32]

As a child of God, you can rest in the knowledge that you are surrounded by a loving Father who cares for you. Jesus said, *Look at the birds of the air, for they neither sow nor reap nor gather into barns; yet your heavenly Father feeds them. Are you not of more value than they?* (Matthew 6:26 NKJV). Trust in God without fear or anxiety about what tomorrow may bring. The same Creator who placed each star in the sky is watching over you.

The beginning of anxiety is the end of faith; and the beginning of true faith is the end of anxiety.

An Angel in Deed

> Do not forget to entertain strangers,
> for by so doing some people have
> entertained angels without knowing it.
> HEBREWS 13:2

The hospital room was quiet. Natalie, who was new to the area, was facing an emergency operation in the morning. Knowing only a few people in this small town added to her fear. She was alone in the hospital room, unable to sleep, and as the night dragged along, she became more and more nervous. The quietness of the room closed in on her.

She was ready to cry when she heard the creaking of the door. She looked toward it and saw a kind young face.

"Hi," the young woman said. "Are you lonely?"

"I sure am," Natalie replied.

"I'm a nursing student and have been observing here for a couple of weeks. I've caught up on all my paperwork. Do you feel like talking?" she asked.

"I sure do," Natalie replied gratefully. She straightened her pillow and slowly propped herself up in bed.

The compassion in the student's eyes comforted Natalie as their conversation soon turned to God and His wonderful and amazing grace. During the conversation, the heavy burden of fear in Natalie's heart began to lift. After a couple of hours, she finally drifted off to sleep. The young woman quietly left the room.

Natalie never saw the student nurse again. She couldn't even remember her name. But she never forgot the comfort and peace that settled over her as the young woman shared her love of Jesus Christ. The next morning, Natalie asked about the student nurse, but no one on the new shift had a clue as to her identity.

What had started out as one of the darkest nights of her life ended in peaceful contentment and sweet dreams, thanks to a young student with a kind heart. Whether the young woman was a celestial angel or an earthly angel of mercy, she was an angel in deed. She brought peace to Natalie's heart and joy to her soul. Isn't that precisely what God sends His angels to do?

Someone
WHO MIGHT
HAVE BEEN AN
ANGEL IN MY
LIFE WAS . . .

Around our pillows golden ladders rise,
And up and down the skies,
With winged sandals shod,
The angels come and go,
the Messengers of God!

Double Blessing

In your godliness, brotherly kindness, and in your brotherly kindness, Christian love.

2 PETER 1:7 NASB

What SIMPLE ACT OF KINDNESS CAN I PERFORM TODAY? HOW WOULD I FEEL IF SOMEONE DID THE SAME FOR ME?

British statesman and financier Cecil Rhodes, whose fortune acquired from diamond mining in Africa endowed the world-famous Rhodes Scholarships, was known as a stickler for correct dress—but not at the expense of someone else's feelings.

Once it was told that Rhodes invited a young man to an elegant dinner at his home. The guest had to travel a great distance by train and arrived only in time to go directly to Rhodes' home in his travel-stained clothes. Once there, he was distressed to find that the other guests were gathered in their finest evening clothes. But Rhodes was nowhere to be seen. Moments later, he appeared in a shabby old blue suit. The young man later learned that his host had been dressed in evening clothes but put on the old suit when he heard of his guest's embarrassment.

Rabbi Samuel Holdenson captured the spirit behind Rhodes' gesture, saying: "Kindness is the inability to remain at ease in the presence of another person who is ill at ease, the inability to remain comfortable in the presence of another who is uncomfortable, the inability to have peace of mind when one's neighbor is troubled."

The simplest act of kindness not only affects the receiver in profound ways but brings blessings to the giver as well. It makes us feel good to make others feel good.

You cannot do a kindness too soon
because you never know
how soon it will be too late.

Masterful Touch

The Lord your God in your midst, the Mighty
One, will save; He will rejoice over you with
gladness, He will quiet you with His love,
He will rejoice over you with singing.
ZEPHANIAH 3:17 NKJV

Polish composer and pianist Ignace Jan Paderewski stood in the wings, listening as the orchestra warmed up in preparation for his grand entrance. He was about to perform in a great American music hall, where the social elite of the city had gathered.

Waiting in the audience that night were a woman and her young son. After sitting for longer than his patience could stand, the boy slipped away from his mother. He was fascinated by the beautiful Steinway piano awaiting the perform-ance, and he made his way toward it. Before anyone knew what was happening, he crept onto the stage and climbed up on the piano stool to play a round of "Chopsticks."

The audience was horrified. What would the great Paderewski think? The murmurs quickly erupted into a roar of disapproval as the crowd demanded that the child be removed immediately. Backstage, Paderewski heard the disruption and, discerning the cause, raced out to join the child at the piano. He reached around him from behind and improvised his own countermelody to the boy's "Chopsticks." As the impromptu duet con-tinued, the master whispered in the child's ear, "Keep going. Don't quit, son . . . don't stop."

We may never play alongside a master pianist, but every day in our lives can be a duet with the Master. What joy it is to feel His love wrapped around us as He whispers, "Keep going . . . don't stop . . . I am with you"!

The
THOUGHT
OVERWHELMS
ME: THE
CREATOR OF
THE UNIVERSE
WANTS A
RELATIONSHIP
WITH ME! HOW
CAN I RETURN
HIS LOVE?

We are all strings in the concert of God's joy.

Courageous

Beloved, thou doest a faithful work in whatsoever thou doest toward them that are brethren and strangers withal.

3 JOHN 1:5 ASV

Am I WILLING TO HELP OTHERS WHEN IT'S INCONVEN-IENT FOR ME?

At the funeral service, Kevin's classmates stood up one by one to tell stories about their friendship with him. Soon a recurring theme emerged: his single most outstanding trait was his willingness to serve others, no matter what the need. He was one of those people who are always ready to lend a hand—no matter how big or small the task.

More often than not, when we hear the word *courage,* we think of heroic acts in times of crisis. But in our everyday lives, we shouldn't overlook the courageousness of simply being there. Lives are changed when we talk about our faith, do the right thing, care for the elderly, or lend an ear to a troubled friend. Persistence in making this world a better place to live—for ourselves and others—is definitely a form of courage.

Albert Schweitzer, the great Christian missionary, doctor, and theologian, was once asked in an interview to name the greatest living person. He immediately replied, "The greatest person in the world is some unknown individual who at this very moment has gone in love to help another."

As you go about your day, remember that you could be someone else's hero.

The greatest work any of us can do for another, whether old or young, is to teach the soul to draw its water from the wells of God.

Your Unique Place

> Since we have gifts that differ according to the grace given to us, each of us is to exercise them accordingly.
>
> ROMANS 12:6 NASB

What ARE MY SPIRITUAL GIFTS? HOW CAN I BEST USE THEM TO SERVE GOD?

Can you imagine a professional football tackle pitching for a major-league baseball game? He might be able to throw the ball with speed because he is strong and in great physical condition, but he won't have a great knuckleball or a split-finger ball that just makes it over the inside corner of the plate for a strike. He isn't equipped to play that position in that setting.

While all athletes go through extensive training to strengthen their God-given talents, each player actually is a specialist in his or her sport of choice. On rare occasions, an athlete can change from one sport to another and still play well. But even that athlete will function better in one particular sport, playing one particular position.

So, too, are our spiritual gifts. Each of us has talents, and God has asked us to be channels of blessing to others. We may be able to do many things—even do them well—but we will find the greatest fulfillment and success when we use our gifts the way God intended them to be used.

Being prepared for the work God has called us to do begins with knowing what our gifts are, and then surrendering our gifts totally to Him. Knowing what we have to offer to our family, friends, and community helps us discover our unique place in God's plan.

Channels only, blessed
Master, But with all
Thy wondrous power
Flowing thro' us,
Thou canst use us
Every day and every hour.

Just Like a Garden

You will be like a well-watered garden,
like a spring whose waters never fail.
ISAIAH 58:11

What CAN I BE THANKFUL FOR IN MY CURRENT CIRCUMSTANCES?

Kaylyn's family moved to a new city, far from family and friends, so her father could accept a new position. Each day when he arrived home from work, his family greeted him at the door with a new complaint: the weather was too hot, the neighbors were unfriendly, the house was too small.

Each afternoon, he would listen to their gripes. "I'm sorry," he would say. "What can I do to help?" Everyone would calm down, only to begin the same scenario the next afternoon.

One evening her dad walked through the front door with a beautiful flowering plant. He found a choice spot in the backyard and planted it. "OK," he said. "Every time you feel discontented, I want you to go and look at the garden. Picture yourselves as that little flowering plant. And watch our garden grow."

Every week he brought home a new tree, flowering shrub, or rose bush for them to plant in the backyard. They cut some flowers from the growing plants and took them to a neighbor. Friendships grew with other families on their block, and they asked them for gardening tips. Soon they were seeking spiritual advice as well.

Our Heavenly Father knows that we must all learn to bloom where we are transplanted. With His wise, loving touch, we will not only flourish, but we can produce the ever-blooming fruit of love, kindness, and contentment.

When life isn't the way you like it,
like it the way it is.

A Solid Foundation for Life

"The rain came down, the streams rose, and the winds blew and beat against that house; yet it did not fall, because it had its foundation on the rock."

MATTHEW 7:25

The world's tallest tower stands in Toronto, Ontario, Canada. The first observation deck rises to 1,136 feet, and the second is even higher at 1,815 feet. A series of photographs taken during construction helps visitors comprehend the enormous undertaking of the project, which involved removing sixty-two tons of earth and shale before workers could begin laying the concrete.

From 1972 to 1974, three thousand people worked at the tower site. Harnessed by safety ropes, some of the laborers dangled on the side of the gigantic tower as they finished the work, but no one was injured or died during construction.

Today a rapid elevator transports visitors upward for a breathtaking view of the city and the surrounding area. Many believe it was worth the money, time, and effort it took to build the CN Tower.

Like the CN Tower, we need a solid foundation for life. As we pray and spend time with our Heavenly Father, we are strengthening our spiritual foundation, our support base for life. When we learn to see life from His point of view, we are not overwhelmed by whatever comes our way. When we feel we're hanging on the edge or suspended in midair, we can take courage in knowing He is holding us—firmly planted—in the palm of His hand. His foundation is strong and sure, and He will not allow us to fall.

What KIND OF FOUNDATION HAVE I BUILT MY LIFE ON?

When God is our strength, it is strength indeed; when our strength is our own, it is only weakness.

Black Mountain

Many are the plans in a man's heart,
but it is the Lord's purpose that prevails.
PROVERBS 19:21

Some
THINGS I NEED
TO FACE IN MY
LIFE ARE . . .

"I will just run away to Black Mountain!" screamed five-year-old Richard.

"Okay, if that's what you want, go ahead," responded his mother, opening the door and ushering him out to the front porch.

The silence descended on him like a cloak. The sun was long gone, and full night had settled upon the landscape. By the starlight he could just make out the dark form of Black Mountain to the north. Somewhere in the darkness, he heard the scurrying of a small animal and then the flap of wings in the night sky.

Suddenly, his small heart was pounding in his chest and his breath was coming quicker. Going to Black Mountain seemed like a really bad idea.

He thought, *Why did I say that?*

He sat on the porch with his knees drawn up to his chest and arms clasped around them. A tear trickled down his cheek as he tried to fight off his fears.

From the kitchen, he heard his father ask, "Richard, would you like to come to supper with the rest of us now?"

Sometimes when we get angry with ourselves, at others, at circumstances, or even at God, we want to run away. We stomp out our anger, and we make threats. We go out on the porch and pout. Yet, the Father waits patiently and even calls to us to rejoin the family. Love chases away fears, and restoration heals hurts.

O God, help us not to despise or
oppose what we do not understand.

The Right Environment

> Those who wait for the Lord will gain new strength.
>
> ISAIAH 40:31 NASB

What ENVIRONMENT DO I NEED IN ORDER TO FLOURISH SPIRITUALLY?

A botanist, exiled from his homeland due to political unrest, took a job as a gardener in a new country in order to support his family. His employer received a rare plant from a friend, but it came with no care instructions. The man put it in a hothouse, thinking it would do well there.

A few days later he noticed the plant was dying. He called in his new gardener, the botanist, and asked if he knew how to save the plant. The botanist immediately identified the plant as one that needed cold weather to survive. He took the plant outside in the frigid winter air and prepared the soil around it so the plant would gradually adjust to its new home. Almost immediately the plant began to flourish.

Unaccustomed to the climate in the hothouse, the little plant must have felt the moisture draining from its small veins. The struggle to hold itself up to look the part of an expensive plant gave way under the weary load. The plant began to wilt and became only a shadow of its original beauty.

When the botanist rescued the plant and placed it in an environment suitable to its unique needs, the bowed-down foliage soaked in the nourishment and experienced renewal. Just like that rare plant, we can lose our spiritual strength if we live in an unhealthy environment. Seek God's help to find the right atmosphere for a joyous and productive life.

Attempt great things for God,
expect great things from God.

Keep Your Eyes on God

As the heavens are higher than the earth,
so are my ways higher than your ways
and my thoughts than your thoughts.
ISAIAH 55:9

What

ARE THE

DISTRACTIONS

THAT TAKE

MY EYES OFF

THE THINGS

OF GOD?

Have you ever tried to read a recipe while you were cracking an egg into a mixing bowl? If you don't keep your eyes on the egg, you'll end up with more egg on the counter than in the mixing bowl. An experienced cook will tell you that you'll have better success if you read the recipe first and then keep your eyes on the eggs.

The Bible agrees. It doesn't talk about recipes, but it does talk about our choices in life. When the Israelites first camped on the edge of the Promised Land, God instructed that twelve men be sent to look the land over and report back to Moses. All twelve had seen God deliver them from slavery. All twelve had heard God's promise of protection and provision. But only two men remembered God and His faithfulness; ten men were distracted by the dangers of Canaan. Ten men turned their eyes away from God and made a mess for the Israelites that took forty years to clean up.

Whenever we focus on our problems instead of on God's promises and possibilities, we're in for a slippery slide too. If we want the recipe of our lives to turn out for the best, we need to stay focused on Him. Let the egg test be your reminder: Whenever you crack an egg, keep your eyes on the egg and remember to ask yourself if your heart is focused on God.

Great thoughts reduced to
practice become great acts.

Voice from the Past

Faith by itself, if it is not accompanied by action, is dead. But someone will say, "You have faith; I have deeds." Show me your faith without deeds, and I will show you my faith by what I do.

JAMES 2:17-18

Laura was mixing cake batter when the phone rang. The voice on the other end said, "Hi. This is a voice from your past."

Since she didn't recognize the voice, Laura quipped, "Whose voice and from which past?"

Laughter broke out on the other end. "This is Carrie," she said. *Of course,* Laura thought. Carrie had been a member of her writer's group. In fact, Carrie had written beautiful and thought-provoking fiction. Her work was good, and she could have been published if she had pursued it. Instead, Carrie chose to end an unhappy marriage and get on with her life, leaving her writing far behind.

Carrie bubbled with excitement. "I'm sailing with friends on a forty-two-foot sailboat from Nova Scotia to Scotland."

Laura listened intently. Was this the same Carrie who had needed lots of support from her friends? The same Carrie who had wrapped herself safely in a little shell?

To Laura's surprise, Carrie had changed. She was now taking control of her life and doing exciting things. She wasn't the least bit apprehensive about crossing choppy waters, battling seasickness, or running from sharks and killer whales.

As Carrie was closing the conversation, she said, "I wanted to make certain my good friends knew I was going on this trip."

Laura's breath caught in her throat. She had never thought of herself as Carrie's good friend. Sure, she'd taken Carrie to the doctor once, visited her apartment, and even lunched at a pizza place with her and her children, but she'd never thought of herself as Carrie's good friend. She couldn't even recall Carrie's last name.

How often do we touch someone's life with a random act of kindness? God uses ordinary people to make an extraordinary difference in the world around them.

A kindness THAT IMPACTED MY LIFE WAS WHEN . . .

✠

Can faith that does nothing be sincere?

Skyrocket to Maturity

He who walks with the wise grows wise.
PROVERBS 13:20

Who ARE THE
PEOPLE I NEED
TO SURROUND
MYSELF WITH?

Michael looked out the window at the trampoline that seemed to take up half the yard. With a smile he grasped his little brother's hand and went out to bounce him. It was an odd sort of pride he took in being able to skyrocket his brother's little body into the air. He outweighed him by a number of pounds, and his weight caused him to go higher than any of his friends could take him. It was just a simple matter of physics, really; the heavier your partner, the higher you go.

It's no different spiritually. The people you surround yourself with will either send you skyrocketing into spiritual understanding and maturity or leave you struggling on the ground.

When you look at those in your life today, who is it that stands out as wise? Who walks with that quiet charisma and peace that you find yourself craving? What would it take to call that person? Keep it simple and comfortable. Sit together at lunch, grab a slice of pizza after school, or simply spend an afternoon talking. Or perhaps you can find an activity you both enjoy. Surround yourself with people who will encourage your growth.

The Bible says in James 1:5, "If any of you lacks wisdom, he should ask God." Ask God to expand your wisdom and your world.

To seek wisdom in old age is like a mark
in the sand; to seek wisdom in
youth is like an inscription on stone.

Destined to Win

> Carry each other's burdens, and in this
> way you will fulfill the law of Christ.
>
> GALATIANS 6:2

Is THERE
SOMEONE
WHO MAY
NEED A CARD,
A THOUGHT,
A PRAYER
TODAY?

Jill could feel the stitch in her side as she drew each ragged breath. Ten more strides, now five, now two. She held her arm out and handed the baton to the runner waiting in front of her. "Go, go, go!" she yelled. Her friend, Anna, took the baton and began to run. Her pace was quick and her prospects good, if only because she was refreshed and ready to run. Jill bent over and filled her lungs in great gasps. She could not have run another step. Thank goodness, Anna was ready.

That's what teamwork is all about. As lovers of God, we carry the weight of responsibility to be there for our friends. We hand off to one another the care and love of our Father. When one is weary, the other is strong; when one is disheartened, the other believes. That's the way God designed the system to work. We're not supposed to run our race alone!

Sheryl experienced this firsthand. After a bout of illness in her family, her church and small Bible study group had taken turns visiting and bringing dinner. Now she had the opportunity to do the same as God blessed her with health and healing.

Like a well-trained, cross-country, running team, we need to be refreshed and ready to run when the baton is handed our way. Yet we also need to be willing to receive when we can't walk on our own. Love and care for one another is the light by which we see our God.

The words of kindness are more healing
to a drooping heart than balm or honey.

Rising Faith

"What shall I compare the kingdom of
God to? It is like yeast that a woman took
and mixed into a large amount of flour
until it worked all through the dough."
LUKE 13:20-21

Has MY FAITH
GROWN IN
THE PAST YEAR?
CAN OTHERS
SEE THE
CHANGE
IN ME?

"What's that, Tanya?" the little girl asked as she watched her big sister carefully mix the ingredients for bread.

"Yeast," her sister replied. "That's what makes the bread rise. We have to cover the dough with a cloth and put it in a warm place if we want our rolls to be light and fluffy."

Not fully understanding the way yeast works, Mary was impatient. She continued to lift the cloth in order to see the round balls of dough that sat in the baking dish. After a while, she realized that they were growing larger.

Finally, Tanya placed the rolls in the preheated oven. Mary watched through the glass window as the tops began turning golden brown.

Tanya thought about the look of amazement on her little sister's face when she saw how the bread had doubled in size. Her faith, she realized, was a lot like that dough. The more she prayed and studied God's Word, the larger her faith grew. And just as the rolls needed to remain warm in order to rise, she needed to keep her heart warm in order to serve God and others.

Today, keep a warm smile on your lips and a glow in your eyes. With the right attitude toward life, we can rise up in the midst of trouble and show others the warmth that only God can provide.

The world is a looking-glass and gives back
to every man the reflection of his own face.
Frown at it, and it in turn will look
sourly at you; laugh at it, and with it,
and it is a jolly, kind companion.

Procrastination Leads Nowhere

> I will hasten and not delay to obey your commands.
>
> PSALM 119:60

Morning is a great time to make a list of "things to do" and plan the day. It's also the best time to tackle those tasks that are the most difficult or we like the least. If we procrastinate as the day wears on, rationalization sets in and sometimes even the tasks we had considered to be the most important are left undone.

Here's a little poem just for those who struggle with procrastination:

How and When

We are often greatly bothered
By two fussy little men,
Who sometimes block our pathway
Their names are How and When.
If we have a task or duty
Which we can put off a while,
And we do not go and do it
You should see those two rogues smile!
But there is a way to beat them,
And I will tell you how:
If you have a task or duty,
Do it well, and do it now.

—Unknown

As part of your morning prayer time, ask the Lord to help you to overcome any tendency to procrastinate and prioritize projects according to His plans and purposes.

Often we ask the Lord, "What do You want me to do?" but then fail to ask Him one of the key follow-up questions, "When do You want me to do this?" When we have a sense of God's timing, and in some cases His urgency about a matter, our conviction grows to get the job done right away.

God's "omnipresence" means He is always with you, and He is always "timely." He's with you in the "now" moments of your life. He is concerned with how you use every moment of your time. Recognize that He desires to be part of your time-management and task-completion process today!

I enjoy
MY LIST
OF THINGS TO
DO MORE
WHEN I . . .

✠

A job worth doing is worth doing right.

Cosmic Wonders

When I consider your heavens, the work of your
fingers, the moon and the stars, which you have set
in place, what is man that you are mindful of him?
PSALM 8:3-4

Lord, THANK
YOU FOR
ALL THAT
YOU HAVE
DESIGNED ME
TO BE AND
TO BECOME!

A number of years ago, IMAX filmmakers produced a movie titled *Cosmos*. In it, they explored the "edges" of creation—both outer space and inner space, as viewed through the most powerful microscope. Viewers saw for themselves that at the far reaches of space, clumps of matter (huge stars) seem to be suspended in fixed motion and separated by vast areas of seemingly empty blackness.

They also saw that the same can be said for the depths of inner space—clumps of matter are suspended in fixed orbits, separated by vast areas of seemingly empty blackness. In fact, the world of the distant stars is almost identical in appearance and form to the world of the tiniest neutrinos! Furthermore, both inner and outer space appear as if they may very well extend into infinity.

In sharp contrast, the created earth as we experience it daily is uniquely suspended between these two opposite poles. It is as if God has placed human beings at the very center of His creation, with the maximum amount of complexity, meaning, and choice. We are "hung in the balances" literally, as well as figuratively—the pivot point between the great and the small, the vastness of outer space and the vastness of inner space.

We are not only fearfully and wonderfully made, but fearfully and wonderfully *positioned* in God's creation. The Lord has a place for everyone—and that includes you. Thank God for your uniqueness today. Delight in all that makes you special in His eyes.

When God conceived the world, that was
poetry. He formed it, and that was sculpture.
He colored it, and that was painting. He
peopled it with living beings, and that
was the grand, divine, eternal drama.

Providence

I have raised you up for this very purpose,
that I might show you my power and that
my name might be proclaimed in all the earth.

EXODUS 9:16

In 1844, the most powerful warship of that time, the *Princeton*, was taking the President of the United States and several other dignitaries down the Potomac. To entertain the guests, the great gun on the *Princeton*, the Peacemaker, was fired. At the second discharge, the gun burst apart, killing the Secretary of the Navy Gilmore and a number of others.

Just before the gun was fired, Sen. Thomas Benton of Missouri was standing near it. A friend placed his hand on Benton's shoulder, and he turned to speak with him. Much to his annoyance, the Secretary of the Navy elbowed his way into Benton's place. At precisely that moment the gun went off and killed Gilmore.

That moment had a great impression upon Benton. He was a man of anger who had recently quarreled with Daniel Webster. But after his narrow escape on the *Princeton*, Benton sought reconciliation with Webster.

He said to him:

> It seemed to me, Mr. Webster, as if that touch on my shoulder was the hand of the Almighty stretched down there drawing me away from what otherwise would have been instantaneous death. That one circumstance has changed the whole current of my thought and life. I feel that I am a different man; and I want in the first place to be at peace with all those with whom I have been so sharply at variance.

Few of us ever know the many times we are spared from death, but in reality each day we live is a gift from God. Never waste a day in anger or unforgiveness. Live each day in peace with God and all people.

Have I WASTED TIME BEING ANGRY TODAY? WHAT CAN I DO TO CHANGE MY BEHAVIOR?

✠

Love is an act of endless forgiveness,
a tender look which becomes a habit.

Help Others, Help Yourself

As the body without the spirit is dead,
so faith without works is dead also.
JAMES 2:26 KJV

What IS
SOMETHING
SOMEONE
ASKED ME TO
DO THAT I
REFUSED TO
DO? CAN I
STILL HELP
THEM?

Charity is never lost. It may meet with
ingratitude, or be of no service to those
on whom it was bestowed, yet it
ever does a work of beauty and
grace upon the heart of the giver.

A tornado rips through a southern town and destroys most of the buildings in its path. Those which remain standing have sustained serious damage, but the owners can't make all of the repairs.

A church in the South has a small congregation, and an even smaller budget. Expenses are met each week, but the funds aren't there to hire someone to do minor but much needed repairs.

Who comes to the rescue? A group of mostly retirees in recreational vehicles. They travel throughout the South during the autumn and winter months, escaping cold temperatures and doing good along the way. Some are experienced in carpentry and construction and some are not, but they all have the same goal: to make their time count by helping others.

The United Methodist Church chooses projects and assigns teams to each site. The workers, who pay all their expenses, meet at the appointed time and get right to work. To keep the jobs enjoyable, everyone works four days and then has three days off to relax and see the sights. The fun part, reported one woman volunteer, is the opportunity to have fellowship with like-minded people.[33]

The same generosity of spirit, on a slightly different scale, is described in the Book of Acts. "All the believers were one in heart and mind. No one claimed that any of his possessions was his own, but they shared everything they had. There were no needy persons among them. For from time to time those who owned land or houses sold them, brought the money from the sales and put it at the apostles' feet, and it was distributed to anyone as he had need" (Acts 4:32,34-35).

When we have the chance to do good, we should jump at it. "So in everything, do to others what you would have them do to you, for this sums up the Law and the Prophets," Jesus said in Matthew 7:12. Jesus asked us to serve, and we will be blessed when we do so.

Penny from Heaven

Some trust in chariots and some in horses, but
we trust in the name of the Lord our God.

PSALM 20:7

Kevin brushed the sandy-colored hair from his eyes. "Mom, I have a chance to be president of the fourth grade!" He reached for a cinnamon roll and poured some milk into a glass.

"You know, son, that it'll be a tough race."

The boy took a swallow of milk and wiped his face with his sleeve. "I know, Mom. But I just know I can do it."

His mother reached into the pocket of her jeans and pulled out a penny. "I tell you what; why don't you take my 'penny from heaven' to keep your spirits up?"

The boy grinned and put the penny in his pocket. He gathered his books and stuck them haphazardly into his book bag, then slung the bag over his shoulder.

Adrienne busied herself with everyday chores, wondering if her little boy would come home disappointed by failure or elated by victory. When 3:15 finally arrived, she was ready with his favorite chocolate chip cookies.

Kevin banged in the back door, his face beaming. He tugged on his baseball cap and cocked his head to one side. "I did it, Mom!" he said. "I'm the new president of the fourth-grade class!"

Kevin caught his breath and settled down in front of his plate of cookies. With his mouth full, he said, "I can't believe it, Mom! I just can't believe it!"

"I can," said his mother.

The boy looked puzzled. "What do you mean?"

"Take out that penny I gave you and read what it says above Abraham Lincoln's head."

A radiant smile spread over her son's face as he read out loud, "In God We Trust!"

What are you putting your trust in? If it's material things, remember, they are only temporary. Instead, put your trust in God and His eternal life. He will never fail you.[34]

Some
THINGS I'M
HOLDING ON
TO THAT I
NEED TO
TRUST THE
LORD WITH
ARE . . .

✠

Let us renew our trust in God,
and go forward without fear
and with manly hearts.

Faith Moves Forward

Men of Galilee, they said, why do
you stand here looking into the sky?
ACTS 1:11

What's
HOLDING ME
BACK FROM MY
GOD-GIVEN
DREAMS?

✚

Not to go forward is to go back.

"Hey! Stop! The sink's going to overflow!" Her father's sharp cry alerted Ginny to the near disaster as he quickly came to her aid and turned off the water. "What were you looking at? Are the squirrels in the bird feeder again?"

Ginny had been staring out the kitchen window, gazing at nothing and yet at everything all at the same time, oblivious to what was going on inside the house. "No squirrels. Just woolgathering, I guess," she replied absentmindedly.

She turned her attention to the dishes in the sink. For days she had been trying to make some sense out of the feelings that were swirling within her. Compared to someone else's problems, Ginny's concerns would seem to be only minor inconveniences, but for her, they were overwhelming. Finances for college. Relationships. Work. Health. Church. No matter where she turned, there were problems, and all of them seemed beyond her control. Tears mingled with the soapsuds as she finished the dishes. Drying her hands, Ginny sat heavily on a kitchen chair and whispered, "Lord, what am I supposed to do?"

And quietly, the answer came. When the disciples witnessed Christ's return to heaven, they stood gazing into the sky, not knowing what to do. They were paralyzed by the overwhelming responsibility that He had placed on their shoulders to share the gospel message with the world. It took a gentle shove from one of God's angels to get them moving down the path that had been placed before them, to turn them away from their fears and back to their faith as they followed God's plan for their lives.

Sure enough, just like those disciples, Ginny had been paralyzed by her dread. She asked forgiveness for her fearful focus, and even before she reached the "Amen," she had a direction . . . a pathway. All she needed to do was faithfully follow God's plan. He'd take care of the rest.

What's holding you back from your God-given dreams? Are you afraid? Remember: Fear stands still, but faith moves forward!

Take Your Time

I delight in your decrees;
I will not neglect your Word.
PSALM 119:16

Kyle was like many Christians. He had been taught that if he truly wanted God to guide his steps each day, he should spend time with Him first thing every morning. He found a copy of a "Through the Bible in One Year" plan and got down to business: three chapters each morning and two each night.

Somehow, though, the inspiration he expected to discover escaped him. He discussed the problem with his Dad. Kyle said, "I wasn't sure how I would find the time to read the Bible every morning, but I manage to squeeze it in. Sometimes I have to rush through the chapters a little, but I always remember what I've read. So why do I feel as if I haven't really read it?"

Dad answered, "It sounds to me as if you're reading the Bible the way you would a textbook. If you want to get into the meaning behind the words, pray before you read, and ask God to reveal things to you. Instead of looking at the Bible as a reading assignment, think of it as a special meeting time with God—time you set aside to sit down and hear what He has to say to you."

"I get it," Frank said. "I was doing the old 'what's in it for me?' and expecting God to reward me for putting in the time."

"Even a few extra minutes can make a big difference. Just remember: the more time you give to God, the more time He gives back to you," Dad suggested. "Your day will go much better if you let *Him* set the pace and listen for what *He* has to say."

While it is important to read the Scriptures daily, it is far more important to read *until you sense in your spirit that God has said something to YOU*. Don't be concerned about reading a specific number of verses or chapters. The key is to read with a listening ear.

My TIME IN THE BIBLE IS MORE SPECIAL WHEN . . .

A lot of kneeling keeps you in good standing with God.

Love and Faithfulness

Proclaim your love in the morning
and your faithfulness at night.
PSALM 92:2

I best KNOW
GOD LOVES ME
WHEN . . .

The psalmist encourages us to proclaim the Lord's love in the morning. This proclamation of love is not a matter of our echoing Elizabeth Barrett Browning in saying to the Lord, "How do I love thee? Let me count the ways." Our love is not a recitation of the reasons why God is worthy of our love. Nor is it a declaration of our love for Him. Rather, our proclamation of love is to be a statement of how the Lord loves us!

As you meditate on the Lord's love for you, certain words come to mind. Certainly the Lord loves you unconditionally . . . gently . . . individually . . . intimately . . . eternally . . . closely . . . warmly . . . tenderly . . . kindly. You are His child. He always has your good in mind.

Proclaiming the Lord's love for you in the morning will give you strength. Because you have a loving Father with you always, you can make it through any day, regardless of the surprises—good and bad—that come your way.

After walking through your day in God's love, at the day's end you can easily recount His faithfulness. He is faithful to provide what you need, deliver you from evil, and lead you into blessings—all of which are expressions of His love. In recognizing God's love first and foremost, and then living in that love all day long, you quickly recognize the power of God's love to sustain you, energize you, and protect you—and you give that love to others.

Accept and expect the Lord to be loving toward you . . . and by tonight, you will surely know He has been faithful!

Faithfulness is consecration in overalls.

True Identity

> Because ye are sons, God hath sent forth the Spirit
> of his Son into your hearts, crying, Abba, Father.
>
> GALATIANS 4:6 KJV

Every day the world challenges your identity by trying to tell you who you are—or ought to be—by shaping your desires, and by telling you what is important, what values you should have, and how to spend your time and resources. What the world is telling you may not be true!

The story is told of a rancher who had been hunting in the mountains of West Texas. Up high on a cliff he came across an eagle's nest. He took one of the eagle's eggs back to his ranch and placed it under one of his hens sitting on her eggs. Eventually the eagle's egg hatched. The mother hen took care of the eaglet along with her baby chicks who hatched at the same time.

The eagle made its home in the barnyard along with the chickens. It ate, slept, and lived just like the chickens. One day an eagle from the nearby mountain swooped down over the barnyard in search of prey. Trying to get her chicks and the eaglet to safety, the mother hen squawked loudly.

As the great eagle swooped low across the barnyard, he also let out a harsh scream—a scream made only by eagles. The young chicks heeded their mother's warning, but the eaglet responded to the call of the eagle. He took flight and ascended, following the eagle to the mountain heights.

What does Scripture tell us about who we are as children of God? We are the apple of His eye (Zechariah 2:8); the flock of His people (Zechariah 9:16); a crown of glory in the hand of the Lord and a royal diadem in the hand of your God (Isaiah 62:3); the temple of God (1 Corinthians 3:16). We are heirs of God and joint heirs with Christ (Romans 8:17). We are kings and priests of our God (Revelation 5:10). We were created to bear His likeness (Genesis 1:27).

Most importantly, we are God's children (1 John 3:1). We belong to Him, and our hearts cry, "Abba, Father!" when He calls to us.

Listen for His call today! Find out who you are and what your purpose is from Him, the One who made you!

I feel MOST LIKE GOD'S CHILD WHEN . . .

✠

The man without a purpose is
like a ship without a rudder—
a waif, a nothing, a no man.

Active Faith

Let us not give up meeting together, as some are in the habit of doing, but let us encourage one another.
HEBREWS 10:25

I think
CHURCH ATTENDANCE CAN STRENGTHEN ME BECAUSE . . .

Philip Haille went to the little village of Le Chambon, France, to write about a people who, unlike other villages, had hidden their Jews from the Nazis. He wondered what caused them to risk their lives to do such extraordinary good.

He interviewed people in the village and was overwhelmed—not by their extraordinary qualities, but by their *ordinariness*. They were not an unusually bright, quick-witted, brave, or discerning people. In the end, the author concluded that the one factor uniting them to do good was their attendance at their little church.

One elderly woman faked a heart attack when the Nazis came to search her house. She told Haille about her personal dramatic ploy, "Pastor always taught us that there comes a time in every life when a person is asked to do something for Jesus. When my time came, I just *knew* what to do."

The strength and courage Haille discovered in the people of Le Chambon was a result of their simple obedience to God—never to stop meeting together to worship and hear His Word. When extreme difficulty came their way, their unity in the faith was a habitual part of their everyday lives.

Thank God today for a church where you can receive strength and courage. If you don't go to church, ask the Lord to lead you to the body of believers just right for you.

Strength and happiness consist in
finding out the Way God is going,
and going in that Way too.

Remembering God

> Choose for yourselves this day whom you will serve.
>
> JOSHUA 24:15

A rabbi once summoned the townsfolk to meet in the square for an important announcement. The merchants resented having to leave their businesses. The farmers could scarcely see how they could leave their fields. The housewives protested against leaving their chores. But obedient to the call of their spiritual leader, the townspeople gathered together to hear the announcement their teacher felt was so important to make at that time.

The rabbi said, "I wish to announce that there is a God in the world." And with that, he departed.

The people stood in silence—stunned, but not bewildered. They understood what he had said, with an understanding born of a heartfelt conviction. They realized they had been acting as if God did *not* exist. While they observed rituals and recited the correct order of prayers, their actions did not comply with the commandments of God. Their daily bread was sought and taken with little thought and reverence for Him.

We may not openly deny God, but instead we may try to confine Him to some remote corner of life. We keep Him away from our daily doings, associations, obligations, experiences, joys, heartaches, and all the commonplace things required to keep body and soul together. The fact is however:

There is a God in the world you call your neighborhood.

There is a God in the world you call your school.

There is a God in the places you frequent, the shops in which you make your purchases, and the dozens of places you walk in the course of a week.

There is a God, and He wants to be a part of *everything* you do.

Recognize He is with you *wherever* you go today. The knowledge that He is with you and that He is interested in every detail of your life will bring joy and peace to every experience.

I can BECOME MORE AWARE THAT GOD IS WITH ME IF I . . .

God of justice, God of mercy,
Make us merciful and just!
Help us see all your creation
As from you a sacred trust.
And when people cry in anguish
For their own or others' pain,
Show us ways to make a difference
O dear God, make us humane!

On Call

O that I had wings like a dove!
I would fly away and be at rest.
PSALM 55:6 RSV

I can BETTER
BALANCE MY
DAY IF I . . .

Porch swings, picnic tables, and handwritten letters almost seem like relics of a bygone age. Symbols of today's fast-paced culture are fast-food drive-thrus, computer games, and E-mail. In spite of the changes in our cultural icons, we actually may not be that much busier than the last generation—after all, we still only have twenty-four hours in a day.

The problem is, however, that we seldom "get away from it all." Experts say that communication technology gives immediate access to anyone, virtually anywhere. We are no more than a beeper or a cellular phone call away from being summoned.

Because of that phenomenon, Dr. Mark Moskowitz of Boston University's Medical Center observes, "A lot of people are working twenty-four hours a day, seven days a week, even when they're not technically at work." That is a precursor to first-class exhaustion.

Government executive Roy Neel quit his job as deputy chief of staff in the Clinton administration and took a slower-paced job. He realized that work "even for the President of the United States" was not worth the price. It hit home for Roy the night he and his nine-year-old son, Walter, were ready to walk out the door for a long-promised baseball game. The phone rang, and it was the president.

Walter was not impressed with a call from the White House. What he wanted was to go to a baseball game with his dad. After the hour-long phone call, Roy discovered his son had found a ride to the game with a neighbor. He commented, "Our society has become schizophrenic. We praise people who want balance in their lives, but reward those who work themselves to death."

When asked his formula for success, physicist Albert Einstein spelled it out this way: "If A is success in life, then A equals X plus Y plus Z. Work is X, Y is play, and Z is keeping your mouth shut." What a genius!

Work, alternated with needful rest,
is the salvation of man or woman.

Seek and Find

*I love them that love me; and those
that seek me early shall find me.*
PROVERBS 8:17 KJV

Who CAN
SHARE I MY
NEEDS WITH
AND KNOW
THEY WILL
PRAY FOR ME?

Terri's parents were struggling with constant calls from the school, the youth director at church, and even other parents in the same community, all complaining about the behavior of their fifteen-year-old. Distraught and discouraged, the parents rose early one morning and sought the Lord on behalf of their child. Although not in the habit of praying together or for their children prior to this, they found the Lord there for them on that morning and every morning after that. This morning prayer time became the one time they longed for all during the day.

Not only was the habit of praying together started, but reading the Bible together as well. Each day the Lord had many new lessons to teach them. They were learning and growing as individuals and as a couple, and soon they noticed positive changes in their daughter's behavior as well. Eventually, what the parents had begun as a united effort—to cry out for help to the Lord on their daughter's behalf—was fast becoming a time when the whole family would get together for devotions and worship.

When Terri saw the transformation in her mother and father, she decided to make some changes in her life too. Today she is a godly young woman who loves the Lord with all her heart.

When we seek the Lord for a specific need, we find He is ready to meet us for all our needs.

*God always answers us in the deeps,
never in the shallows of our soul.*

Dr. Simpson and Dancing

He hath put in his heart that he may teach.
EXODUS 35:34 KJV

A special
TEACHER MADE
A DIFFERENCE
IN MY LIFE
BECAUSE . . .

Lively music filled the air as the college students mingled with one another, shared laughs, and danced together. Just then, Dr. Simpson walked up to Rob and asked him, "Why aren't you out there dancing with everyone else?"

"I don't want anyone to laugh at me," he responded.

"What makes you think that they would be looking at you anyway?" came her quick retort with more than a hint of laughter in her voice. She was like that. Quick to challenge her students' assumptions, but in a way that provoked thought and self-examination rather than pain and embarrassment.

A respected and admired professor of English, Dr. Simpson expected much from every student. She was tough, but her classes were always full. It was exchanges like this one that made it possible for Rob to see his life from a perspective other than his own, and in gaining this insight he became more self-confident and less uptight. She helped—no, she *forced* him to grow as both a student and a person. Dr. Simpson epitomized the role of teacher.

In the words of one author, "The teacher must be able to discern when to push and when to comfort, when to chastise and when to praise, when to challenge and when to hold back, when to encourage risk and when to protect."[35] This, Dr. Simpson did on a daily basis. And this is just the type of teacher we need. God usually provides each of us with our own unique Dr. Simpson—many times with more than one.

Can you recall your favorite teachers? And did they challenge you to become more than you were before? Thank God, they did!

Teachers affect eternity; they can never
tell where their influence stops.

Editing Your Life

> Seeing we also are compassed about with so great a cloud of witnesses, let us lay aside every weight, and the sin which doth so easily beset us.
>
> HEBREWS 12:1 KJV

Disney films are known the world over as the best in animation, but the studio didn't earn that reputation easily. One of the reasons for the level of excellence achieved was the filmmaker himself. Walt Disney was ruthless about cutting anything that got in the way of the unfolding story.

Ward Kimball, one of the animators for *Snow White*, recalls working 240 days on a four-minute sequence. In this scene, the dwarfs made soup for Snow White, almost destroying the kitchen in the process. Disney thought it was funny, but he decided that it interrupted the flow of the picture, so it was edited out.

Often we find ourselves doing "good" things, which are not only unnecessary but also a distraction from the unfolding story of our lives. Like the soup scene, many of these things are worthwhile or entertaining, but they lack the essential element of being the best use of the time and talents God has given us.

The next time you're asked to take on another "good scene," ask yourself the following questions:

- Does this fit in with the plan God has set before me—do I have a lasting inner peace about it?

- Will this task help me or others grow closer to the Lord?

- Can I do this without taking away from the time I've already committed to my family, church, job, or friends?

Be diligent concerning the multitude of *good* things you edit out of your life in favor of the *great* things God wants to do through you!

The wisest thing is Time, for it brings everything to light.

How CAN I DO A BETTER JOB OF EDITING MY LIFE?

The Guide

For such is God, our God forever and ever;
He will guide us until death.

PSALM 48:14 NASB

I need TO ALLOW GOD TO LEAD AND GUIDE ME EACH DAY BECAUSE . . .

In *A Slow and Certain Light,* missionary Elisabeth Elliot tells of two adventurers who stopped by to see her at her mission station. Loaded heavily with equipment for the rain forest, they sought no advice. They merely asked her to teach them a few phrases of the language so they might converse a bit with the Indians.

Amazed at their temerity, she saw a parallel between these travelers and Christians. She writes, "Sometimes we come to God as the two adventurers came to me—confident and, we think, well-informed and well-equipped. But has it occurred to us that with all our accumulation of stuff, something is missing?"

She suggests that we often ask God for far too little. "We know what we need—a yes or no answer, please, to a simple question. Or perhaps a road sign. Something quick and easy to point the way. What we really ought to have is the Guide himself. Maps, road signs, a few useful phrases are good things, but infinitely better is having Someone who has been there before and knows the way." [36]

In the midst of your day, you may face unexpected situations. Trust God to be your Guide and pray, "Lord, I know this didn't take You by surprise! You knew it was coming and have already made a way for me. I thank You for taking me where I need to go and giving me everything I need to get over the rough spots along the way."

Relying on God has to begin all over again
every day as if nothing had yet been done.

Praise Break

> Oh, give thanks to the Lord, for he is good;
> his lovingkindness continues forever.
>
> PSALM 136:1 TLB

Rather than take a coffee break today, take a praise break! Take a pause in your day to acknowledge all the specific ways in which the Lord has been good to you. Thank Him for what He is doing in your life, right now, where you are.

Nothing is too large or too small to be worthy of your praise. Every good thing you have and experience in life ultimately comes from the Lord. Sometimes blessings come directly from Him, and sometimes through the talents or skills of others who are inspired or empowered by Him. Give praise for the things you see at hand! Your praise list may include the following:

Help with homework

A window through which to view the world

Microwave ovens

Walking shoes

Budding trees

Ready access to vital data

Computer repair people

The postal worker being five minutes late, which gave you time to find a stamp

A completed phone call

Spell-check

Good health

Fulfilling work

A loving family and circle of friends

Look around, look down, and look up. You'll never run out of things to be thankful for!

Remember the day's blessings;
forget the day's troubles.

Lord, I WILL
PRAISE YOU
TODAY FOR . . .

Take Cover

He will cover you with His pinions, and
under His wings you may seek refuge;
His faithfulness is a shield and bulwark.
PSALM 91:4 NASB

What CAN
I DO TO REPEL
THE NEGATIVES
THAT COME
MY WAY
EACH DAY?

Bouncing back from disappointment, loss, or
an irritating situation can take time. When you're
hurting, the thing you need to do is nurse your
wounds for a little while, regroup, then go back
out and face the world. What a relief it would be
if angry words, dirty looks, and cruel actions had
no power to hurt us.

Many of us have frying pans coated with
Teflon because food doesn't stick to it. The scientists at Dow Chemical have come up with what
might be called the next generation of Teflon: a
fluorocarbon formula that can be sprayed or
brushed onto a surface. It's been suggested it might
be used to repel graffiti on subway walls, barnacles
on ships, dirt on wallpaper, and ice on aircraft. Its
"base" sticks to whatever it's applied to, but its
"surface" repels moisture.

This is a little like being in the world, but not
of it. "I pray not that thou shouldest take them out
of the world, but that thou shouldest keep them
from the evil," Jesus prayed for His disciples in
John 17:15 KJV. "As thou has sent me into the
world, even so have I also sent them into the
world" (v. 18).

We have to come into contact with a lot of negatives throughout our lives, but we don't have to
absorb them or let them become part of us. With
the help of the Holy Spirit, we can stick to God.

Kind words don't wear out the tongue.

Morning Praise!

Come before Him with joyful singing.

PSALM 100:2 NASB

Some WAYS I CAN PRAISE GOD WHOLE-HEARTEDLY ARE . . .

A young graduate moved away from her home to New York City. She rented a room from an elderly lady who had migrated to the United States years before from Sweden. The landlady offered a clean room, a shared bathroom, and use of the kitchen at a reasonable rate.

The little white-haired Swedish woman made the rules of the house very clear. There would be no smoking or drinking, no food in the bedrooms, etc. Pausing mid-sentence, the landlady asked, "Do you sing? Do you play? Music is good! I used to play the piano at the church, but not now. I'm too old. My hearing isn't good, but I love to praise God with music. God loves music."

Later that evening, after a full day of moving into her new room, the young tenant heard horrible noises coming from somewhere downstairs.

Cautiously making her way down the stairway, she followed the sounds to the kitchen door. There she discovered her new landlady standing at the stove, joyfully "singing" at the top of her lungs!

Never had the young woman heard such a horrible voice. Yet she heard that voice, precious to God, every day for as long as she rented the room just over the kitchen.

The tenant moved on, married, and had her own family. Every morning she stands in front of the stove and sings off key and loud, but joyful, praising the Lord!

What a glorious way to start the day!

Joy rises in me like a summer's morn.

A New Look

Happy are the people who are in such a state;
Happy are the people whose God is the Lord!

PSALM 144:15 NKJV

Who HAS SMILED AT ME LATELY? WHAT MESSAGE CAME THROUGH?

In 1998, twenty-one-year-old Se Ri Pak became the newest "wonder kid" of women's professional golf, winning the United States Open and later becoming the first woman to shoot a 61 in an LPGA event. Having played golf for only six years before turning professional, her amazing ascent was attributed not only to talent but also to a fierce mental focus based in the Asian tradition.

Onlookers are awed at the young player's ability to ignore distractions on the course. Even her caddy was asked if they were fighting because she walks alone and does not talk with him. But he explained that it's because she is intensely focused all the time.

In fact, her control is such that Se Ri broke into tears for the first time in her life upon winning the U.S. Open. Emotional display is that unusual for her. But she explains how she's working to change that habit:

> I usually look very serious, but after I started playing golf at fourteen, I saw Nancy Lopez on TV. I didn't know she was a great golfer—all I knew was that she always smiled. My goal is to be that way too. Now when I sign autographs, I always put a smile by my name. . . . Even if I don't win, I want to give people a smile.[37]

It is said a smile is the best way to improve your appearance. It's also one of the nicest things you can do for others.

A smile costs nothing but creates much.

Perfect Harmony

Do not forsake your friend.
PROVERBS 27:10

The late Leonard Bernstein—conductor, composer, teacher, and advocate—may well be the most important figure in American music of the twentieth century. With his personality and passion for his favorite subject, he inspired generations of new musicians and taught thousands that music should be an integral part of everyone's life.

As a public figure, Bernstein was larger than life—his charm and persuasiveness infectious. While his career progressed, he was constantly sought after for performances, lectures, and other appearances.

But it's said that in his later years, one way his personal life eroded was in his friendships. There came a time when he had few close friends. After his death, a comment from one of his longest acquaintances was that "you wanted to be his friend, but so many other people sought his attention that, eventually, the friendliest thing you could do was leave him alone."

Scientific evidence now shows us how important friendships are, not only to our emotional health, but to our physical and mental health as well. These most cherished relationships are a two-way street. The following are a few tips for keeping friendships on track:

Be aware of your friends' likes and dislikes.

Remember your friends' birthdays and anniversaries.

Take interest in your friends' children.

Become sensitive to their needs.

Keep in touch with them by phone.

Express what you like about your relationship with another person.

Serve your friends in thoughtful, unexpected ways.[38]

What CHARACTERISTICS ARE MOST IMPORTANT IN A FRIEND?

Friendship is a plant that must often be watered.

Fine China

Behold, like the clay in the potter's hand,
so are you in My hand, O house of Israel.
JEREMIAH 18:6 NASB

What
ATTITUDES
SHOULD I
CHANGE TO
MAKE MY
HEART MORE
PLIABLE IN
GOD'S HANDS?

Antique hunting one day, a collector noticed a lovely teacup and saucer. The delicate set stood out from the other china pieces in the display. She picked up the cup and examined it carefully. Discovering a small imperfection on the bottom, she lovingly held it in her hands as she thought about what might have caused the cup's flaw.

A few years earlier while visiting a pottery shop, she had watched as the potter chose a lump of clay to work and began to punch and slam it over and over again until it was just right. He shaped it, painted it, and fired it into a beautiful piece of earthenware that would be looked upon admiringly and be a serviceable item as well.

The clay, useless in its original form, had become beautiful, strong, and useful in the potter's hands. The woman thought of her own life with all its flaws, yet Jesus was willing to sacrifice himself so that she could have a good life with Him. Many lumpy places had existed in her heart prior to her salvation, but Jesus Christ, the Master Craftsman, began His work of shaping and molding, lovingly concentrating on even the finest details. This human vessel was then made fit for His service as He gently filled it to overflowing with the refining work of the Holy Spirit.

Grace is the love that gives, that loves
the unlovely and the unlovable.

By Your Fruit

Love, joy, peace, patience, kindness, goodness,
faithfulness, gentleness and self-control.
Against such things there is no law.

GALATIANS 5:22-23

With these words, Mother Teresa explained a lifetime of service: "I can love only one person at a time. I can feed only one person at a time. Just one, one, one. So you begin . . . I begin. I picked up one person—maybe if I didn't pick up that one person I wouldn't have picked up 42,000."

When she died, the entire world mourned.

Sometime before her death, a college professor asked his students to name people they considered truly worthy of the title "world leader." Although many different names appeared on the class list, the one name most commonly agreed upon was Mother Teresa.

The students wrote the following statements about her:

- She transcends normal love.

- She has a capacity for giving that makes me ashamed of my own self-centered actions.

- The most remarkable thing about her is that she never grows tired of her work. She never experiences "burnout" like so many other people. I just hope that I can be as satisfied with my life as she is with hers.

Although none of the students had ever met her, they acknowledged that Mother Teresa had had a profound impact on each of their lives. How? By her love. She welcomed the opportunity to fulfill her duties. Can we do any less?

Next time you have a chance to be kind, remember her words: "It is not how much we do but how much love we put in the doing."[39]

Take away love and our earth is a tomb.

What WAYS
CAN I GIVE
OF MYSELF
FOR THOSE
IN NEED
AROUND ME?

May I Take Your Order?

Then shall ye call upon me, and ye shall go
and pray unto me, and I will hearken unto you.
JEREMIAH 29:12 KJV

A special
DESIRE OF MY
HEART THAT I
HAVE NEVER
SHARED WITH
ANYONE IS . . .

Sometimes, the only solution for a difficult day is a nice double-dip ice cream cone—that is, if you love ice cream. One fan described a recent trial in ordering her treat at a drive-thru window.

She drove up to the speaker to place her order. This ice cream franchise carried too many flavors to list them all on the menu, so customers had to ask if a special flavor was in stock. The attendant answered: "May I take your order?"

"Do you have butter brickle today?" she asked. It was her favorite since childhood, and it was becoming increasingly difficult to find.

"No, I'm sorry . . . can we get you anything else?"

Oh, the frustration of drive-thru communication. "What else do you have?" she asked.

The attendant paused and said, "Well . . . what do you *want?*"

She couldn't help herself. "I *want* butter brickle!"

It was useless. But, determined to find that flavor, she drove two miles to the next franchise store. She approached the speaker with optimism. "May I take your order?" he asked.

"Yes, do you have butter brickle today?"

After a long pause, the attendant responded, "Butter brickle *what?*"

It is so disheartening to feel that no one hears our needs. How fortunate that God not only understands our every desire, but also knows them even before we do. Philippians 4:6 ASV encourages, "In nothing be anxious; but in everything by prayer and supplication with thanksgiving let your requests be made known unto God."

**Those who know when they
have enough are rich.**

Basket of Love

Gray hair is a crown of splendor;
it is attained by a righteous life.

PROVERBS 16:31

What HAVE
I BEEN
SHARING?
WHAT IS IN MY
HAND THAT I
COULD SHARE?

Every Saturday morning Tristen, a senior in high school, hustled off to visit the people on her list. Some resided in nursing homes; others were lonely at home. Tristen's mother filled a wicker basket with bananas or flowers and sometimes included a cassette tape of their church's Sunday service. Most of all, she packed her basket with lots of love and concern for others.

Tristen often sat at the bedside of one feeble lady. Although the woman did not respond, Tristen treated her tenderly as though she heard and understood every word. She chatted about current happenings, read Scripture, prayed, then kissed her goodbye at the end of the visit and said, "I'll see you next week."

Like a sturdy basket used for a variety of practical needs, Tristen filled her heart and life with love for others. With time and heavy use, baskets may wear out, but God continues to use His children to help others as long as we are willing to carry around His love. Whether we minister to others through praying, meeting physical needs, sending cards, or just calling them on the phone, we can still serve.

Tristen didn't just believe in God; she lived her faith by sharing her basket of God's love with all those around her.

With every deed you are sowing a seed,
though the harvest you may not see.

Book Me, Papaw!

Children's children are the crown of old men;
and the glory of children are their fathers.
PROVERBS 17:6 KJV

I can

HELP LAY A
FOUNDATION
FOR SOMEONE
ELSE'S LIFE BY ...

His eyes moistened with unbidden tears as Nicole climbed into his lap and settled comfortably against his chest. Her hair, freshly shampooed and dried, smelled of lemons and touched his cheek, soft as down. With clear blue-green eyes, she looked expectantly up at his face, thrust the trusted and well-worn book of children's stories at him, and said, "Book me, Papaw, book me!"

"Papaw" James carefully adjusted his reading glasses, cleared his throat, and began the familiar story. She knew the words by heart and excitedly "read" along with him. Every now and then he missed a word, and she politely corrected him, saying, "No, Papaw, that's not what it says. Now let's do it again so that we get it right."

She had no idea how her purity of heart thrilled his soul or how her simple trust in him moved him. James had a far different childhood—a harsh existence, made harder still by a distant and demanding father. His father ordered him to work the fields from dawn to dusk beginning at age 5. Most memories of his childhood bring back feelings of anger and pain.

This first grandchild, though, has brought joy and light into his life in a way that supersedes his own childhood. He returns her love and faith with a gentleness and devotion that makes her world secure and safe beyond measure. Theirs is a relationship made for a lifetime. For Nicole, it lays a foundation for life. For James, it heals a past of pain.

The world moves forward
on the feet of little children.

Touching Life

Preserve my life according to your love.
PSALM 119:88

The sounds of the delivery room receded to a quiet murmur of post-delivery activities and near-whispered comments between the parents. The father, gowned, with a hair net and masked face, leaned forward and touched their child who was cuddled to the mother. She looked down on the baby who was scowling, eyes tightly shut. With a sense of awe, the mother stretched forth one finger to gently smooth the child's wrinkled forehead. The need to touch her daughter was urgent, yet she was careful.

Developmental psychologists who have examined the process of childbirth and witnessed thousands of deliveries inform us that the need to gently touch one's newborn is a near-universal impulse crossing all cultural boundaries. Obviously, we have been created with an innate need to physically connect with our offspring. In this sense we are very much like God.

In *The Creation of Adam,* one of Michelangelo's famous frescoes that decorate the ceiling of the Sistine Chapel, he portrays the hand of Adam outstretched with a finger pointed. Opposite to it you see the hand of God in a similar pose reaching toward man. The two fingertips are nearly touching. No image more clearly reveals the Father's heart. He is always reaching out His hand to touch, with gentleness and love, those who are created in His own image.

Mothers and God share a common bond then, do they not? Both yearn to touch those made in their image.

If I TOUCHED THE HAND OF GOD, I THINK IT WOULD FEEL . . .

The love of a mother is the veil of a softer light
between the heart and the heavenly Father.

A Heart for Art

Do good, O LORD, to those who are good,
and to those who are upright in their hearts.
PSALM 125:4 NASB

HOW WOULD
I REPAY A TRUE
KINDNESS
FROM
ANOTHER'S
HEART?

Nguyen Van Lam began selling coffee from a cart in 1950. Several years later, he bought a building near an art school. Many of his customers were struggling art students who could barely afford to put food in their stomachs, much less buy art supplies. Lam, an impassioned art lover, loaned them money so they could practice their craft.

Several of the artists—who later became quite famous—repaid Lam's generosity with paintings, prints, and drawings. Over the years, his collection grew to more than a thousand pieces of art. Only a small portion of the collection is displayed in the Café Lam in Hanoi, but it covers almost every square inch of wall space.

Lam's extensive collection is a precious treasure. To protect the art during the war, he stored the art in an air-raid shelter. These days, he hopes to turn his building into a museum to permanently display his collection for future generations to enjoy.

Lam loves artists as much as he loves art. He admires their generous spirits, their ability to find beauty in everything, and the way they pour themselves into their work without demanding something back.[40]

Time with Jesus can be time spent in a lovely art gallery, where He shows you all the colors and patterns of your life. Just as Lam cared for the struggling artists, Jesus cares for you. He is your Comforter, Friend, Protector, and the Source of all creativity and beauty.

God's love for us is proclaimed with each
sunrise.

Pass It On

In truth I perceive that God shows no partiality.

ACTS 10:34 NKJV

Through the years, kitchens have played a major role in Connie's life. When she was growing up, she lived on a farm surrounded by aunts, uncles, cousins, siblings, her mother, and her grandmother. She often remembered the hot summer days when the kitchen would be steamy because they were canning. Canning was a family affair. The men raised and harvested the crops; the children peeled, chopped, and prepared the produce; and the women cooked and did the actual canning. There was much lively discussion over recipes, techniques, and timing.

At some point during the day, Grandma would sneak Connie under the table and give her a taste of whatever was being canned. Grandma would warn her to keep this their special secret. In fact, it was such a secret that Connie didn't find out until a few years ago that Grandma did this for all her cousins and siblings.

Because of it, Connie always thought she was Grandma's favorite grandchild, and that knowledge sustained her through many rough times. When she found out that everyone in her generation thought they were Grandma's favorite grandchild, it didn't diminish that special feeling. She was awed by the love that Grandma gave to the whole family. Her grandmother became the model for the kind of person she wanted to be.

God is the same way. He loves each one of us as if we were the only person in the universe. We are individually and personally His own special children.

God loves a cheerful giver.
She gives most who gives with joy.

I know GOD LOVES ME ESPECIALLY BECAUSE OF THE TIME HE . . .

Redirected Anger

A gentle answer turns away wrath,
but a harsh word stirs up anger.
PROVERBS 15:1

Someone

HAS CHEATED
ME, HOW
COULD I TURN
IT INTO A
BLESSING?

A Salvation Army officer stationed in New Zealand tells of an old Maori woman who won the name Warrior Brown for her fighting ability when she was drunk or enraged. After her conversion to Christianity, she was asked to give her testimony at an open-air meeting. One of her old enemies took the opportunity to loudly make fun of her. He ended his harangue by throwing a large potato at her, which hit her with a nasty blow.

The crowd grew deadly silent. A week earlier, the cowardly insulter would have needed to sprint into hiding to salvage his teeth. But what a different response they witnessed that night!

Warrior picked up the potato without a word and put it into her pocket. No more was heard of the incident until the harvest festival came around, when she appeared with a little sack of potatoes to share. She explained she had cut up and planted the potato and was now presenting it to the Lord as part of her increase.

Warrior had learned how to live in peace with her neighbors and yet be a strong spiritual "warrior" for the Lord's cause. What a beautiful example of taking the bad things that people do and turning them into praise for the Father in Heaven!

The heart benevolent and kind
the most resembles God.

Homebound

> Encourage one another and build each
> other up, just as in fact you are doing.
>
> I THESSALONIANS 5:11

Do I APPRECIATE WHAT "HOME" MEANS IN MY LIFE? HOW CAN I BE A BLESSING TO THE MEMBERS OF MY FAMILY?

Prior to his conversion, the apostle Paul persecuted scores of Christians. But God met this ruthless Pharisee in a special vision on the road to Damascus and changed his heart.

Yet wherever Paul went after his conversion, he caused controversy. The book of Acts tells us that many Christians were unwilling to accept Paul's conversion as a real change of heart. They feared that his supposed love for Christ was mere play-acting and would ultimately result in their imprisonment. Jews were angry at his new message too. Death threats against him were commonplace, and the increasing threats of violence prompted the church leaders in Jerusalem to take Paul to the seacoast, place him aboard a ship, and send him back to his hometown of Tarsus.

For several chapters, the book of Acts is silent about the life of Paul. But when he reappears in the narrative in Acts 11, no one questions his change of heart. No one misunderstands his intentions. No one criticizes his involvement in missionary endeavors. Something is different about Paul.

While the Bible does not tell us what happened to Paul during that time, perhaps he went home to his family. When the world is pressing in too closely on us, the four walls of home become a place to regenerate and renew. And when it comes time to move on again, we are refreshed and ready—just like Paul.

Tell a man he is brave, and
you help him to become so.

A Kite's Tale

Just as each of us has one body with many members . . . these members do not all have the same function.
ROMANS 12:4

Of ALL THE PEOPLE I WORK WITH, I AM INSPIRED BY . . . WHY?

A preacher told the following story:

On a breezy March day, the town mayor happened through the park where a small boy was flying the largest, most beautiful kite he had ever seen. It soared so high and floated so gently, the mayor was sure it must be visible from the next town. The mayor decided to award a "key to the city" to the one responsible for setting this spectacle aloft.

"Who is responsible for flying this kite?" the mayor inquired.

"I am," said the boy. "I made the kite with my own hands. I painted all the beautiful pictures and constructed it with scraps I found in my father's workshop. I fly the kite," he declared.

"I am," said the wind. "It is my whim that keeps it aloft and sets the direction it will go. Unless I blow, the kite will not fly at all. I fly the kite," the wind cooed.

"Not so," exclaimed the kite's tail. "I make it sail and give it stability against the wind's whims. Without me, the kite would spin out of control and crash to earth. I fly the kite," declared the tail.

"Now who flies the kite?" the pastor asked the children of the congregation.

"They all do!" said several kids in concert. Smart kids!

Take a moment to consider each of your coworkers. Ask yourself, *How would our progress be changed if that person's job didn't exist?* Next time you pass their work area, tell them you're glad they are part of the team.

The heart hungers for a kind word.

The Gift of Words

There are different kinds of gifts, but
the same Spirit. There are different
kinds of service, but the same Lord.
1 CORINTHIANS 12:4-5

Melissa wanted more than anything to be able to sing and play the piano! Unfortunately, she simply had no musical talent, no matter how hard she tried or how much she practiced. She finally came to the conclusion that she had no sense of rhythm and no ability to carry a tune.

As the daughter of a preacher with a beautiful voice, it didn't help matters. Most people expect a pastor's daughter to play the piano. She had never seen it written in any book, but she saw it written on every church member's face.

For years she prayed, "God, give me the ability to sing," but during the congregational hymns, she realized that nothing had happened. Her voice was just as bad as it was before she prayed. She took piano lessons until a well-meaning teacher kindly told her that she was wasting her father's money. Many times she wondered why God didn't answer her prayer in the way she would have liked.

Finally, Melissa gave up on the idea of being an accomplished pianist or soloist. She sang in the shower after everyone had left for the day and hummed as she cooked before anyone arrived back home in the evening.

She helped with Sunday school and later started writing. She discovered that God had given her the gift of words.

God does not give everyone the same talents. We're all unique and special in His eyes. Discovering her talent gave Melissa an entirely different outlook on life.

A bit of fragrance always clings
to the hand that gives you roses.

What TALENTS DO I SEE IN MYSELF THAT I'VE OVERLOOKED?

Circadian Meetings

To everything there is a season, a time
for every purpose under heaven.
ECCLESIASTES 3:1 NKJV

A favorite
MEMORY OF
A BYGONE
FRIEND IS . . .

A business consultant once advised executives to follow this pattern for scheduling their meetings and appointments:

Have breakfast meetings to set agendas, give assignments, and introduce new projects.

Have lunch meetings to negotiate deals, give advice to key staff members, and discuss mid-course corrections.

Have afternoon meetings to interview prospective employees, clients, or vendors, to return phone calls, and to resolve personnel issues.

From this consultant's perspective, morning hours are best spent in task activities, midday hours in problem-solving, and afternoon hours in people-intensive activities. The reason has little to do with management and much to do with biology. Our "circadian rhythms" seem to put us at a high-energy time in the morning and a low-energy time in the afternoon. Meeting with people requires less energy than attention to task and detail.

This afternoon, perhaps you can meet a friend for refreshments and conversation. Take time out for a brief end-of-the-day conversation with a parent, sibling, or friend. Allow time for light conversation about your dreams and accomplishments.

Jesus no doubt spent full days in ministry, preaching, teaching, and healing those who flocked to Him. But at the close of His ministry-intensive hours, Jesus spent time with His friends. We are wise to follow His example!

Hast thou a friend, as heart may wish at will?
Then use him so, to have his friendship still.
Wouldst have a friend, wouldst know
what friend is best? Have God thy
friend, who passeth all the rest.

When Faith Flutters

> You who are spiritual should restore him gently.
>
> GALATIANS 6:1

Early one morning, Jill sat at her desk, enjoying the warm rays of spring sunshine as they streamed through her bedroom window. Just outside the window, Jill noticed a small, brownish butterfly go by—or so she thought. A few seconds later, she turned to look at the window and saw that same butterfly had not landed on a plant; yet it seemed strangely suspended in midair. Its wings fluttered helplessly, but the flying insect could not move.

Puzzled, Jill walked outside to get a closer look. Glistening in the sun, like a ladder of dew-dropped pearls, hung an almost invisible net. During the night, another one of nature's creatures had spun a magical web to trap its victims.

Jill observed the struggle briefly until she watched the butterfly's wings grow motionless. She reached over and very gently plucked the winged insect from the spider's deadly threads. At first, the butterfly seemed stunned and fell to the ground. Jill gingerly picked it up and lifted it toward the sky, releasing its wings again. This time, it soared into the air and over the fence.

Anyone can tumble into tangled webs of deception—believing a lie, following the wrong leader, or confusing priorities. Disillusionment sets in. With faith fluttering, we can easily lose the strength to fight. At that point, a gentle, steady hand may be all we need to help free our fragile wings and send us soaring again on our Heavenly way.

A lie travels around the world while
truth is putting her boots on.

Some OF THE PEOPLE WHO HAVE HELPED ME KEEP FLYING ARE . . .

A Reason to Rise

Arise, shine, for your light has come,
And the glory of the Lord has risen upon you.

ISAIAH 60:1 NASB

A memory

I CHERISH

IS . . .

While camping deep in the woods, the first sense to attract our attention each morning is smell. The aromatic whiffs of food cooked over an open flame are a wonderful treat to awakening senses. The savory aroma of bacon, sausage, and especially a fresh pot of coffee, gently moves through the forest and rests overhead just long enough to rouse the sleeping camper and produce a memory like no other. Years later campers talk about that experience as if they were reliving it, almost capable of smelling the coffee right then. It's a wake-up call campers fondly cherish.

Each of us has moments like these that provide a platform for memories past that are special to us. These classic times of pleasure linger in our minds, much like the smells of a delicious breakfast on a long ago camping trip. The first call of the morning brings us into the new day and helps to set the pace and tone for the tasks ahead.

Could it be that as followers of Christ, we experience wake-up calls in our lives that are for more than just reminiscing? Our wake-up calls, lessons learned, and "deserts crossed" with God's help and presence, can turn these experiences into opportunities that allow God's loving plans for our lives to shine through us to a lost and depraved world.

Isaiah shouted, "Arise, shine!" Share the joy of knowing Christ with others.

A candle loses nothing by
lighting another candle.

Kitchen-Sink Legacy

"Do to others as you would have them do to you."

LUKE 6:31

Corinna's grandmother never went to seminary, but she sure could preach. From her kitchen-sink pulpit, Grandma would sermonize while she scrubbed the supper dishes. Her congregation of assembled relatives labored alongside her, clearing the table, drying the dishes, and putting away the pots and pans.

Corinna wanted to be like the neighbor children who gulped down their meals and left their dishes on the table as they flew out the back door to play. But Grandma would have none of that. By the time Grandma finished her sermonizing, it would be dark outside, and Corinna would have to wait until the next day to play with her friends. She quickly learned to do her chores without excuse or complaint; otherwise Grandma would remind her to "do everything without grumbling or complaining."

It seemed Grandma had a saying for every situation. If someone were upset about the treatment they had received from a friend, a clerk, or a neighbor, Grandma answered with, "Do to others as you would have them do to you." Or if she overheard one of the kids hinting that they were considering mischief, she quickly countered with, "Be sure your sin will find you out."

Only much later did Corinna discover that Grandma's gems of wisdom came from God's Word. Grandma's example demonstrates that everyday chores can be used as an opportunity to share God's love.

We should behave to our friends as
we would wish our friends to behave to us.

A time
WHEN I WAS

TREATED WITH

UNUSUAL

KINDNESS

WAS . . .

As Time Goes By

This is the day which the LORD has made;
We will rejoice and be glad in it.

PSALM 118:24 NKJV

Today, I
SHOULD TAKE
TIME TO . . .

True happiness comes from
the job of deeds well done,
the zest of creating things new.

"Where does the time go?" we ask. Here it is—a new day on the horizon—and we can't remember how it arrived so quickly. Why, last week seems like yesterday, and last year flew by like a video in fast-forward.

And worse, it's hard to remember what we spent it on.

Shouldn't I have more great memories? we wonder. *What did I accomplish?*

Singer Jim Croce mused in his hit song "Time in a Bottle" that "there never seems to be enough time to do the things you want to do, once you find them." We search so hard for happiness. But often, we don't understand that happiness is not a goal to be won, but a by-product of a life well spent.

This "Old English Prayer" offers simple instruction for enjoying the day that the Lord has made:

Take time to work, it is the price of success.

Take time to think, it is the source of power.

Take time to play, it is the secret of perpetual youth.

Take time to read, it is the foundation of wisdom.

Take time to be friendly, it is the road to happiness.

Take time to dream, it is hitching your wagon to a star.

Take time to love and be loved, it is the privilege of the gods.

Take time to look around, it is too short a day to be selfish.

Take time to laugh, it is the music of the soul.

The Art of Caring

Now these three remain: faith, hope and
love. But the greatest of these is love.

1 CORINTHIANS 13:13

This was the first meeting of a support group
for middle school youngsters who had suffered significant losses in their lives. The group leader was
unsure of what to expect, so the question really
caught him by surprise.

"Why does God kill babies?"

The question hung in the air for an eternity,
and two young faces stared intently at the group
counselor, waiting for an answer. He gazed at the
two brothers' faces as he contemplated how to
respond. He wished to reassure them that God
does not kill babies, yet, for the moment, the
answer to the question seemed far less important
than what prompted it.

"Something really sad must have happened for
you guys to ask such a question," he finally
responded.

The two brothers shared the sad story of how
their entire family had hoped for a new baby. The
boys wanted to become uncles in the worst way.
Finally, their older sister became pregnant, but the
baby was stillborn. They could not understand
why this would happen.

With careful encouragement and much listening, the counselor found a way for the two brothers to come to grips with the loss of their niece.
Although they eventually understood that the loss
of their niece was not a direct act of God, they still
struggled with why it happened.

As the other group members shared their own
stories of loss and sadness, a kinship developed
among the group that lifted the sadness.

Take time to care every chance you get!

The capacity to care gives life
its deepest significance.

Who
NEEDS MY
ENCOURAGE-
MENT TODAY?

Holy Hush

You, O LORD, are a compassionate and gracious God,
slow to anger, abounding in love and faithfulness.
PSALM 86:15

A PIECE
OF GOD'S
ARTWORK
THAT I
ADMIRE IS . . .

All is still as a man sits at his dining room table, allowing the pages of a well-worn Bible to slip slowly through his fingers and basking in the peace of the moment. The pages have a comfortable feel, and the soft plop they make as they fall barely disturbs the quiet. Early morning always brings with it a hush of holiness for him. In his mind's eye he remembers another such morning.

The new dawn air is tangy and sharp as the two brothers turn onto a gravel road bordered by wheat fields. Early in the growing season the wheat is about two feet high and a brilliant green. Suddenly one boy catches his breath. From the edge of the wheat field, a ring-necked pheasant comes into view just as a bright ray of sunshine creates a natural spotlight. As if showing off for God himself, the pheasant stops and strikes a pose.

Time stands still, sound ceases, and God paints an image on the young boy's mind that will remain for a lifetime. The beautiful hues of the pheasant, with its shining white collar glistening in the sunshine against the vivid green of the wheat, remain sharply etched in his memory. Whenever he relives that day, he experiences anew the presence of God and a supernatural sense of contentment.

All around us are awesome reminders of a big God who created everything in a matter of days. Isn't it great to know the Artist firsthand?

When God makes his presence felt through
us, we are like the burning bush; Moses never
took any heed what sort of bush it was—
he only saw the brightness of the Lord.

Daily Bread

> We do not have a High Priest who cannot sympathize with our weaknesses, but was in all points tempted as we are, yet without sin.
>
> HEBREWS 4:15 NKJV

When Jesus instituted the Last Supper, He told His disciples to "do this in remembrance of me" (Luke 22:19). Remembering someone is to allow them to shape and influence our lives. Jesus was asking His disciples to remember Him in the Lord's Supper so that even when He was no longer physically present with them, He would still be shaping and guiding their lives. When we go to the Lord's Table, we give witness to the fact we are depending upon Jesus.

As we remember Jesus, we have the picture of Him giving himself to us to nurture and feed our souls. A song written by Arden Autry describes how He lovingly gave—and continues to give—His life for us:

As you eat this bread, as you drink this cup,
Let your heart give thanks and be lifted up.
Your soul can rest in this truth secure:
As you eat this bread, all I am is yours.
All I am is yours. All I am I gave,
Dying on the cross, rising from the grave,
Your sins to bear and your life restore:
As you eat this bread, all I am is yours.
In delight and joy, in the depths of pain,
In the anxious hours, through all loss and gain,
Your world may shake, but my Word endures:
As you eat this bread, all I am is yours.[41]

Throughout your day, remember Jesus. Let Him direct your thoughts and ways.

The mind grows by what it feeds on.

I feel
CLOSEST TO
GOD WHEN
I AM IN . . .

Make Hay While the Sun Shines

This is what the Lord says: "Stand at the crossroads and look; ask for the ancient paths, ask where the good way is, and walk in it, and you will find rest for your souls."

JEREMIAH 6:16

I Would

LIKE TO TRY . . .

Medicine—what a glamorous profession! High salaries, prestige, respect, travel, speaking engagements, curing the sick, and discovering new drugs.

Medicine—occasional tedium, exposure to a host of diseases, making an incorrect diagnosis, watching patients die, long hours, no sleep, no family time, and malpractice suits.

Medicine—maybe not so glamorous after all.

When doctors spend most of the year trying to help their patients sort out various physical and mental ailments, while trying not to become emotionally involved, where do they go to heal their own wounded spirits?

One doctor in Michigan goes back home to Vermont to help her father and brother with the haying. "It's elegantly simple work," she says. The job has a set of basic steps that, when followed, result in neatly bound bales of hay that are then trucked off the fields and sold the following winter. Haying is hot, sweaty, tiring work, but it has a satisfying beginning, middle, and end . . . unlike medicine.[42]

All of us need an activity that is the antithesis of what we do all day. We need a cobweb-clearer, a routine-shaker. Crafts and hobbies for those in mental work. Puzzles or reading for those who perform manual labor. Gardening for workers with high stress. People activities for those who work alone.

We each need to be completely out of our normal work mode for a little while every day—and for a week or two when we can manage it. It's a crucial part of living a balanced life!

Take rest; a field that has rested
gives a bountiful crop.

A "Body of Work"

Christ Jesus . . . gave Himself on our behalf
that He might redeem us (purchase our freedom)
from all iniquity and purify for Himself
a people [to be peculiarly His own].

TITUS 2:13-14 AMP

Sixty-five years has within it exactly 569,400 hours. If you subtract the number of hours that a person spends growing up and receiving a basic high-school education, and then subtract the hours that a person normally spends eating, sleeping, and engaging in recreation, you will still have 134,000 hours for work between the ages of eighteen and sixty-five.

That's a lot of time! Yet, many people reach retirement age, look back over their years, and conclude: "I was only putting in time and drawing a paycheck."

Take a different approach, starting today. Choose to create a "body of work" with the time that you have!

A body of work is more than a career or a pile of achievements, awards, and accomplishments. A "body" of work is just that—physical and human. A body of work is people.

Get to know the people with whom you work. Spend time with them. Value them. Share experiences with them. Be there when they face crises and when they celebrate milestones. Count your colleagues—and also those above and below you on the organizational ladder—among your friends, and treat them as friends. Build relationships that endure through the years, regardless of who is transferred, promoted, or laid off. People are what will matter to you far more than possessions when you reach your retirement years.

See everything; overlook a
great deal; correct a little.

A close

FRIENDSHIP

THAT I HAVE

MADE

THROUGH MY

WORK IS . . .

In Progress

He who has begun a good work in you
will complete it until the day of Jesus Christ.

PHILIPPIANS 1:6 NKJV

To BE
CHRISTLIKE
I WILL HAVE
TO CHANGE. . .

A sign in a hotel lobby that was being remodeled stated, "Please be patient. Renovation in progress to produce something new and wonderful." Perhaps we all need to wear a sign like that! We are all unfinished projects under construction, being made into something wonderful. Being mindful of this, we might have greater grace and patience for others, as well as for ourselves, while the work is underway.

Hope is the anticipation of good. Like the hotel lobby in the disarray of renovation, our hope is often in spite of our present circumstances. What is the basis for our hope?

For the Christian, hope is not simple optimism or a denial of reality. The Reason for our hope is Jesus Christ, the solid Rock of our faith. As the hymn writer wrote, "My hope is built on nothing less than Jesus' blood and righteousness." We are never without hope for our lives if we know the Lord Jesus.

The focus of our hope is to be like Jesus. This goal may seem too great and way beyond our ability to achieve, and it is.

The Scriptures tell us it is "Christ in you" that is our hope. (See Colossians 1:27.) The transformation of our lives into Christlikeness is a goal that is larger than life. As Paul wrote to the Corinthians, to have hope only for this life is to be miserable. (See 1 Corinthians 15:19.) The Christian hope is for this life and for eternity.

Our hope lies, not in the man
we put on the moon, but in
the Man we put on the cross.

Knowing God's Will

I pray You, if I have found favor in
Your sight, show me now Your Way.

EXODUS 33:13 AMP

Saint Ignatius of Loyola saw the doing of God's will as not only our command in life, but also our reward:

Teach us, good Lord, to serve thee as thou deservest: to give and not to count the cost; to fight and not to heed the wounds; to toil and not to seek for rest; to labor and not to ask for any reward save that of knowing that we do thy will.[43]

It is as we know we are doing God's will that we find true meaning in life and a deep sense of accomplishment and purpose.

How can we know that we are doing God's will? One of the simplest approaches is this:

Commit yourself to the Lord each day, and periodically throughout the day, by simply saying, "Lord, I put my life in Your hands. Do with me what You will."

Trust the Lord to send you the work and the relationships you need for His purpose in your life to be accomplished.

As Roberta Hromas, a noted Bible teacher, once said, "Simply answer your door, answer your phone, and answer your mail. The Lord will put in your path the opportunities that He desires for you to pursue."

God's will is not a mystery you try desperately to unlock. The key is to seek His will, to listen to the Holy Spirit, and to read and study His Word. Then you can know what He has planned for you!

A man's heart is right when
he wills what God wills.

Some OF
GOD'S PLANS
FOR ME
INCLUDE . . .

Whose Strength?

When I am weak, then I am strong.

2 CORINTHIANS 12:10 NKJV

The MOST STRETCHING EXPERIENCE OF MY LIFE HAS BEEN . . .

In the springtime, it's fun to watch tiny baby birds with downy crowns begin to find their way around. They make their way to the edge of their nest and take a peek over to view the very large, unexplored world around them.

At first they may look into the abyss and then shrink back to the familiar security of their nest. Perhaps they imagine the strength of their own untried wings is all that will save them from a fatal fall—and they know how weak and unproven those little wings are! Yet, when they are either pushed out of the nest or gather courage to launch out on their own to try that first flight, they find the air supports them when they spread their wings.

How often do we allow unfamiliar situations and circumstances to loom large and threatening in our imagination? Sometimes when we look at circumstances that lie outside our familiar "nest," we may feel just like a baby bird. We take a look at our own weakness, and we may want to turn around and head back to safety.

In times of crisis—either real or imagined— what is it that God has called us to do? He may be trying to push us out of our nest and "stretch our wings," so we can grow in our faith.

Let us not pray for lighter burdens,
but for stronger backs.

The Hand of Blessing

> He gives you something you can then give away . . .
> so that you can be generous in every way,
> producing with us great praise to God.
>
> 2 CORINTHIANS 9:10-11 THE MESSAGE

Glen patted the wallet in his back pocket. He had landed a job after school as grocery checker at Fergeson's Supermarket and had just cashed his paycheck. In a few weeks, he would be able to make the down payment for that 1985 Chevrolet at Bud's Used Car Lot.

Times were tough for Glen and his mom. His father, an alcoholic, had died in a drunken brawl when Glen was only ten. His mom suffered with chronic asthma but ironed clothes to pay the bills. Glen delivered papers for several years to supplement their income, but this new job promised more: a future. The thought of managing his own store someday made Glen swell with pride.

Upon leaving, Glen heard a commotion in the checkout line. A shabbily dressed woman pleaded with the checker: "But I must feed my babies! I don't have enough money!

People grumbled in line. The checker looked angry.

Glen sighed deeply and walked over to the lady. "Excuse me," he said, pulling her away from prying eyes. Without hesitation, he reached into his pocket and placed the bills into her trembling hands. "Sshh! Now go buy your groceries." Glen tore loose from the woman's grateful embrace and rode home.

A few days later, Glen found an envelope from Mr. Fergeson in his time card slot. Inside it read, "Promoted to assistant manager. I need people with unselfish hearts in my business." In the envelope was a $200 advance.

Trouble knocks at every door, but we can always find someone who suffers more. In God's plan of economy, we are blessed so that we can bless others. In the process, He always meets our own needs.

Generosity lies less in giving much than in giving at the right moment.

God's Promise

"I am with you all the days (perpetually, uniformly, and on every occasion), to the [very] close and consummation of the age."
MATTHEW 28:20 AMP

I can SAFELY
TRUST GOD
BECAUSE
HE HAS . . .

A person who conducted an informal survey about the prayers of people in his church found that most people pray one of two types of prayers. The first was an SOS—not only "Save Our Souls," but also "O God, help us now."

The second was SOP—"Solve Our Problems." People asked the Lord to eliminate all needs, struggles, trials, and temptations. They wanted carefree, perfect lives, and they fully believed that is what God had promised them. He concluded from his survey: "Most people want God to do it all."

God has not promised, however, to live our lives for us—but rather, to walk through our lives with us. Our part is to be faithful and obedient; His part is to lead us, guide us, protect us, and help us. In her poem, "What God Hath Promised," Annie Johnson Flint recognized the true nature of God's promise:

> God hath not promised
> Skies always blue,
> Flower-strewn pathways
> All our lives through;
> God hath not promised
> Sun without rain,
> Joy without sorrow,
> Peace without pain.
> But God hath promised
> Strength for the day,
> Rest for the labor,
> Light for the way,
> Grace for the trials,
> Help from above,
> Unfailing sympathy,
> Undying love.[44]

Do what you know you can do today—and then trust God to do what you cannot do!

You cannot control the length of your life, but you can control its width and depth.

Stop and Think

God . . . richly furnishes us with everything to enjoy.
1 TIMOTHY 6:17 RSV

I can SEE SEVEN WONDERFUL THINGS OUT MY WINDOW. WHAT ARE THEY?

Have you ever noticed that when we're in a hurry, we hit nothing but red lights? Although they are annoying when we're racing to an appointment, stoplights are there for our protection.

We need stoplights throughout our day too. Hard work and busy schedules need to be interrupted with time for leisure and reflection. Without it we can become seriously sick with stress-induced illnesses. Time set aside for recreation or relaxation can rejuvenate our spirits. This poem by W. H. Davies tells us to take time to "stop and stare":

> What is this life if, full of care,
> We have no time to stand and stare?
> No time to stand beneath the boughs
> And stare as long as sheep or cows.
> No time to see, when woods we pass,
> Where squirrels hide their nuts in grass.
> No time to see, in broad daylight,
> Streams full of stars, like stars at night.
> No time to turn at Beauty's glance,
> And watch her feet, how they can dance.
> No time to wait till her mouth can
> Enrich that smile her eyes began.
> A poor life this if, full of care,
> We have no time to stand and stare.[45]

There are two ways of making it through our busy life. One way is to stop thinking. The second is to stop and think. Take time to contemplate what life is for and to what end you are living. The word Sabbath literally means, "stop doing what you are doing."

A happy life consists of tranquility of mind.

Balm

Is there no balm in Gilead,
Is there no physician there?

JEREMIAH 8:22 NKJV

My FAVORITE
SONG OF
WORSHIP IS . . .

In centuries past, groves of balsam trees were planted on terraces in the hills south of Jerusalem. They were also planted in fields east of the Jordan River, in the area known as Gilead. The sap from the trees was harvested to create a balm that was considered to have great medicinal value in helping wounds to heal. The balm was used especially to treat scorpion stings and snake bites. Since scorpions and snakes abounded in the wilderness regions of Judea and throughout the Middle East, the balm was extremely valuable and was an important export item along ancient trade routes.[46]

The "balm of Gilead" is identified with Jesus. He is the One who heals our wounds.

Every day holds the potential for us to experience stings and bites, both literal and figurative. While not always life-threatening, these "jabs" from the enemy are hurtful nonetheless. How can we apply the balm of Jesus Christ to them?

The foremost way is through praise. Any time we find ourselves under attack or wounded, we can turn our minds and hearts to Him with a word, a thought, or a song of praise.

For example, if we feel attacked by a swarm of stinging problems, we can say, "Praise You, Jesus, You are my Deliverer, my Rescuer, my sure Help."

As you praise Jesus, you will find the pain associated with an incident or situation soothed. He is the Lord of Lords—including anything that tries to "lord" it over you!

We increase whatever we praise.
The whole creation responds
to praise, and is glad.

The Person in the Mirror

Looking unto Jesus the author and finisher of our faith; who for the joy that was set before him endured the cross, despising the shame, and is set down at the right hand of the throne of God.

HEBREWS 12:2 KJV

As Christ's nature grows within us, the selfish nature with which we were born begins to recede into the background. Our attitudes toward others change along with our behavior.

Away on a business trip, a man's wife and little daughter stayed at the home of a friend. On the bedroom wall just over the head of the bed in which they slept was a picture of the Lord Jesus, which was reflected in the large mirror of the dressing table standing in the bay of the bedroom window.

When the little girl woke on her first morning there, she saw the picture reflected in the mirror and exclaimed, "Oh, Mummy, I can see Jesus through the mirror!" Then she quickly kneeled up to take a better look, but doing so brought her own body between the picture and the mirror, so that instead of seeing the picture of Jesus reflected, she now saw herself.

So she lay down again, and again she saw the picture of Jesus. She was up and down several times after that with her eyes fixed on the mirror.

Finally, she said, "Mummy, when I can't see myself, I can see Jesus; but every time I see myself, I don't see Him."

When self fills our vision, we do not see Jesus. This afternoon, when the events of the day and your personal concerns are heavy on your mind, turn your eyes to Him.

Before us is a future all unknown,
a path untrod; beside us a friend well
loved and known—that friend is God.

I Want

TO SEE JESUS
IN MY LIFE
BECAUSE . . .

The Key Ingredient

This is the day the LORD has made;
let us rejoice and be glad in it.
PSALM 118:24

Do I HAVE ALL THE INGREDIENTS FOR A FUL-FILLED LIFE?

Caroline's son, Brad, had left home for college a few months earlier, leaving her home much too quiet and empty. The phone hardly ever rang, and the doorbell remained silent. Now he was coming to visit.

Excitedly, Caroline changed the sheets on Brad's bed, fluffed his pillow, and straightened up his bedroom. Then she breezed into the kitchen to bake his favorite dessert—a buttermilk pound cake.

All the ingredients were on hand, and she almost had the recipe memorized. She measured them out carefully and made every effort to mix it as directed, but before all the flour was mixed in, the phone rang. After a brief conversation, she returned to the cake. She poured the batter into the baking pans and hurriedly placed them in the pre-heated oven.

About halfway through the baking time, she looked into the mixing bowl. Oh, no! She had left out a large portion of the flour! A quick glance into the oven confirmed her fears; the cake was not rising. She was so disappointed. Despite her good intentions, she had left out most of an important ingredient. The cake might have tasted okay, but it was flat and gooey.

Life is a lot like that cake. Some experiences may seem to be good and offer happiness, but without Christ, the most important element of life is missing.

Be simple; take our Lord's hand
and walk through things.

Fire!

Be pleased, O LORD, to deliver me;
O LORD, make haste to help me!
PSALM 40:13 NKJV

Putting MY
DAY IN GOD'S
HANDS WILL
HELP ME . . .

It's usually about lunchtime when we realize that the clock's been moving faster than we have. So we break into a mental sprint to see if we can beat the clock to the day's finish line. It's usually about this time of day when everyone and everything need immediate attention. Sometimes we end the day thinking all we did for the last few hours was "put out brush fires." Consequently, the primary objectives of the day stand waiting for attention.

With the usual candor of children, one kindergartner shed some light on this late-afternoon dilemma. He was on a class field trip to the fire station to take a tour and learn about fire safety. The fireman explained what to do in case of a fire. "First, go to the door and feel it to see if it's hot. Then, if you smell or see smoke coming in around the door, fall to your knees. Does anyone know why you ought to fall to your knees?"

The little boy piped up and said, "Sure! To start praying to ask God to get you out of this mess!"

What a good idea for those brush fires that break out in the heat of the day! If we mentally and spiritually fall to our knees, we move our thoughts to God's presence around us and His authority over the circumstances we are facing.

Sometimes your lunchtime becomes a "falling on your knees" time!

Speak to Him thou for He hears,
and spirit with spirit can meet—
Closer is He than breathing,
and nearer than hands and feet.

Seventy Times Seven

"Forgive, and you will be forgiven."
LUKE 6:37 NKJV

IF SOMEONE
HURTS ME,
HOW CAN I
FORGIVE AND
STILL PROTECT
MYSELF?

When one boy hit another during Sunday school class, the teacher's aid took the offending child outside for discipline. She then assigned a crafts project to the rest of the class so she could talk to the child who had been hit. "You need to forgive Sam for hitting you, Joey," she said.

"Why?" Joey asked. "He's mean. He doesn't deserve any forgiveness."

The teacher said, "The disciples of Jesus may have felt that same way. They asked Jesus how many times they had to forgive someone who was mean to them, and Jesus said seventy times seven." (See Matthew 18:21-22.) Joey sat thoughtfully, and the teacher continued, "Do you know how many times that is, Joey?"

Joey had just learned how to multiply, so he took a nearby pencil and piece of paper and worked this math puzzle. Upon getting his answer, he looked up at the teacher and said in shock, "Do you mean to tell me that Sam is going to hit me 489 more times! I'm going to be black and blue for forgiving him all year!"

To forgive does not mean another person's behavior has not hurt us or that they were justified in their actions. But forgiving means saying, "I choose to let you go. I will not hold the memory of this inside me. I will not seek revenge." We may have to "let go" 490 times. But in the end, we will be free, and the other person will be in God's hands.

"I can forgive, but I cannot forget,"
is only another way of saying,
"I cannot forgive."

Rewards

Surely there is a reward for the righteous.

PSALM 58:11 NKJV

The writer of Hebrews encourages us to believe two things about God: First, He exists, and second, He is a "rewarder of those who diligently seek Him" (Hebrews 11:6 NKJV). Among those rewards are reconciliation to God, forgiveness of sins, peace of heart and mind, provision and help, and power to overcome evil. All of these are wonderful rewards—but they are also intangible ones.

Like children who live in a material world, we often desire a "God with skin on." We long to see, feel, and touch our rewards. We long to feel appreciation, to be hugged and kissed, and to receive tangible gifts from our loved ones.

Is there a link between the intangible rewards that come from God and the tangible rewards of the "real world"? There may be! Research has revealed that those who have less stress in their lives—a by-product of peace, forgiveness, reconciliation, and spiritual power—enjoy these rewards:

Fewer illnesses, doctor's appointments, need for medication, and overall health care expense.

Fewer repairs on appliances and machinery. Apparently when we are at peace on the inside, we use machines with more precision and patience. We break things with less frequency.

Fewer automobile accidents. When we are feeling peace and harmony with God and people, we are less aggressive and more careful in driving.

Diligently seek the Lord today. Make your relationship with Him your number one concern. And enjoy the rewards He will bring your way!

God is never found accidentally.

I have
STRESS IN
MY LIFE CON-
CERNING . . .

That Loving Touch

He hath said, I will never
leave thee, nor forsake thee.
HEBREWS 13:5 KJV

God HAS
ENCOURAGED
ME IN BLEAK
TIMES BY . . .

A minister told of a certain family in his church who had waited a long time for a child. The couple was overjoyed when at last a son was born to them, but they were crushed when they learned he had a severe handicap. He would go into extremely violent seizures without warning. Nevertheless, as he grew, they tried to make his life as normal as possible.

Whenever the church doors were open, this family could be found in attendance. As time passed, the child developed a deep love for the same Jesus his parents loved, and he counted on Him to bring him through each of his life-threatening episodes.

The minister tells of the father's love as reflected on one particular Sunday:

I remember the father always holding the little boy during worship at our church. I remember one particularly hard seizure when the father gently but firmly held the little guy and went to the back of the sanctuary. There he held him to his chest, gently whispering into his ear. There was no hint of embarrassment or frustration on that father's face. Only calm, deep, abiding love.

That is a picture of our Heavenly Father's love for us. In spite of our deep imperfections, He is not embarrassed to call us His children. He tenderly holds us through the deepest, hardest part of our struggles and whispers words of assurance and encouragement while He clutches us to himself and supports us with His loving care.

He prayeth best, who loveth best,
All things both great and small; For the dear
God who loveth us, He made and loveth all.

After the Uproar

> After the uproar was ceased, Paul called unto him the disciples, and embraced them.
>
> ACTS 20:1 KJV

For a small child, the most comforting place in the world is in the secure arms of his mother or father. It's not really very different for grown-ups. The embrace of caring arms is a wonderful place to be. Even a brief hug from a casual friend can lift one's spirits.

At the end of a busy or frustrating day, "after the uproar has ceased," grown-ups may long for a pair of loving parental arms to assure them everything's going to be all right—to hear a voice that says soothingly, "I'm here, and I'll take care of you."

Take this little poem as a "hug" this evening from One who loves you without measure, and who watches over your every move with tenderness and compassion:

When the birds begin to worry
And the lilies toil and spin,
And God's creatures all are anxious,
Then I also may begin.
For my Father sets their table,
Decks them out in garments fine,
And if He supplies their living,
Will He not provide for mine?
Just as noisy, common sparrows
Can be found most anywhere—
Unto some just worthless creatures,
If they perish who would care?
Yet our Heavenly Father numbers
Every creature great and small,
Caring even for the sparrows,
Marking when to earth they fall.
If His children's hairs are numbered,
Why should we be filled with fear?
He has promised all that's needful,
And in trouble to be near.[47]

Our ground of hope is that
God does not weary of mankind.

My HUG
IN RETURN
TO JESUS
TELLS HIM . . .

In His Eyes

The eyes of the Lord are upon the righteous.
PSALM 34:15 KJV

I think THAT
    GOD SEES
    ME AS . . .

In *The Upper Room,* Sandra Palmer Carr describes a touching moment she experienced with one of her sons. When her younger son, Boyd, was four years old, she was rocking him in a high-backed wooden rocking chair, as was her habit. But this time he was facing her, straddling her lap with his knees bent.

Suddenly, he sat up straight, lifted his head, and stared intensely into her eyes. He became very still, and Sandra stopped rocking. He cupped her face in his little hands and said in a near-whisper, "Mommy, I'm in your eyes."

They stayed that way for several long moments, staring into one another's eyes. The rocking stopped, and the room grew quiet. Then Sandra whispered back, "And I'm in yours." Boyd leaned his head against her contentedly, and they resumed their rocking.[48]

How can we be assured we are always in God's eyes? The Bible has many, many verses to indicate He is continuously thinking of us, attending to us, and doing all He can to bless us. Certainly, Jesus' death and resurrection are constant reminders of how dear and precious we are to Him.

Your Heavenly Father desires to comfort you with His love, letting you stop now and then to call to mind a verse of Scripture that tells you how much you mean to Him.

You should never doubt you are the focus of God's tender care and attention. You can have a grateful and confident heart knowing you are always in His eyes.

The only important decision we have to make
is to live with God; He will make the rest.

God Is Awake

He will not let your foot slip—he who watches
over you will not slumber; indeed, he who
watches over Israel will neither slumber nor sleep.

PSALM 121:3-4

Anna and her mother were alone in her new home for the first time. Her father's new job meant they would someday be able to buy a home of their own in a safer part of town. But for now, they could only afford a rental in a less secure area.

When her father left on a business trip, he admonished her mother to be sure all the windows and doors were locked before Anna and she went to bed. "We'll be okay," she assured him. "God has always taken care of us."

Later, however, as her mother checked the last door lock, she thought she heard people yelling somewhere down the street. When she reached Anna's room, she found Anna sitting in a little ball in the middle of her bed. Her wide eyes told Anna that she had heard the yelling too.

"Mom, do we have to turn out the lights tonight?" Anna pleaded. Her mother had not left the lights on for Anna since she was four-years-old. The bright country moon had provided enough light to wean her away from the night light. But God's lamp, as they had called it, was nowhere to be seen in this smoggy city atmosphere.

"Sweetie, God never sleeps. Even when you can't see His lamp, He's up there watching over you."

"Well," Anna replied, "as long as God is awake, there is no sense in both of us staying awake!"

God is awake! He's always watching over you, ready to protect you from harm.

**God is protecting because
He is proactively detecting!**

When I FEEL
AFRAID,
I REMIND
MYSELF OF THE
FACT THAT . . .

Family Devotions

"When you pray . . . pray to your Father who is in the secret place; and your Father who sees in secret will reward you openly."
MATTHEW 6:6 NKJV

A prayer
THAT I
REMEMBER
ASKING OF
GOD AS A
CHILD WAS
ABOUT . . .

Bedtime prayers are often limited to reciting a poem or saying a little memorized prayer. However, bedtime prayers can become family devotions if the entire family gathers at the bedside of the child who retires first.

Each member of the family says a heartfelt prayer that is spontaneous and unrehearsed. A verse or two of Scripture might be read prior to prayer. The point of such a devotional time is not that children are obedient to say a prayer before sleep, but that the children's hearts are knit to the heart of God and to the hearts of other family members.

Albert Schweitzer once commented on the need for parents to provide an example in devotion:

From the services in which I joined as a child I have taken with me into life a feeling for what is solemn, and a need for quiet self-recollection, without which I cannot realize the meaning of my life. I cannot, therefore, support the opinion of those who would not let children take part in grown-up people's services till they to some extent understand them. The important thing is not that they shall understand but that they shall feel something of what is serious and solemn. The fact that a child sees his elders full of devotion, and has to feel something of devotion himself, that is what gives the service its meaning for him.[49]

Give family devotions a try soon!

When I am with God my fear is gone;
In the great quiet of God my troubles
are as the pebbles on the road,
my joys are like the everlasting hills.

Stargazing

He brought [Abram] outside and said,
"Look now toward heaven, and count the stars
if you are able to number them." And He
said to him, "So shall your descendants be."

GENESIS 15:5 NKJV

A father decided to take his young daughter for an evening walk along a country road. The family lived in a large city, where walking at night was not the custom or considered safe. The father could hardly wait to see how his daughter would respond to a star-filled sky.

As dusk turned into dark, the little girl became fearful and clung to her father's hand. Then suddenly, she looked toward the sky and exclaimed with surprise, "Daddy, somebody drew dots all over the sky!"

Her father smiled. His young daughter had never seen a night sky away from the city lights. He was glad the moon had not yet risen so the stars appeared even closer and more distinct. "Daddy," she continued in her enthusiasm, "if we connect them all, will they make a picture?"

What an interesting notion, the father thought. "No," he replied to his daughter, "the dots are there for another purpose. Each one is a hope God has for your life. God has lots of hopes that your life will be filled with good things. In fact, there are more hopes than you or I can ever count!"

"I knew it!" the little girl said. "The dots do make a picture." And then she added more thoughtfully, "I always wondered what hope looked like."

Stargazing is one of the best ways to get your earthly life back into perspective and realize that in God's infinite universe, He has a specific plan for you.

Eternity is the divine treasure house, and hope is the window, by which mortals are permitted to see, as through a glass darkly, the things which God is preparing.

The LAST
TIME I LOOKED
AT THE STARS
IN THE SKY, I
THOUGHT . . .

The Dinner Table

He took bread, gave thanks and
broke it, and gave it to them.

LUKE 22:19 NKJV

For A SPECIAL
MEAL, I WOULD
PREPARE . . .
AND SERVE
IT IN AN
ATMOSPHERE
OF . . .

Elton Trueblood has written eloquently about family dinnertime. Perhaps it's time we reinstitute this practice in our lives! She writes:

The table is really the family altar! Here those of all ages come together and help to sustain both their physical and their spiritual existence. If a sacrament is an actual conveyance of spiritual meaning and power by a material process, then a family meal can be a sacrament. It entwines the material and the spiritual in a remarkable way. The food, in and of itself, is purely physical, but it represents human service in its use. Here, at one common table, is the father who has earned, the mother who has prepared or planned, and the children who share, according to need, whatever their antecedent participation may have been.

When we realize how deeply a meal together can be a spiritual and regenerating experience, we can understand something of why our Lord, when he broke bread with his little company toward the end of their earthly fellowship, told them, as often as they did it, to remember Him. We, too, seek to be members of His sacred fellowship, and irrespective of what we do about the Eucharist, there is no reason why each family meal should not take on something of the character of a time of memory and hope.[50]

When was the last time your family gathered together for a meal?

The family circle is the supreme
conductor of Christianity.

What Do You Want?

I thank You and praise You, O God of my fathers,
Who has given me wisdom and might and has
made known to me now what we desired of You.
DANIEL 2:23 AMP

Father,

I HAVE A NEED

TO BRING

TO YOU . . .

Children are quick to respond to their environment. Babies immediately cry when they are hungry, thirsty, tired, sick, or wet. Toddlers are not at all bashful in communicating what they do and do not want. However, as we grow older, maturity teaches us to use discernment in making our desires known and to give way to the needs of others in many situations.

The Lord nevertheless tells us we are wise to always come to Him as little children—telling Him precisely what we need and want. While looking directly at a man whom He knew was blind, Jesus asked him, "What do you want Me to do for you?" Without hesitation he replied, "Master, let me receive my sight" (Mark 10:51 AMP).

Jesus could see he was blind, yet He asked him to make a request. In like manner, God knows what you need "before you ask Him" (Matthew 6:8 AMP). Yet He says in His Word, "by prayer and petition (definite requests) . . . continue to make your wants known to God" (Philippians 4:6 AMP).

Why pray for what seems to be obvious? Because in stating precisely what we want, our needs and desires become obvious to us.

State your requests boldly before the Lord tonight. He'll hear you. He'll respond to you. And just as important, you'll hear yourself and respond in a new way to Him.

Our prayers must mean something to us
if they are to mean anything to God.

Serenity

I have [expectantly] trusted in, leaned on, and relied on the Lord without wavering and I shall not slide.
PSALM 26:1 AMP

What

SITUATION
DO I NEED
COURAGE TO
CHANGE?

Many people are familiar with the *Serenity Prayer,* although most probably think of it as a prayer to be said in the morning hours or during a time of crisis. Consider again the words of this prayer: "God, grant me the Serenity to accept the things I cannot change, Courage to change the things I can, and Wisdom to know the difference."

Can there be any better prayer to say at day's end? Those things that are irreversible or fixed in God's order, we need to relinquish to Him. True peace of mind comes when we trust that God knows more about any situation than we could possibly know.

Those things we can change, we must have the courage to change. Furthermore, we must accept the fact that in most cases we cannot change things until morning comes! We can rest in the interim, knowing the Lord will help us when the time comes for action.

The real heart of the *Serenity Prayer* is revealed in its conclusion: that we might know the difference between what we need to accept and what we need to change. That takes wisdom. James tells us, "If any of you is deficient in wisdom, let him ask of the giving God [Who gives] to everyone liberally and ungrudgingly, without reproaching or faultfinding, and it will be given him. Only it must be in faith that he asks with no wavering" (James 1:5-6 AMP).

Ask the Lord to give you true serenity tonight!

The invariable mark of wisdom is to
see the miraculous in the common.

Shalom

"Peace I leave with you, my peace I give unto you."

JOHN 14:27 KJV

A word that appears throughout the Old Testament is *shalom*. It is often translated "peace," but shalom means far more than peace in the aftermath of war or peace between enemies. Shalom embodies an inner peace that brings wholeness, unity, and balance to an individual's life. It describes a harmonious, nurturing environment with God at its center.

In creation, God brought order and harmony out of chaos. He created shalom. It was people's sin that destroyed shalom, but it has always been God's plan that it be restored—first to the human heart and then, flowing from that, to heart-to-heart relationships.

God has given us many promises for peace in His word. Meditate on His promises of shalom, and as you do, they will flood your heart and mind with peace.

Since we have been justified through faith, we have peace with God through our Lord Jesus Christ (Romans 5:1).

Great peace have they who love your law, and nothing can make them stumble (Psalm 119:165).

When a man's ways are pleasing to the LORD, he makes even his enemies live at peace with him (Proverbs 16:7).

May the God of hope fill you with all joy and peace as you trust in him, so that you may overflow with hope (Romans 15:13).

The peace of God, which transcends all understanding, will guard your hearts and your minds in Christ Jesus (Philippians 4:7).

First keep the peace within yourself,
then you can also bring peace to others.

I can MAKE
MY HOME A
PEACEFUL
PLACE BY . . .

Come Home

"This son of mine was dead and is alive again; he was lost and is found."
LUKE 15:24

What PLACE
DO I THINK
OF AS A
TRUE HOME?

Once there was a widow who lived in a miserable attic with her son. Years before, the woman had married against her parents' wishes and had gone to live in a foreign land with her husband. Her husband had proved irresponsible and unfaithful, and after a few years he died without having made any provision for her and their child. It was with the utmost difficulty that she managed to scrape together the bare necessities of life.

The happiest times in the child's life were when the mother took him in her arms and told him about her father's house in the old country. She told him of the grassy lawn, the noble trees, the wild flowers, the lovely paintings, and the delicious meals. The child had never seen his grandfather's home, but to him it was the most beautiful place in all the world. He longed for the time when he would go to live there.

One day the postman knocked at the attic door. The mother recognized the handwriting on the envelope, and with trembling fingers she broke the seal. There was a check and a slip of paper with just two words: "Come home."[51]

Like this father—and the father of the Prodigal Son—our Heavenly Father opens His arms to receive us back into a place of spiritual comfort and restoration at the end of a weary day.

Nor can we fall below the arms of God,
how low soever it be we fall.

Step Right Up

Blessed are those who hear the joyful
blast of the trumpet, for they shall
walk in the light of your presence.
PSALM 89:15 TLB

"Getting away from it all" takes on a whole new meaning when you decide, as a young Scottish girl did, to walk around the world. A troubled home life convinced her she needed a change of scenery, as well as a challenge that would test her mettle.

How does one go about walking around the world? In Ffyona's case, she spent eleven years and covered more than nineteen thousand miles walking from northern Scotland to southern England; New York to Los Angeles; Sydney to Perth, Australia; and South Africa to Morocco. Along the way, she fought disease, poisonous insects, bad weather, blisters, stonings, and loneliness.

To keep herself going, she had to come up with a way to motivate her often tired feet. She quickly discovered that if she could focus her mind on doing what had to be done to make it through each phase of the walk, her body would do the rest. The stronger her mind, the better her body performed.

Another of Ffyona's important discoveries was that she needed to take one day at a time. Building in breaks and small rewards along the way made it much easier for her to stay committed to her bigger goal.[52]

Oh, the power of a walk! Even when we have no particular destination, our feet can take us to a new place and give us both a physical and a psychological break from where we've been.

When we are obedient,
God guides our steps and our stops.

Where WOULD I LOVE TO GO FOR A WALK? WHAT MIGHT I SEE THERE?

The Plaster Solution

A man hath joy by the answer of his mouth: and
a Word spoken in due season, how good is it!
PROVERBS 15:23 KJV

I can

IMPROVE THE

WAY I HANDLE

DISAGREE-

MENTS BY . . .

Disagreements are a natural part of relationships—and different points of view are critical to creative and problem-solving processes. Still, the friction caused when differing opinions arise can cause needless pain and waste valuable time and energy. Occasionally, the best way to convince someone of your point of view while maintaining clear lines of communication is just to keep quiet and "start plastering."

Benjamin Franklin learned that plaster sown in the fields would make things grow. He told his neighbors, but they did not believe him, arguing that plaster could be of no use at all to grass or grain.

After a little while, he allowed the matter to drop. But he went into the field early the next spring and sowed some grain. Close by the path, where people would walk, he traced some letters with his finger and put plaster into them.

After a week or two, the seed sprang up. His neighbors, as they passed that way, gasped at what they saw. Brighter green than all the rest of the field, sprouted Franklin's seeded message in large letters, "This has been plastered."

Benjamin Franklin did not need to argue with his neighbors about the benefit of plaster any longer!

The answer to some disagreements may be to stop talking and try out several solutions together, measure them against like standards, and then resume the selection process. Meanwhile, tempers cool, objectivity returns, and new options can surface.

The best way to keep people
from jumping down your throat
is to keep your mouth shut.

Run With Perseverance

Since we are surrounded by such a great cloud of
witnesses, let us throw off everything that hinders
and the sin that so easily entangles, and let us run
with perseverance the race marked out for us.

HEBREWS 12:1

Jenny Spangler won the women's marathon at the United States Olympic Trials in February 1996, earning the right to compete at the Summer Olympic Games in Atlanta, Georgia.

At the time of the trials, Spangler was qualifier number 61, which meant that sixty runners had entered the race with faster times than hers. No one had ever heard of her—and no one thought she could maintain a winning pace when she passed the leaders at the sixteen-mile mark.

Spangler had few successes to her credit. She had set an American junior record in the marathon during college, but then she left the sports scene after a stress fracture dashed her hopes in the Olympic Trials of 1984. Abandoning the sport after she ran poorly in 1988, she returned to school and earned a master's degree in business administration. She ran only two marathons between 1988 and 1996.

The favorites in February's race expected Spangler to fade, but she never did. Somewhere inside herself, she found the courage and stamina to finish strongly. Not only did she make the Olympic team, but she also took home first prize—forty-five thousand dollars.

Does the day ahead of you look as grueling as a marathon? Run the race God has marked out before you. Keep moving! You can end each day with the satisfaction of knowing you are that much closer to the goal!

I find IT
EASIER TO KEEP
RUNNING
WHEN . . .

Today, whatever may annoy,
the word for me is Joy, simple Joy.

Revolving Door

*Come to me, all you who are weary
and burdened, and I will give you rest.*
MATTHEW 11:28

How CAN I
SLOW THE
REVOLVING
DOOR IN MY
LIFE? ARE
THERE SPE-
CIFIC THINGS
I CAN DO
TO CHANGE
MY ROUTINE?

Aimee felt like her life was caught in a revolving door. Each day seemed like the day before, with no way out of the routine. She pulled herself out of bed each morning and headed to the kitchen for that necessary pick-me-up called coffee. After gobbling breakfast, she caught the bus to school.

Once she arrived at school, she had tests to take and math problems to work out. Stress crowded out the pleasure her teen years were supposed to bring. Trapped in that revolving door, she just went around and around, doing the same things day after day. She had to find a better way of getting through the day! Aimee realized that the only thing she could change was her attitude.

The next morning when she woke, she took time to pray, the first step out of that revolving door. She sang in the shower, ate with her siblings, hugged her mom good-bye, and noticed a new blossom on the rosebush by the driveway. At school, she thanked God for the teachers He'd given her and the friends she'd made. The revolving door began slowing down.

If your life is stuck in a revolving door, step out and enjoy the peace that God offers. He'll be with you all along the way as you pray, sing, and change your tune.

*True peace is found by man in
the depths of his own heart—
the dwelling place of God.*

Hide and Seek

Then Barnabas went to Tarsus to look for Saul.
ACTS 11:25

When Lucy was young, she enjoyed playing hide-and-seek in the dark with her brothers and sisters. The old country kitchen with its cavernous cupboards and deep recesses contained many good places to hide. On one such occasion, one of their cousins—the smallest one, in fact—curled up into the back of the cupboard where Momma kept her baking pans. With the pans arrayed in front of him, he was virtually invisible. It was an ideal hiding place.

With a shout of "Ready or not, here I come!" the game started. One by one, the hiding places and hidden children were found. But the littlest cousin, curled up in the baking pan cupboard, evaded discovery. Lucy would have been thrilled. But this younger child didn't see things that way. Sipping a cup of tea in the darkened kitchen, Momma heard a tiny voice whimper, "Isn't anyone going to come looking for me?" That little voice was all it took for the rest of the children to locate their cousin. Though the others congratulated him on his hiding place, he was just glad someone had found him.

Though we may not play hide-and-seek anymore as grown-ups, we can sometimes feel buried under responsibilities and schedules that close in on us and hide us from time with friends and family. Do you know someone who needs to be found? Reach out—with a note, a phone call, a prayer, or a visit—and do a little seeking, not hiding, today.

Kindness in words creates confidence.
Kindness in thinking creates profoundness.
Kindness in giving creates love.

I would
LIKE A NEW
FRIEND
WHO WAS . . .

Ultimate Worth

You are Christ's, and Christ is God's.

I CORINTHIANS 3:23 NKJV

What KIND
OF VALUE DO
I PLACE ON
MY FRIENDS?

The bidding was over, and the auctioneer's gavel fell. The winning bid for a rocking chair that had been valued between $3,000 and $5,000 was $453,500.

This had been the case through the duration of the auction. A used automobile valued between $18,000 and $22,000 was sold for $79,500. A set of green tumblers valued at $500 sold for $38,000. A necklace valued at $500 to $700 went for $211,500. For four days articles of common, ordinary value were sold for wildly inflated prices. Why? The items auctioned were from the estate of Jacqueline Kennedy Onassis.

As in the sale of the items of the Kennedy estate, some things are valuable solely because of the one to whom they belong.

We may inflate a person's worth because of their financial status, their influence, or their potential to benefit us; or we may say a person has no value because they have few assets or cannot help us. But the Scriptures tell us that when we were still sinners, Jesus Christ died for us. (See Romans 5:8.) When we had no value and were even opposed to God, He paid the price to redeem our lives.

Whenever you feel depressed and worthless, meditate on this: your value is determined by God. He loved and valued you so much, He sent His Son to die so you could become His child. Never doubt your importance and worth!

All I could never be, all men ignored
in me—this, I was worth to God.

Discretionary Time

In all your getting, get understanding.

PROVERBS 4:7 NKJV

If MY APPLIANCES SAVED ME AN HOUR A DAY, I COULD SPEND IT ON . . .

Twenty-year-old college student Amy Wu wrote about her aunt who "tends to her house as if it were her child." The house is spotlessly clean and usually smells of home-cooked meals. Roses from the garden are artfully arranged in beautiful vases. Her aunt could afford a housekeeper, but she truly enjoys doing her own housework.

Amy went on, "I'm a failure at housework. I've chosen to be inept and unlearned at what my aunt has spent so much time perfecting. Up to now, I've thought there were more important things to do." But those "more important things" didn't turn out to be all that important.

One day she decided to make a meal for her family. While the dinner was cooking, she wrote a letter to her cousin. Then she made a chocolate cake to celebrate her sister's birthday. It was a success: "That night I grinned as my father and sister dug into the pasta, then the cake, licking their lips in appreciation. It had been a long time since I'd felt so proud. A week later my cousin called and thanked me for my letter, the first handwritten correspondence she'd received in two years."

She concluded, "Sure, my generation has all the technological advances at our fingertips. We're computer-savvy, and we have more time. But what are we really saving it for? In the end, we may lose more than we've gained by forgetting the important things in life."[53]

The great rule of moral conduct is, next to God, to respect time.

Kitchen Friends

Share with God's people who
are in need. Practice hospitality.
ROMANS 12:13

If I COULD
CHANGE MY
HOME, I
WOULD MAKE
IT . . .

How wonderful to see the goodness of God in my own room! Jennifer thought as she browsed through her CD collection. God had provided abundantly for her and her family and the new house offered so much more space. Not only did she enjoy a room all her own, He had provided a place for everything—a bigger closet, a new CD player. He also had given her a talent she loved— singing—a blessing to her and her entire family.

Friends loved to visit around her homework table, probably because her yellow walls were bright and cheerful. Her room was much like her mother's kitchen where everyone seemed to feel warm and accepted there. Over the years, her table had been the scene of a lot of sharing, delight, heartbreak, good times, games, food, and plenty of fellowship. On holidays, everyone trooped in and out of the kitchen, helping with the cooking, visiting, carrying cups of coffee or other drinks to family members, stirring, laughing, and bumping into each other.

She was thankful for a happy home and many friends and family to share all of it with.

Is your home the kind of place where everyone feels comfortable and welcome? If not, how can you make it a spot that binds you closer to your family, friends, and God? It might be as easy as planning a pizza night or baking chocolate chip cookies together. Give it a try!

Happy is the house that shelters a friend.

A Heart of Hospitality

> When Priscilla and Aquila heard him,
> they invited him to their home and explained
> to him the Way of God more adequately.
>
> ACTS 18:26

Because of Jeff's father's profession, their family relocated many times over the years. However, one of the relocations was memorable, not because of something that happened, but rather because of something that *didn't* happen.

His father was required to begin his position in a new city before their home was ready for occupancy. A woman from a local church heard about his predicament and offered the family the use of her family's guest house until their home was ready.

When they finally moved into their new house, Jeff's mother wanted to show her gratitude to the woman for her kindness to their family. She called and asked her to stop by for tea, apologizing that she might have to sit on a few packing boxes but assuring her that she would be most welcome. There was a slight pause before the woman replied, "No, dear. I'll wait until you have things the way you want them. Then we can have a nice visit."

The woman was no doubt only trying to give Jeff's mother some extra time to settle in. But time passed and his mother never seemed to get things "the way she wanted them." Soon, nine months had gone by, and Jeff asked his mother about it. She said she was too embarrassed to re-extend her invitation of hospitality.

Hospitality asks us to open our hearts to others, whether our homes are picture perfect or not. And when we refuse hospitality, we may be hurting the heart of a stranger. Let's keep our hearts open to give and receive hospitality.

When there is room in the heart,
there is room in the house.

When HAVE I VISITED SOMEONE AND FELT WELCOME? WHAT MADE IT HOSPITABLE?

Fear Not

Those of steadfast mind you keep in peace—
in peace because they trust in you.
ISAIAH 26:3 NRSV

When HAVE
I BEEN IN
A FEARFUL
SITUATION?
HOW DID I
HANDLE IT?

Driving across the country by herself, a young woman recorded this experience:

I was on the second leg of a three-leg journey, and all I wanted to do was fall into bed for a good eight hours. But I couldn't stop, because I was still more than two hours from Tucumcari, New Mexico, and tired though I was, I was determined to get as close to the Texas border as I could.

What I hadn't reckoned on was bad weather. California and Arizona had been sunny and warm, and I wrongly assumed that New Mexico in late March would hold no unpleasant surprises.

The sun was sinking fast behind me, and soon disappeared altogether. On cross-country trips, I prefer not to drive at night—especially on unfamiliar roads—but I pushed on.

A quarter hour or so after sunset, I saw snow gliding past the glow of my headlights. Soon it was coming down fast and furiously at a slant, directly into my windshield, having a kaleidoscopic effect.

Panic took hold. There were few cars on the interstate, no lights along the route, no parking lots to pull into and wait it out.

Since I couldn't see where I was going as well as I would have liked, I had to put all my faith and trust in Someone who could.

I made it safely to my destination that night because I learned a long time ago Who it is who really keeps my car on the road.

Fear knocked at the door.
Faith answered.
No one was there.

The Better Way

> Since, then, you have been raised with
> Christ, set your hearts on things above,
> where Christ is seated at the right hand of God.
>
> COLOSSIANS 3:1

Martha was a dedicated homemaker. She was an expert at entertaining her guests while preparing a scrumptious meal at the same time. One day when Jesus was passing through the village, Martha opened her home to Him. Her house was spotless, and the aroma coming from her kitchen was delightful. As a wonderful hostess, she made sure that Jesus felt welcome in her home.

Her sister, Mary, also was there. While Martha opened her home to Jesus, Mary opened her heart to Him and sat at His feet. She knew that true wisdom would be hers if she listened to His teachings and applied them to her everyday life.

Meanwhile, Martha began to grumble. She felt that Mary should be more involved in the work at hand. She went to Jesus to ask Him to send her sister to help her in the kitchen.

Jesus' response probably surprised her. He taught Martha some things about priorities, while sharing with her a better way to serve Him. Mary, He said, had chosen the better way, and it would not be taken away from her.

While working and serving are vital parts of living, they cannot be the most important parts. Seek God's guidance today through prayer and Bible study. The wisdom that you gain will benefit not only you, but others as well, for your life will serve as a shining example for Him.

Deep in your heart it is not guidance
that you want as much as a guide.

In THE LAST FEW DAYS, GOD HAS BEEN TEACH- ING ME . . .

Sunbeam Blessings

"I am the light of the world. Whoever follows me will never walk in darkness, but will have the light of life."

JOHN 8:12

Five THINGS I HAVE TO BE THANKFUL FOR TODAY ARE . . .

As Gloria sat alone at the dining table, a single sunbeam shone through the closed blinds. At the point where the light entered the window, it was just a tiny speck, but as it spread across the room, all the colors of the rainbow burst into an array of splendor. It highlighted the old shadowbox that hung on the wall, and reflected on the glass that protected her treasures from dust and grime.

She spotted the golden tree figurine covered with her birthstones and thought of how her mother often spoke of what a glorious day it was when she was born. She saw the animal figurines that resembled her pets from long ago. The angel standing over the small boy and girl on the bridge reminded her of her childhood years, as she and her brother played together.

The baby figurine took her back to the days when her children were small. The fellow pointing to a carving in a tree that said, "I Love You," made her smile. It had been a gift from her husband on one of their anniversaries. Many fond memories came alive as Gloria spied the tiny angel holding the Bible, and she thanked God for the many blessings in her life.

Even in the midst of difficult circumstances, try to remember the good things God has done for you, no matter how small or insignificant. It will get your eyes off your problem and on the Solver of problems instead.

There are no days when God's fountain does not flow.

Perseverance

I will praise You, for You have answered me and have become my salvation.

PSALM 118:21 NKJV

With

PERSEVERANCE

AND GOD'S

HELP I CAN . . .

Rafael Solano, a diamond prospector in Venezuela, was one of many impoverished natives and fortune seekers who came to sift through the rocks of a dried-up riverbed reputed to have diamonds. No one, however, found any diamonds in the sand and pebbles for some time. One by one, those who came left the site—their dreams shattered, and their bodies drained.

Discouraged and exhausted, Solano had just about decided it was time for him to give up too. Then Solano stooped down, scooped up a handful of pebbles, if only so he could say he had personally inspected every pebble in his claim. He pulled out one that seemed a little different. It seemed heavy. He measured it and weighed it on a scale. Could it be?

Sure enough, Solano had found a diamond! New York jewelry dealer Harry Winston paid Solano $200,000 for that stone. When it was cut and polished, it became known as the Liberator, the largest and purest unmined diamond in the world.

The Scriptures teem with examples of men and women who, on the verge of disaster or failure, experienced God's creative work in their lives. Remind yourself . . .

God's Word is true.

God can do the impossible.

God can heal the incurable.

God can conquer your enemies.

God loves you.

You may have been plugging away at a project for weeks, even months or years, without seeing much progress. Today may be the day. Don't give up!

Perseverance is the rope that ties the soul to the doorpost of heaven.

Scheduled Rest

[Jesus] said to them, "Come with me by yourselves to a quiet place and get some rest."
MARK 6:31

I can FIND REST IN MY DAILY CIRCUM-STANCES THIS WEEK BY . . .

Researchers say that Americans today are plagued with more stress-related health problems than any other generation in history. Stress is a contributing factor to heart disease and high blood pressure and has been linked to an increase in bad cholesterol and the worsening of arthritis.

How can we keep the daily pressures of life from becoming debilitating stress? God's solution has always been to take a day of rest. Return to the simple pleasures of the kitchen. The kitchen in our great-grandmothers' time was both the center of family activity and the center of rest. Family meals were made and shared around a common table. Conversation was the primary form of entertainment—not the television, radio, or compact disc player with headphones. Comforting aromas greeted family members throughout the day. And nothing could beat the smell of a chicken roasting in the oven for Sunday dinner.

Plan a day of rest and relaxation. Find some time on your calendar when you don't have to be anywhere and no projects are due. Then anticipate your enjoyable day. Chat with a friend, go for a walk, help with a garden or something special to your parents that you can share in.

Take rest; a field that has rested
gives a bountiful crop.

Comfort in the Valley

> Even though I walk through the valley of the
> shadow of death, I fear no evil; for Thou art
> with me; Thy rod and Thy staff, they comfort me.
>
> PSALM 23:4 NASB

After the untimely death of her father, Fran had to learn about trusting God. Sometimes she felt forsaken, lonely, and at times even angry when she felt God had allowed her seventeen-month-old little brother to succumb to bacterial meningitis. Everything medically possible was done to no avail.

With time, God comforted her and called Fran to encourage others, even in the midst of her own pain and doubt, and help them understand that while our loved ones will always be in our hearts, our focus remains on the Lord Jesus Christ.

Fran had often read Psalm 23, but she never actually understood it until she visited Israel during a Bible tour with her Christian school and saw the rugged terrain traversed by David and the shepherds. Many of the crevices on the rocky hills are so narrow and deep that the sun never shines all the way to the bottom. It remains in a constant shadow. Certain death would result if anyone should fall in, because rescue would be virtually impossible. David's staff helped him walk with sure footing, and the rod defended him from wild animals. Most of all, he became acutely aware of God's provision.

Through the valley times in our lives, we, too, can be sure that we are not alone. His presence is real. Jesus will still be there through all the pain and the changes in our life situations. Nothing is more comforting.

God is closest to those whose
hearts are broken.

What PROMISE HAS GOD MADE TO ME THAT HAS GIVEN ME GREAT COMFORT?

Sunrise

The Sunrise from on high shall visit us.

LUKE 1:78 NASB

Something

I SAW THAT

HAD BEEN

HIDDEN

WAS . . .

Sunrise, shining its beams through the window on a cold winter's morning, is a welcome sight. Even if the air outside is icy cold, sunrise gives the illusion of warmth. With the rising sun, the city opens its shutters and makes preparations for the day; in the country, the farm animals are let out to pasture. Kids are off to school, adults are on their way to work, and each has a different perspective of the sunrise.

Sunrise happens whether we see it or not. Clouds may cover the sky so totally that we can't experience the beauty of the sunbeams making their way to the earth. No matter what the climate, the sun still rises in the eastern horizon and sets over the west. Sunrise is set by God's clock, and it is ours to enjoy in the early mornings when we can see it clearly. It is just as much there for us to enjoy when the cloud shadows cover it. We can trust it to be there—although it may be hidden for a while.

We can also trust God to be there every morning because He is the one, irrefutable reality in this life, and He remains constant and true!

Life is a mixture of sunshine and rain,
Laughter and teardrops, pleasure and pain—
Low tides and high tides, mountains and plains,
Triumphs, defeats and losses and gains.
But there never was a cloud
That the Son didn't shine through
And there's nothing that's impossible
For Jesus Christ to do!

Giving Thanks

Do not be anxious about anything, but in everything, by prayer and petition, with thanksgiving, present your requests to God.

PHILIPPIANS 4:6

The Thanksgiving table stood ready, a plump turkey in the center and a myriad of side dishes that seemed to cover every remaining square inch. The aroma of stuffing wafted from the oven door as Susan set out the deviled eggs.

The combined smells brought back memories of the first Thanksgiving that Susan could remember. She had been a five-year-old then. That year she had contracted strep throat, which developed into rheumatic fever. She was sick for days. Her mother handled the sickness matter-of-factly, although she probably knew the risk of heart damage. Throughout the day and night, Susan would hear her mother slip into her room to check on her.

After the danger passed, Susan went to the doctor and learned that for the next year, she would not be allowed to run, exercise, or even walk fast, in order to prevent heart damage. That fall, as brightly colored leaves skittered to the ground, Susan walked slowly to school and back home again.

November arrived, and her kindergarten teacher prepared a Thanksgiving skit. Susan was excited as she dreamed of becoming one of the Indians who danced around the stage. But instead, she was told she would have to play the part of an oak tree. It was disappointing, but her mother taught her to be thankful anyway. At least she was part of the play.

Standing at the stove, Susan stirred the gravy. Other Thanksgivings came to mind—a smile graced her lips when she thought of the Thanksgivings when her children were toddlers. She could almost hear the kids sitting on the floor banging on pots and pans with wooden spoons.

Susan brought her mind back to the present as her family began arriving. Her grandchildren burst through the back door, and she hugged each one. And looking heavenward, she thanked God for all the memories yet to be made.

Special
MEMORIES I
HAVE ARE . . .

I awoke this morning with a devout thanksgiving for my friends, the old and the new.

Grace for Today

All have sinned and fall short of the glory of God, and are justified freely by his grace.
ROMANS 3:23-24

I know

I HAVE FORGIVEN WHEN I NO LONGER FEEL . . .

In *The Grace of Giving*, Stephen Olford gives an account of Peter Miller, a Baptist pastor who lived in Ephrata, Pennsylvania, during the American Revolution. He enjoyed the friendship of George Washington.

Michael Wittman also lived in Ephrata. He was an evil-minded man who did all he could to oppose and humiliate the pastor. One day Michael Wittman was arrested for treason and sentenced to die. Peter Miller traveled the seventy miles to Philadelphia on foot to plead for the life of the traitor.

"No, Peter," General Washington said, "I cannot grant you the life of your friend."

"My friend!" exclaimed the old preacher. "He's the bitterest enemy I have."

"What?" exclaimed Washington. "You've walked seventy miles to save the life of an enemy? That puts the matter in a different light. I'll grant your pardon."

Peter Miller took Michael Wittman back home to Ephrata—no longer an enemy, but a friend.

Miller's example of grace and forgiveness flowed from his knowledge of God's sacrifice for the human race. Because God forgave him and sacrificed His Son for him, he found the grace to sacrifice for his enemy. Although most of us know God's grace and love for us is great, sometimes we have to be reminded that His love never fails—even when we do!

At the beginning of each day, take a deep breath and say, "Even if I blow it today, my God will still love me."

A mother's love endures through all.

On a Clear Day

You will go out with joy, and be led forth
with peace; the mountains and the hills will
break forth into shouts of joy before you, and
all the trees of the field will clap their hands.

ISAIAH 55:12 NASB

Many people end their workday with a trip to the gym. Doing so helps them to clear their head of the day's frustrations, gives them more energy to face the evening ahead, calms them down, and improves their mood. It is also a complete departure from sitting at a desk all day.

While any exercise can be helpful, research has shown that where you exercise can make a big difference in the benefits derived from a workout session. A psychologist at an East Coast university tracked hormonal and mood changes in a group of runners who participated in three different jogs:

- Outdoors
- Indoors, on a treadmill, while listening to "sounds of nature" tapes
- Indoors, on a treadmill, while listening to tapes of their own heartbeats

Can you guess which jog proved to be the most beneficial? The outdoor jog. Levels of the positive mood hormones adrenaline and noradrenaline were up, while the levels of the stress hormone cortisol were down in those who had exercised outside.

It seems environment really matters. Whether you're exercising or just taking a few moments to relax with a cup of tea, where you do it can be nearly as important as why and how you do it. Find a delightful, stimulating spot for your getaway and make the most of your break.

As children we often asked our neighborhood friends, "Can you come out and play?" It's still a good question to ask!

**Those who do not find time for exercise
will have to find time for illness.**

My FAVORITE PLACE OUTDOORS IS ...

Personal History

I will instruct you and teach you
in the way you should go.
PSALM 32:8

I Would
LIKE TO ASK
MY PARENTS
OR GRAND-
PARENTS
ABOUT . . .

Twelve-year-old Sarah sat in rapt attention, listening to her great-grandpa's stories. He told her about growing up in a family so poor that he received only oranges for Christmas presents. He explained how when his parents couldn't afford to buy him a bicycle, he tried to make one out of spare parts he found in a junkyard. When he told her about how he rode his horse, King, to school she was bewildered.

"Your family didn't even have a car?" she asked. "When were you born, Popaw?"

He chuckled, crossed his arms around his round belly, and said with pride, "In 1910."

"Wow," Sarah exclaimed. Her mouth dropped open in amazement.

"Pretty old, huh?" he grinned. He named some the technological inventions that had come into existence during his lifetime. Electric lights, cars, planes, radios, telephones, televisions, computers, and cell phones were a few things that he listed.

"Yeah, I've sure seen a lot of changes," he explained. "Some were good and some were bad. But through it all, I've learned that the one constant in this world is God. Whenever I'm worried or frightened, I stop to talk to Him. God is unchanging and completely dependable. You will probably face a lot of changes in your life, too, honey. But no matter what happens, remember to hold on to the Lord, for you can always count on Him to stay the same."

Her grandfather understood that the history that would affect Sarah the most was the history of his personal walk with God. What about you? Have your parents and grandparents shared this most important part of your history with you?

Christ, once crucified, now living,
Bids us faith and love to share.

What Does Love Look Like?

> Cast your bread upon the waters, for
> after many days you will find it again.
>
> ECCLESIASTES 11:1

Someone
WHO TAUGHT
ME WHAT
LOVE LOOKS
LIKE IS . . .

Brad and his brother loved their grandparents dearly. The boys spent as much time as possible with them after they retired. Grandma and Pop adored them, as well. The relationship among the four of them was indescribably rich. Pop spent hours teaching the boys important truths about life and love.

When Brad moved away from home to attend college, he initially lived in their grandparents' basement. Their relationship grew even closer during the months that they lived in the same house together.

Shortly after retirement, his grandfather became ill. The family was forced to place Pop in a nursing home so he could receive proper care.

Brad met the love of his life. A few months later, he bought her an engagement ring. When Brad picked it up, he drove straight from the jewelry store to the nursing home to show it to Pop first. Pop smiled, as he understood what the ring meant. Although he couldn't verbalize his feelings, his smile said everything that needed to be spoken.

Unfortunately, Pop didn't live long enough to attend Brad's wedding. Brad relished the fact, however, that his loving grandfather was the first to know that he was engaged and that he was also the first to see the ring that would be placed on his bride's finger. Because his grandfather had invested time and love into Brad's life, Brad wanted to share this most important event with him.

Spend time with your family and learn what love looks like.

Love sings as a father looks upon his son.

Sowing Seeds

You will always reap what you sow!
GALATIANS 6:7 NLT

Whose

LIFE CAN I
SOW SEEDS
OF UNCONDI-
TIONAL LOVE
INTO TODAY?

Michael sat in the nursing home room spoon-feeding his grandfather ice cream. A nurse's aide noticed that he came to visit on a regular basis. One day she asked him about his obvious dedication to his grandfather.

"My grandfather never could find his glasses," Michael explained. "He always remembered the time I rolled his new Cadillac down the driveway into the neighbor's trashcans, however. He was always ready and willing to share the story with others. Grandpa remembered every one of my birthdays too. Although five dollars doesn't go very far anymore, I could count on getting the gift he had to offer. My grandmother was a lot like him. At Christmas she remembered to bring us gifts. But she often forgot that very few of us like to wear homemade sweaters.

"When I was a little kid, my grandparents came to my baseball and soccer games," Michael continued. "I can see them now sitting in their lawn chairs and big goofy hats waving at me. They made it to every church production, school play, and high school debate championship. They attended my college graduation and my wedding. They have met all three of my sons. They gave me their time and their unconditional love. Now it is my turn to give something back in return."

The principles of seedtime and harvest, of sowing and reaping, of giving and receiving, always stand true and will last for generations to come.

Love expands and grows before us to eternity,
until it includes all that is lovely,
and we become all that can love.

The Matchmaker

> Keep yourselves in God's love as you
> wait for the mercy of our Lord Jesus
> Christ to bring you to eternal life.
>
> JUDE 1:21

A farmer posted a sign "puppies for sale." Early the next morning he spotted a young boy walking slowly up the dusty trail to his farm.

"Hello, son," the farmer announced, "What can I do for you?"

"I heard you have some puppies for sale, and I've got 45 cents to spend."

The farmer scratched his head. These puppies were purebred and could be sold for a lot more than 45 cents. The freckle-faced boy looked up and grinned. The farmer thought of his own grandson's pleasure with the many litters of puppies they'd had on the farm over the years. He found himself calling the puppies over.

"Skipper, Skipper." Soon the pile of fur, teeth, and lolling tongues came rolling out in a pile. The young boy squealed with delight and tried petting them all simultaneously. Just behind the heap of dogs, came the last pup, a runt, who didn't scamper but slowly trudged along.

The boy gasped, "That's the one!"

"No, son, something's wrong with this puppy's legs. He wouldn't be a good choice." The boy pulled up his own pant legs and exposed the steel braces that glistened in the sun.

"But, sir, there is something wrong with my legs, too, so we're a perfect match."

The farmer fingered the 45 cents in his hand as he watched the two new friends walk down the driveway. The two of them were a match made in heaven.

God is a matchmaker. He unites men and women together. He joins orphans with parents. He brings families together. And He even creates the perfect matches with kids and grandparents. Thank Him for the way He has matched you with the special people in your life.

I am
THANKFUL
GOD HAS
MATCHED ME
WITH . . .

God is the ultimate matchmaker.

The Greatest Love

May the Lord make your love increase
and overflow for each other.
I THESSALONIANS 3:12

Someone
I WOULD LIKE
TO GIVE MORE
TO IS . . .

True love is the gift which God has given
To man alone beneath the heaven.

Evan's older sister needed a blood transfusion. He had recently recovered from the same rare disease that his pale, small sister now struggled to defeat. The only treatment for this rare disease was a blood transfusion from a person who had already overcome the affliction. Since they both had the same rare blood type, her brother seemed to be the perfect donor.

When the parents asked Evan if he would like to give his blood to his sickly sister, he hesitated, stared off into space for just a moment, and then said, "Sure."

The next day Evan and his sister went to a large medical center to perform the life-saving blood transfusion. On the way, Evan and his sister giggled and fidgeted together. As soon as the nurse began to prepare for the procedure, however, they both settled down.

For someone so young and full of energy, the young boy seemed to be very quiet during the whole process. The nurse was concerned about his quietness and allowed his parents and grandfather into the room.

"Are you okay, Evan?" his grandfather inquired.

Even slowly nodded. Then he whispered, "When do I die, Grandpa?"

The grandfather smiled and looked deeply into his grandson's eyes. "Son, you're not going to die. They won't take all your blood. Your sister only needs a little bit of your blood to help her get better. You will be just fine."

Evan's mother reassured him with a nod of her head and a hug.

Evan's grandfather slowly slipped out of the room with his own son. Tears clouded his eyes as he spoke to him, "Evan was willing to die so that his sister could live."

Jesus loved us enough to die for us. While few on this earth are called to that level of commitment, we are called daily to give to others.

The Empty Tomb

Be honest in your judgment and do not decide
at a glance (superficially and by appearances);
but judge fairly and righteously.

JOHN 7:24 AMP

Philip was born with Downs syndrome. He was a happy child, but as he grew older he became increasingly aware that he was different from other children.

Philip went to Sunday school with boys and girls his own age. The class had wonderful experiences together—learning, laughing, playing. But Philip remained an outsider.

As an Easter lesson, the Sunday school teacher gave each student a large egg-shaped plastic container. Each child was to explore the church grounds and find something that symbolized new life to them, put it in their "egg," and bring it back to share with the class.

The children had a grand time running about the church yard collecting symbols. Then they gathered back in the classroom, put their eggs on the table, and watched with great anticipation as the teacher opened each egg. In one egg, there was a flower, in another a butterfly. The students responded with great glee and enthusiasm as the teacher revealed the contents of each egg . . . a branch, a leaf, a flower bud.

When the teacher opened the next egg, there was nothing in it. As could be expected, the eight-year-olds responded, "That's not fair—that's stupid! Somebody didn't do it right."

Philip went up to the teacher, tugged on her sleeve, and said, "It's mine. That egg is mine." The children laughed and said, "You never do anything right, Philip. There's nothing there."

Philip replied, "I did so do it. I did do it. It's empty—the tomb is empty!"

The classroom fell silent. From that day on things were different. Philip became a full-fledged part of the class. The children took him into their friendship. Philip had been freed from the tomb of his being different and given a new life among his peers.[54]

My BEING DIFFERENT IS GOOD BECAUSE . . .

✠

You must look into people,
as well as at them.

Strangers and Pilgrims

There will be no more death or mourning or crying or pain, for the old order of things has passed away.
REVELATION 21:4

I envision
MY FINAL
DESTINATION
AS A PLACE
OF . . .

Day in and day out, the details of everyday life can cause our attention to be focused on only the here and now. When change comes—the birth of a child, the first day of school, a new job, the death of a parent—it can be exciting, bittersweet, or even sad.

The first line of a hymn written by Albert E. Brumley gives us the perspective we should have toward the time we spend on this planet. "This world is not my home, I'm just a passing through."

In his book *Strangers and Pilgrims*, W. R. Matthews describes how we should see ourselves. While he doesn't recommend a total detachment from the life that swirls around us, he advises:

"We should live in this world as if we did not wholly belong to it. It is wise to remind ourselves that even our most cherished ambitions and interests are passing; the soul will grow out of them or at least must leave them behind.

"To the pilgrim these passages should not be wholly sad. He may feel regret, but not desolation; they do not cause him to rebel. These phases of life are incidents of the journey, but it is the way that matters, not the accidents of the road. The time has come to move on? Then break up the camp with a good heart; it is only one more stage on the journey home!"[55]

By heaven we understand a
state of happiness infinite in
degree and endless in duration.

The Quiet Touch of Stillness

In repentance and rest is your salvation,
in quietness and trust is your strength.

ISAIAH 30:15

A late-night snowfall blanketed the city one Saturday. When everyone awoke on Sunday morning, evergreens were layered with sparkling white icing. The roofs of houses looked as if someone had draped each one with a fluffy quilt.

But more striking than the beautiful white-wash was the pervasive stillness. The city noises were gone. No horns honking or dogs barking. No cars screeching or boom boxes blaring. No doors slamming or machines running. Just still-ness—quietness.

The quiet didn't last long, however. Soon city snowplows were out, clearing and salting the streets. The sounds of shovels and snowblowers mixed with window scrapers and revving car engines as neighbors began to dig out from the storm. It was not the first snowstorm of the season, nor would it be the last.

But amazingly, the quiet start to the morning left its imprint on the entire day. The pace slowed for a moment, granting people an opportunity for reflection and allowing neighbors time to connect with others. And when normal activities resumed, some people were even able to hold on to the still-ness for a while.

When Monday came, it brought with it all the noise of a busy week. But it also brought the remembrance of God's words to His people—that in quietness and trust they would find strength. Let God's quietness fill a corner of your heart today and find the joy that can be found in stillness.

The great mind knows the
power of gentleness.

I enjoy

QUIETNESS

BECAUSE . . .

The Kingdom Family

"Whoever does the will of my Father in heaven is my brother and sister and mother."
MATTHEW 12:50

Who IS
THE SPECIAL PERSON GOD ADDED TO ME?

Charlene walked down the hallway alone. This had been the moment she was supposed to share with her father—the precious time when he would give her his undivided attention as she made the transition from girl to young lady. It was a special tea. He had gone to her sister's promotion.

Yet her father was not there. Nor was her mother or sister. Her family had a previous commitment, a convention they had to attend, and that convention had been more important than her coming of age tea at her boarding school. It had been a tough blow, and Charlene could feel the pain clouding this special moment.

There, waiting near the reception line, was her pastor—her shepherd. His warm and tender smile received them into his presence. Charlene felt her longing subside as she looked into his kind face. The pastor and his wife had always been family since she was a small child. They often served as substitute parents in her own parents' absence. They had counseled, laughed, and cried with Charlene as she worked through pre-teen jitters. They had prayed with her and held her hand. They had always been dependable.

Charlene smiled from the depths of her heart. This was a time to celebrate the new, and God had been faithful in surrounding her with special friends that were part of His kingdom.

Your family doesn't have to come from the same womb or share the same blood. Allow God to give you the gift of His family. We are meant to be that for each other.

The Lord gives his blessing when
he finds the vessel empty.

God's Light

> "Let your light shine before men in such a way that they may see your good works, and glorify your Father who is in heaven."
>
> MATTHEW 5:16 NASB

HOW CAN I BE SURE MY LIGHT IS BURNING BRIGHTLY?

The menorah, a candelabra with four candles on each side and one in the middle, actually represents a miracle. It is used during the winter Jewish holiday known as Hanukkah, or the Festival of Lights. Hanukkah, which means dedication, commemorates the revolt against the Syrian Greeks in 167-164 BC, when the Jews recaptured the temple and rededicated it to God's service.

The Greeks had extinguished the great seven-branched candelabra in the temple and only enough oil remained for the light to burn one day. It took eight days for the priests to consecrate more oil. Nevertheless, the Jews lit the lampstand, and it continued to burn for eight full days!

Thus the Feast of Dedication, also called the Festival of Lights, was established. In Jewish homes the miniature menorah candles are lit, one each day to represent the eight days. The center candle is the *shamash*, a Hebrew word meaning servant, and it is used to light the other candles. From Scripture, Christians know that Jesus is the Light of the World, God's *shamash*.

The Jerusalem temple has been destroyed, but when we receive Christ, we become the temple of God, and the *shamash* shines in our hearts. We become lights in a dark world. Through His Holy Spirit we have a never-ending supply of oil to keep our lamps burning brightly.

I don't have to light all the world,
but I do have to light my part.

A Smile Makes the Difference

DECEMBER 3

A glad heart makes a cheerful countenance.
PROVERBS 15:13 AMP

Something

THAT ALWAYS

MAKES ME

SMILE IS . . .

✚

Better by far you should forget
and smile than that you
should remember and be sad.

Charles Smith, grandfather to four and great-grandfather to ten, always wore a smile on his face. He greeted everyone with a smile. He offered a friendly smile before parting with others. Charles even smiled when he talked on the telephone. Unbelievably, this smiling man came from what many people would consider a childhood of terror.

Charles, the oldest of five brothers, grew up poor in an abusive family in the early 1900s. His father, an alcoholic, beat his wife regularly. The boys lived in fear that he might kill her. One day when Charles and his brothers were in school, a tornado ripped through their town, killing two-thirds of their classmates. This abruptly ended their schooling. The tornado destroyed his own home except for the wall that stood beside the stove, where his mother was cooking.

All five of the Smith brothers lived during the Depression. They all served in the armed forces and contributed to service-oriented careers. Charles was the only one who came out smiling, however. One brother drank. Two of them physically abused their wives. The other one suffered with poor health.

Charles attributed his positive outlook to his godmother who took him to church each Sunday. It was his relationship with God that allowed him to keep his smile although he faced some of life's worst circumstances.

His only daughter recalled, "Every night before he went to bed, I saw my father kneel down next to his bed to say his prayers."

Two of his grandsons often speak of the times they shared their problems with their grandfather. He always smiled and encouraged them to talk to God about their problems. He declared that God is the "Man with the answers."

Charles' family agrees that a kneeling man is a cheerful man.

Early to Bed

> O God, You are my God; early will I seek You.
>
> PSALM 63:1 NKJV

Most of us are familiar with the old saying: "Early to bed and early to rise, makes a man healthy and wealthy and wise." And there are numerous references in the Bible to the joys and benefits of rising early. The psalmist said,

"My heart is steadfast, O God, my heart is steadfast;
I will sing and give praise. Awake, my glory!
Awake, lute and harp! I will awaken the dawn."

PSALM 57:7-8 NKJV

The clear implication is that the psalmist had a habit of getting up before dawn and "singing in" the morning. But what does this have to do with our sunset hours?

Very practically speaking, in order to be able to rise early in the morning, we have to get to bed early. There is no substitute for sleep. According to modern sleep research, most people need seven to ten hours of sleep a day, and lost hours can never be made up.

Sufficient sleep is the foremost factor in a person's ability to sustain a high performance level, cope with stress, and feel a sense of satisfaction in life. Getting enough sleep directly impacts our moods and emotions, our ability to think creatively and respond quickly, and our ability to sustain exertion. It is as vital to our health as what we eat and drink.

More good news about sleep and our health is that every hour of sleep we get before midnight is twice as beneficial as the hours after midnight!

A good night's sleep is one of God's blessings to you. Sufficient sleep was a part of His design for your body and His plan for your life. When you make a habit of retiring early, you put yourself in a position to receive this blessing. You'll find it easier to rise early and seek the Lord for wisdom and strength for the day ahead.

When I GET A GOOD NIGHT'S SLEEP, I FEEL . . .

Sleep recreates. The Bible indicates that sleep is not meant only for the recuperation of a man's body, but that there is a tremendous furtherance of spiritual and moral life during sleep.

Is There Room?

She wrapped him in cloths and placed him in a manger, because there was no room for them in the inn.

LUKE 2:7

I can KEEP MY
DOORS OPEN
TO LOVE
OTHERS IF I . . .

In some places at Christmas, people place lanterns, or *farolitos,* along walls and paths or flat adobe roofs. Candles are set in sand inside paper bags and symbolize the journey of Joseph and Mary. These lanterns help the couple in their search for an empty room and reflect the starry light of Bethlehem that welcomed the Christ child's birth.

Rev. Douglas Showalter remembered the story of Mary and Joseph's search in a profound way one Christmas. In their white-steepled New England church, his parishioners always looked forward to the Christmas Eve service each year. In the dim auditorium, a group of young people fully presented the Nativity tableau.

This particular year, Rev. Showalter's church council realized Christmas Eve fell on the same night as the Alcoholics Anonymous large public meeting in their church fellowship hall. Would there be enough parking space? Would the AA group even attend or would they want to spend the night with friends and family? Ultimately, the church leaders decided to let the AA group meet, regardless of the inconvenience.

The church parking lot overflowed as both AA and church members arrived. In the restroom that night, Rev. Showalter overheard a stranger—a young, sad-eyed teenage boy—talking to an older man: "I'm glad there's a meeting tonight. It's Christmas Eve, and I didn't have anywhere else to go." The older man from AA agreed.

Rev. Showalter watched the Nativity scene that night with a lump in his throat, grateful they had kept their "Inn" open to the ones who needed it.[56]

Our lives are like lanterns lighting the way to hope. When others come to us, looking for a safe place to shelter their hearts, will we cry "no room" or will we, like Rev. Showalter's church, keep our doors open to all who need the Savior's love?

When there is room in the heart, there is room in the house.

A Permanent Companion

> Surely I am with you always,
> to the very end of the age.
> MATTHEW 28:20

What little girl wouldn't love to see a new doll waiting for her under the Christmas tree? One that eats, wets, talks, walks—or one that is nothing but a silent bedtime companion. Every year the toy shelves burst with new models, just waiting to be dubbed the child's favorite doll.

Author Dale Galloway shares a story by R. E. Thomas that makes us rethink just what constitutes a "favorite" among some children.

"Do you like dollies?" the little girl asked her houseguest.

"Yes, very much," the man responded.

"Then I'll show you mine," was the reply. Thereupon she presented one by one a whole family of dolls.

"And now tell me," the visitor asked, "which is your favorite doll?"

The child hesitated for a moment and then she said, "You're quite sure you like dollies, and will you please promise not to smile if I show you my favorite?" The man solemnly promised, and the girl hurried from the room. In a moment she returned with a tattered and dilapidated old doll. Its hair had come off; its nose was broken; its cheeks were scratched; an arm and leg were missing.

"Well, well," said the visitor, "and why do you like this one best?"

"I love her most," said the little girl, "because if I didn't love her, no one else would."[57]

The beauty of Christmas is that God knows our condition: tattered lives, broken hearts, blind eyes, missing parts. If He didn't love us, no one else would. That's why He sent Jesus, not just as a babe in Bethlehem, but as a permanent companion for us—anytime, day or night.

I am
THANKFUL TO
GOD FOR . . .

God is in all things and in every place. There is not a place in the world in which He is not most truly present. Just as birds, wherever they fly, always meet with the air, so we, wherever we go, or wherever we are, always find God present.

Who's in Control?

Peace I leave with you; my peace I give you.
I do not give to you as the world gives. Do not
let your hearts be troubled and do not be afraid.
JOHN 14:27

A fear I
NEED TO GIVE
TO GOD IS . . .

Wendy jumped at the opportunity—two full weeks at a writers' camp. Looking forward to her "writers' retreat," she eagerly packed her suitcase with everything she would need and boarded a bus headed for camp. Finally she and the other campers reached their destination—a retreat with separate cabins on a deserted road, almost hidden by overgrown bushes.

That first evening, after a morning of class and an afternoon of writing, Wendy watched the sun dip behind the hardwood forest, leaving in its wake blackness so dense that, without moonlight, she couldn't see her hand in front of her face. Inside the cabin she refused to think about being alone in the middle of the woods and calmly stacked her writing books, dictionary, and paper next to the computer she had brought along.

Later, she worked on a poem, then stretched out on the loveseat. Picking up a novel, she began to read. Yawning sleepily, the words on the page blurred, and she dozed off. Some time later, a noise in the attic awakened her. She bolted upright, her heart pounding in her ears. *Lord,* she thought, *please take this fear from me.*

Her breathing quickened as she walked silently to the front door and peered onto the porch. Easing up each narrow step, she felt a lump in her throat. Listening at the door, she realized to her great relief that the sound was merely mice scurrying across the wooden floor.

The next morning, Wendy thanked God for His ever-present help in time of trouble. Holding a mug of coffee, she walked down a pathway to the breakfast hall. Sun-dappled wildflowers greeted her, and lizards raced under rhododendron bushes. Around the next turn was a hidden waterfall. She sat down on a boulder and prayed, turning all her fears over to God, trusting Him to take care of her. During the rest of her stay at camp, her writing flowed as easily as the rush of water over river rocks.

Tonight, if you need peace, seek God's.
Drop thy still dews of quietness,
Till all our strivings cease;
Take from our souls the strain and stress,
And let our ordered lives confess
The beauty of thy peace.

God's Treasures

> Come to me, all you who are weary
> and burdened, and I will give you rest.
> MATTHEW 11:28

Up on the hillside in a quiet community stands a quaint little country church. Its steeple stands proud, and its stained-glass windows provide a welcoming atmosphere to everyone who passes by. As the wind blows, the tall trees bow down over the church, as if they are protecting the outside walls of the magnificent but small structure.

On Wednesday nights and Sunday mornings, the church comes alive with enthusiasm and laughter, as its dedicated members come to worship God. During that time, love is evident as friends and family members embrace each other with warm hugs and handshakes.

During the week, the church is normally quiet. Periodically, someone will stop by to walk around the yard, while admiring the beauty it bestows. This place is truly God's house, a holy and sanctified building. Many times a passerby will slow his pace and see the beauty it holds, but sadly too many people speed by without even acknowledging its existence.

Unfortunately, these people regard God in the same manner as they do His church building. Their days are too busy. They speed through life without seeking His Will for their life or enjoying His everlasting love for them. As God looks upon the earth, He probably sheds a tear knowing that some of His children are simply surviving life rather than living an abundant life. He offers a life full of hope and peace.

God will not force a person to stop to smell the roses, to ponder the history of His house or to worship Him. But when a passerby glances toward the church and lifts a few words to Him, He rejoices with the angels in Heaven. Like salvation, the opportunity to stop, to rest in His hands, and enjoy the treasures that God gives is available to all who will take the time to accept His gift.

✟

What TREASURES IN MY LIFE HAVE I BEEN OVER-LOOKING?

You wake up in the morning with twenty-four hours of the unmanufactured tissue of the universe of your life. It is yours. It is the most precious of possessions. No one can take it from you. It is unstealable. And no one receives either more or less.

Extra Encouragement

Little children, let us not love in word or speech but in deed and in truth.
1 JOHN 3:18 RSV

I experience

MUCH
ENCOURAGE-
MENT FROM . . .

Scott was fortunate to grow up in a house three doors down from his grandparents' home. His grandparents were like a second set of parents to him. In many ways Scott considered them wiser than his own parents. When Scott wanted to quit Boy Scouts, his mother left the decision up to him. His grandpa, however, told him that he would like to see him stick it out for the entire year. Scott learned that quitting is not always the answer and stayed with the troop for the remainder of the year.

Scott was disappointed when he didn't make the cut for the high school football team. His father promised to talk to the coach. But his grandfather told him a story from his own life when he didn't make the baseball team. Scott understood that everybody couldn't be successful at everything. Instead of playing baseball, Scott took a photography class. Photography became his passion and his livelihood for forty years.

Scott had the desire to go to a college out of state. His parents were insistent that he should attend the local junior college. His wise grandmother, who rarely voiced an opinion, spoke up and said, "Let the boy go. He needs to experience life." Scott's parents took her advice and allowed him to go.

When Scott proudly showed his grandmother the engagement ring that he picked out for his bride-to-be, Grandma hugged him warmly. With tears in her eyes said, "Honey, I am so proud of you."

Love always shines through with a small ray of encouragement from special people in your life.

We need to encourage members of this next generation to become all that they can become. . . . You and I can't even begin to dream the dreams this next generation is going to dream, or answer the questions that will be put to them.

Night Glories

Let my prayer be set forth before thee as incense;
and the lifting up of my hands
as the evening sacrifice.
PSALM 141:2 KJV

Some of the most fragrant flowers in the garden stay tightly closed, or "sleep," during the day. They open only later in the afternoon and evening, perfuming the night air with their sweet scents.

The most magnificent of these late-bloomers is the moonflower. Moonflowers look like white morning glories, except that their blossoms are enormous—up to eight inches across. Each bloom lasts for only one night, but the scent more than makes up for the short performance.[58]

Just as nature lends itself to day and night creations, so there are "morning people" who feel their best in the early hours of the day and "night people" who seem to bloom after dark. If you are a late bloomer, fill the night air with the sweet fragrance of prayer before God this evening.

The Lord looks forward to your companionship and is waiting to hear from you. Give Him your attention and listen to what He wants to tell you. Treat God as you would a dear friend.

Review your schedule to find time you can commit to God. Have no time? You may be overlooking some ready-made times, such as your ride to and from school. Perhaps you need a place of isolation without distractions.

Jesus said, "Enter your closet" (Matthew 6:6 KJV). This "closet" can be any place, any time you can be alone with Him. Or you may want to designate one special place where you pray.

As you spend time seeking God during the night, you will bring a sweet fragrance into the throne room of God. The Bible describes this beautifully in Revelation 8:3 KJV: *And another angel came and stood at the altar, having a golden censer; and there was given unto him much incense, that he should offer it with the prayers of all saints upon the golden altar which was before the throne.*

Enjoy your night glories.

Some TIMES
I COULD
SPEND WITH
THE LORD
INCLUDE . . .

✠

All the Christian virtues are locked up
in the word prayer.

Power Naps

With him is an arm of flesh; but with us is the LORD
our God to help us, and to fight our battles.
And the people rested themselves upon
the words of Hezekiah king of Judah.

2 CHRONICLES 32:8 KJV

Some

THINGS IN MY
MIND THAT I
NEED TO TURN
OFF ARE . . .

Have you ever considered trading in your afternoon break for a quick nap?

Medical students are usually adept at taking power naps. They fall asleep immediately upon lying down, sleep for fifteen to twenty minutes, and then awake refreshed. Researchers have discovered these short naps are actually more beneficial than longer midday naps. The body relaxes, but does not fall into a "deep sleep," which can cause grogginess and disorientation.

Only one thing is required for people to sleep this quickly and benefit fully from a power nap—the ability to "turn off the mind." We quiet our minds by not thinking about all that remains to be done, worrying about all that might happen, or fretting over events in the past.

Power nappers are experts at inducing a form of inner peace that comes from knowing all will be well with the world while they check out for a few minutes. What they believe with their minds actually helps their bodies relax.

When King Hezekiah told the people the Lord was with them and would fight their battles, they *rested* upon his words. His words gave them inner peace, confidence, and a rest for their souls. We can take those same words to heart today.

The Lord is with us also, to help us and to fight our battles. These simple lyrics from a Bible-school chorus say it well:

You worry and you wonder how you're gonna get it done,
from the rising of the moon 'til the setting of the sun.
Plenty to do when your rest is through,
Let Him have the world for a turn or two.
There will be plenty to do when you wake up . . .
so sleep on for a few minutes.
Not without design does God write the music of our lives. Be it ours to learn the time, and not be discouraged at the rests. They are not to be slurred over, not to be omitted, not to destroy the melody, not to change the keynote. If we look up, God himself will beat the time for us. With the eye on him, we shall strike the next note full and clear.

Gifts from the Heart

"Freely you have received, freely give."

MATTHEW 10:8

HOW CAN I FREELY GIVE TO OTHERS WHAT GOD HAS FREELY GIVEN TO ME?

As the department store shoppers elbowed their way through the holiday crowd, Patricia Moss stopped to listen to her children whine and cry about the toys they wanted for Christmas. After examining her family's values, she decided to adopt a friend's tradition based on the song "The Twelve Days of Christmas."

Twelve days before Christmas, she and her family would begin slipping anonymous gifts onto the front porch of a needy family. They wrote clever rhymes to accompany each gift, which ranged from twelve candy canes on December 13 to eleven fancy bows on the eleventh day before Christmas to a tin of ten giant homemade cookies on the tenth day before Christmas. They continued to leave gifts through Christmas Day.

One year the Moss family chose an elderly man who had suffered a stroke. He and his wife had decided not to put up a tree that year—that is, until the "twelve days" gifts started arriving. Another year the Mosses selected two families to cheer up, since both of the Moss sons had friends whose families needed their love and care.

Patricia said that even after her sons were grown and had moved away, they still participated in this tradition when they returned home for Christmas.

Patricia taught her children well, allowing them a hands-on opportunity not only to see good but also to do good, moving them beyond their own problems as they gave generously of themselves to others.

Every gift which is given, even though it be small, is great if given with affection.

Expectant Hearts

Before honour is humility.

PROVERBS 15:33 KJV

HOW CAN
I BETTER
APPROACH
GOD WITH AN
EXPECTANT
HEART?

During the Coolidge administration, an overnight guest at the White House found himself in an embarrassing predicament. At the family breakfast table he was seated beside the President. To his surprise, he saw Coolidge take his coffee cup, pour the greater portion of its contents into the deep saucer, and leisurely add a little bit of cream and sugar.

Wanting to do as the President did, the guest hastily poured his own coffee into his saucer. But he froze with horror as he watched Coolidge place his own saucer on the floor for the cat!

We've all been in uncomfortable situations where we were unsure of ourselves and the proper etiquette for the occasion. Scripture describes the proper protocol for entering the presence of God: "Enter into His gates with thanksgiving, *and* into His courts with praise" (Psalm 100:4 NKJV). We go into the Lord's presence with gratitude and joy for all He is and does in our lives.

The writer of the book of Hebrews said that Jesus made a way to God for us. We can approach His throne with confidence and "receive mercy and find grace to help us in our time of need" (Hebrews 4:16).

We don't have to worry about *how* we come to the Lord when we approach with pure and expectant hearts, understanding that before honor comes humility.

Christ is not one of many
ways to approach God, nor
is He the best of several
ways; He is the only way.

A Sip at a Time

> My servants will sing out of
> the joy of their hearts.
> ISAIAH 65:14

The great moviemaker Cecil B. DeMille once remarked on the importance of happiness in one's life and how to savor it:

"The profession one chooses to follow for a livelihood seldom brings fame and fortune, but a life lived within the dictates of one's conscience can bring happiness and satisfaction of living far beyond worldly acclaim. I expect to pass through this world but once, and any good therefore that I can do, or any kindness that I can show to any fellow creature, let me do it now. Let me not defer or neglect it, for I shall not pass this way again. Happiness must be sipped, not drained from life in great gulps—nor does it flow in a steady stream like water from a faucet. 'A portion of thyself' is a sip of happiness as satisfying as it is costless."[59]

DeMille's slow-sipping metaphor reminds us that one may sit for quite some time with a mug of hot tea resting warmly between one's hands. The warm, fragrant steam helps to revive one's attitude and generally gives a feeling of contentment. In those moments, it is easier to agree with Paul: "I have learned in whatever state I am, to be content" (Philippians 4:11 NKJV).

One of the ways in which we may experience true happiness is to "sip" from the supply of talents and abilities God gives us and use them to benefit others. "Sipping" doesn't require spending great amounts of time. Neither does it require extraordinary or professional helping skills.

Use a gift or talent you have to serve others. Volunteer for a committee at work, teach Sunday school, join a choir or musical group, help someone with schoolwork, or simply make an effort to get better acquainted with those you meet but don't know well.

Helen Keller, blind and deaf from the age of 19 months, had remarkable sight when it came to viewing life's priorities. She said, "Many persons have a wrong idea about what constitutes true happiness. It is not attained through self-gratification, but through fidelity to a worthy purpose."

How miraculous it is that God has built an automatic measure of happiness into every act of self-sacrifice. Take a sip of happiness by serving others!

A big SIP OF HAPPINESS I'D LIKE TO TAKE RIGHT NOW IS . . .

✚

He stands erect by bending over the fallen.
He rises by lifting others.

"Easy, Albert!"

A wrathful man stirreth up strife: but he that is slow to anger appeaseth strife.
PROVERBS 15:18 KJV

I need

TO WORK ON NOT BECOM-ING ANGRY ABOUT . . .

Even the well-controlled temper can find itself sorely tested on days when nothing seems to go according to plan. As the shadows lengthen, occasionally the fuse gets shorter.

One young father with a new baby discovered a secret to handling his temper. Desiring to take full part in the raising of his infant son, he cared for the baby on his days off, while his wife worked a part-time job. On one particular day, his son seemed to scream constantly. The father thought a visit to the park might distract the child.

He pushed the child's stroller along at an easy pace and appeared to be unruffled by his still crying baby. A mother with her baby strolled near them and she heard him speaking softly, "Easy, Albert. Control yourself." The baby cried all the louder. "Now, now, Albert, keep your temper," he said.

Amazed at the father's calm, the mother said, "I must congratulate you on your self-control. You surely know how to speak to a baby—calmly and gently!" She patted the crying baby on the head and asked soothingly, "What's wrong, Albert?"

"No, no!" explained the father, "The baby's name is Johnny. I'm Albert!"

Albert had stumbled onto something that actually works better with adults than with babies and children. When others lose their temper or seem to be baiting you intentionally, practice speaking in your most calm, quiet voice. In most cases, your tranquil demeanor will help the other person to calm down. And practicing self-control in frustrating circumstances lengthens your own fuse—as well as diffuse strife.

Hard to do? Sure! But try this: allow the other person to finish speaking his thoughts. Then, before you reply, take a deep breath. As you exhale say to yourself, *Jesus, I love You.* Keep it up every time you respond. The powerful name of Jesus can calm even the angriest seas of temper!

A man who can't control his temper is like a city without defenses.

Yule Log

Thy name, O Lord, is everlasting, Thy remembrance,
O Lord, throughout all generations.

PSALM 135:13 NASB

> IF MY FAMILY
> COULD
> POSSESS SUCH
> AN OBJECT OF
> TRADITIONAL
> MEANING,
> WHAT WOULD
> IT BE?

It took place around the second week of December every year. Mother would open her cedar chest and gingerly begin to sort through her most prized material possessions. She took such care as she reached inside and one by one removed items that held great meaning to her. Bubble lights, ornaments, tinsel, and many things shiny and fragrant renewed the season year after year.

One special item was always placed on the mantel, transforming the home. It was a Yule log, covered in artificial hyssop and man-made holly berries. It had a place in the center for a candle. A bright red satin ribbon was attached with a metal staple on the end to enhance its beauty.

Each year, the family had a tradition of discussing the yule log and remembering what each part of the decoration meant. The log signified a celebration, the birth of Christ. Hyssop, a fragrant herb, was used in ancient Hebrew sacrifices. The lovely red satin ribbon signified the blood of Christ that was shed for our sins. The holly berries represented growth, a bountiful supply. And the candle glowed as a loving reminder that Christ is the Light of the World.

Sometimes in the ordinary, sometimes in our traditions, sometimes in our celebrations, we can find the foundation of our faith. Here, a plain log, a few faded green leaves, some old berries, and a tattered ribbon tell the ageless story of God's infinite love.

**God's love for us is proclaimed
with each sunrise.**

Opposites Balanced

The day is Yours, the night also is Yours;
You have prepared the light and the sun.
You have set all the borders of the earth;
You have made summer and winter.
PSALM 74:16-17 NKJV

Something

I WOULD LIKE

TO FIND TIME

TO DO MORE

OFTEN IS . . .

Much of our life seems to be suspended between opposites. We grow up learning to label things as good and bad, hurtful and helpful, naughty and nice. People are kind or mean. The thermostat can be adjusted to avoid extremes of heat and cold. We look forward to the changing of seasons from summer to winter. Time is divided by day and night.

Not only are these opposites helpful to us in defining or "bordering" our lives, but they can also help us release stress.

Very often people who are engaged in physical, muscle-intensive work all day choose a "mental" activity with which to relax and unwind. Those who have idea-intensive jobs often enjoy relaxing with hobbies that make use of their hands, such as wood carving or needlework. Those in sterile, well-ordered environments look forward to coming home to weed their gardens.

Structured tasks and routines are good relaxation for those involved in the creative arts. The musician runs home to his computer. The surgeon delights in growing orchids in a hothouse. The factory worker enjoys crossword puzzles. The executive unwinds in the kitchen, preparing gourmet meals.

The Lord created us for this rhythm of opposites. God told Noah as he and his family left the ark that Noah would experience "seedtime and harvest, cold and heat, winter and summer, and day and night shall not cease" (Genesis 8:22 NKJV). Mankind was set in a world of opposites.

When you feel stressed out at day's end, try engaging in an activity that is opposite in nature to what you have been doing. If you have been using your mind, turn to an activity that is physical. If you have been exerting physical energy, turn to an activity that is mental.

Let the pendulum swing back to rest in a central location!

People who cannot find time for
recreation are obliged sooner or
later to find time for illness.

Explore the Scenery

The earth is full of the goodness of the LORD.

PSALM 33:5 NKJV

Every day has moments worth savoring and enjoying to the fullest. It may take some effort to search out those moments, but the reward is a sense of enriched meaning in life which is, in turn, motivating and satisfying.

Play freely in a warm spring rain shower. Take your brown-bag lunch to the park and watch the geese circle on the pond or the elderly men bowl on the green. Gaze out a window and watch the birds making their nest on a ledge or the careful balancing act of window washers at work on the building across the boulevard. Enjoy a steaming cup of cappuccino in a garden-room cafe while a string ensemble plays in the background. Watch puppies tumble about in their play or kittens toying with a ball of yarn. Linger at a balcony rail with a glass of tangy lemonade and watch the sun set in golden glory.

Harold V. Melchert once said, "Live your life each day as you would climb a mountain. An occasional glance toward the summit keeps the goal in mind, but many beautiful scenes are to be observed from each new vantage point. Climb slowly, steadily, enjoying each passing moment; and the view from the summit will serve as a fitting climax for the journey."

God's creation is all around us. Take time today to enjoy what God has done and is doing! You'll enjoy what *you* are doing more.

HOW CAN I SHARE SOME OF THE SIMPLE THINGS IN LIFE WITH THOSE AROUND ME?

The kiss of the sun for pardon,
The song of the birds for mirth,
One is nearer God's heart in a garden
Than anywhere else on earth.

You Are One of Us

Be ye kind one to another, tenderhearted,
forgiving one another.

EPHESIANS 4:32 KJV

I can

DEVELOP A
FORGIVING
ATTITUDE BY
TAKING THIS
FIRST STEP . . .

"It's all right; sometimes I don't know why I do things either. You are part of our group, and we support you." With that one statement, the tension evaporated from the room, and other teens expressed their support to Sara.

The setting was a community meeting of adolescents in a mental health treatment facility. Sara suffered from chronic schizophrenia, and she often did not comprehend her actions or control them. The previous evening, upon returning from a visit home, she had promptly set a small fire in her bathroom that created major problems for the unit, including an evacuation as well as the canceling of evening activities.

The next morning, the staff and patients met to work through the problems of Sara's actions and the anger it created among the other teens. For nearly an hour she sat mute in the group, refusing to meet anyone's eyes.

But when Sam, another patient, came across the room, knelt down before her, looked up into her face, and expressed his support for her, she responded. Sara told how her mother had become angry with her and screamed at her, "Why don't you just stop being schizophrenic?"

"I just wanted to die; that's why I started the fire," Sara said in a barely audible voice.

Sam's willingness to forgive her in spite of this error in judgment made it safe for Sara to share her heart with the group.

Forgiveness is not an occasional act,
it is a permanent attitude.

Talk with the Creator

> Wisdom begins with respect for the Lord; those who obey his orders have good understanding.
>
> PSALM 111:10 NCV

"There is literally nothing that I have ever wanted to do, that I asked the blessed Creator to help me do, that I have not been able to accomplish. It's all very simple if one knows how to talk with the Creator. It is simply seeking the Lord and finding him." These are the words of the great scientist, George Washington Carver, the American botanist who literally rebuilt the Southern agricultural economy after the Civil War.

Born a slave, Carver eventually became head of the Agriculture Department at Tuskegee Institute in Alabama. He developed more than three hundred uses for the peanut and dozens of products from the sweet potato and the soy bean. Much of Carver's research was conducted in his laboratory, which he called "God's Little Workshop."

"No books are ever brought in here," he said, "and what is the need of books? Here I talk to the little peanut and it reveals its secrets to me. I lean upon the 29th verse of the first chapter of Genesis. 'And God said, Behold I have given you every herb bearing seed which is upon the face of all the earth, and every tree in which is the fruit of a tree yielding seed; to you it shall be for meat.'"

Carver had a habit of seeking the Lord early in the morning. He rose at four o'clock every day and went into the woods to talk to God. He said, "There He gives me my orders for the day. I gather specimens and listen to what God has to say to me. After my morning's talk with God, I go into my laboratory and begin to carry out His wishes for the day."

You can begin each day asking your Creator what He would have you do that day and how He would have you do it! If you are facing a challenge, God can reveal a new perspective. If you need inspiration, God can stir you up. If you feel you are in a dead-end situation, God can show you His way out.

Seek your Creator today! He desires your fellowship and He wants to give you the answers you need.

✝

My ORDERS FROM GOD TODAY ARE TO . . .

There He gives me my orders for the day. I gather specimens and listen to what God has to say to me. After my morning's talk with God, I go into my laboratory and begin to carry out His wishes for the day.

Miracles Still Happen

> With man this is impossible, but
> with God all things are possible.
> MATTHEW 19:26

Something

THAT
HAPPENED
IN MY LIFE
THAT I THINK
WAS A MIRACLE
HAPPENED
WHEN . . .

A small preschooler waited impatiently as the long "North Pole" line snaked its way to the department store to see Santa. Finally, the child arrived at the head of the line. He climbed onto Santa's lap, eager to express his wish list.

Santa's blue eyes twinkled as his burly arms wrapped around the young child. "And what do you want Santa to bring you?" he asked. "A toy truck? A new football? A bike?"

The little boy shook his head no. "I want a new daddy," he whispered.

"What do you mean, 'a new daddy'?"

"I want my daddy to act different. My daddy does drugs." A tear trickled down the preschooler's face.

Santa tried to console the child and promised his best, knowing he could not provide this impossible request.

Jim Cymbala, author of *Fresh Wind, Fresh Fire,* and pastor of the inner-city Brooklyn Tabernacle in New York, shows a video of one young man in his church. In that clip, the young man explains how he often left his wife and children for days, living in a literal doghouse while nurturing his crack addiction.

One night his wife and children had gone to Pastor Cymbala's church where many of the people began to pray earnestly for the woman's husband. That night, as if drawn by some unseen power, the young addict made his way to the church. As he walked down the aisle of the massive building, he heard his name spoken aloud in a petition to God. He knelt at the church altar and gave his life to Christ. He abandoned his habit and soon began singing in church and ministering to others.

Two stories—different endings. What seems impossible for us, is always possible for God. Miracles still happen—and not just at Christmastime.

A miracle, my friend, is an event
which creates faith.

Never Give Up

> Let us not become weary in doing good,
> for at the proper time we will reap
> a harvest if we do not give up.
>
> GALATIANS 6:9

Again, the young teacher read the note attached to the fresh green ivy.

"Because of the seeds you planted, we will one day grow into beautiful plants like this one. We appreciate all you've done for us. Thank you for investing time in our lives."

A smile widened the teacher's face as grateful tears trickled down her cheeks. Like the one leper who expressed gratitude to Jesus for healing him, the girls she had taught remembered to say thanks to their Sunday school teacher. The ivy plant represented a gift of love.

For months the teacher faithfully watered that growing plant. Each time she looked at it, she remembered those special teenagers and was encouraged to continue teaching.

But after a year, something happened. The leaves began to turn yellow and drop—all but one. She started to discard the ivy, but decided to keep watering and fertilizing it. One day as she walked through the kitchen, the teacher noticed a new shoot on the plant. A few days later, another leaf appeared, and then another. Within a few months, the ivy was well on its way to becoming a healthy plant again.

Henry Drummond says, "Do not think that nothing is happening because you do not see yourself grow, or hear the whir of the machinery. All great things grow noiselessly."

Few joys exceed the blessings of faithfully investing time and love into the lives of others. Never, never give up on those plants!

God does not pay weekly,
but he pays at the end.

I refuse
TO GIVE UP
ON . . .

Polished Thanks

In all you do, give thanks to God.

COLOSSIANS 3:17 NCV

I Was

RESENTFUL
AND NOW
HAVE A
REASON TO BE
THANKFUL
ABOUT . . .

As the pipe organ thundered out the notes to a favorite Christmas carol, stained glass windows reflected the flickering of tiny candles at the church's Christmas Eve program. It should have put Maggie in the Christmas spirit, but all she could see was the dust and dirt and mess she would have to help clean up after this late-night service.

Maggie's grandfather was the church custodian. He needed extra help to keep the church clean at Christmastime, so Maggie and her siblings had been drafted to work with him. Trash would have to be collected, floors washed, and the white pews wiped clean of dirty handprints and boot marks before services the next day. Here Maggie was, stuck in an emptying church with a polishing cloth in her hand, wishing she could be anywhere else in the world. With a sigh, she began to polish the pews.

Grandpa noticed her work and said with a smile, "God must be hearing a lot of thanksgiving from you." When she didn't reply or look up from her polishing, Grandpa continued, "With every push of the broom or every shovel of snow I thank God for my job, don't you?"

Maggie didn't want Grandpa to know that she was more resentful than thankful that night. But she knew in her heart that he was right. "I'm sorry, God," she muttered. And by the time Maggie finished polishing the row, she had found that she could thank God—even for a job polishing pews. The next morning, as the sun blazed through the colored windows and reflected off her polished pews, Maggie said "thanks" once more—and smiled.

A single thankful thought towards heaven
is the most perfect of all prayers.

Shining Lights and Singing Angels

Surely goodness and mercy shall follow
me all the days of my life: and I will
dwel lin the house of the LORD forever.

PSALM 23:6 KJV

A U.S. Air Force sergeant in Thailand let his light shine. When others were out partying and chasing women, he stayed in, talked to other soldiers, relaxed, and read.

One day, a young soldier asked him why. The sergeant shared his faith in God with the young man and told him that his relationship with Jesus meant he made different lifestyle choices. The two began reading Scriptures together and praying on a regular basis. The older soldier had the joy of leading the younger man to his Lord.

Christmas was approaching, and the young man celebrated his new birth as the world celebrated Christ's birth. Due to seniority, the sergeant went home for holiday leave, while some of the others in the unit stayed behind, including the younger soldier. When the sergeant returned, the men in his unit met his plane with unhappy news. The young soldier had been killed in battle the day before.

Though deeply saddened by the passing of his young friend, the sergeant comforted the other soldiers with the truth of good news: "This year, he really did get to go 'home' for Christmas."

A great crowd of witnesses worships at God's throne. In endless praise, those who have gone on to be with our Lord in Heaven ahead of us can inspire hope in our hearts. Christmas is a special time to join in the heavenly celebration of joy.

God is my strong salvation,
What foe have I to fear?
In darkness and temptation,
My light, my help is near.

Someone
I'D LIKE TO
SHARE THE
GOOD NEWS
WITH IS . . .

Joy—From the Inside Out

But the angel said to them, "Do not be afraid.
I bring you good news of great joy
that will be for all the people."
LUKE 2:10

The BEST
CHRISTMAS
I REMEMBER
WAS WHEN . . .

✚

Carry Christmas in your heart year 'round.

Who hasn't read the famous Dr. Seuss story of *How the Grinch Stole Christmas?* When the wicked Grinch heard all the hoopla of Christmas celebrations in Who-ville, he determined to destroy every shred of joy in town. He plotted carefully, assembled a sleigh, and tied reindeer horns to his dog, Max, to represent Rudolph. Then as Christmas Eve approached, the Grinch swept into every home, sucking up all the trees, gifts, stockings, and toys left by Santa for every boy and girl.

When little Cindy-Lou-Who caught the Grinch in the act of stealing, the devilish robber thought up a lame excuse to satisfy the child: he claimed the tree lights were in need of repair. He would quickly return the tree in working order.

The Grinch roared through town, up one chimney and down another, until he had stolen every reminder of Christmas in Who-ville. To his dismay the next morning, the Grinch listened to the townspeople of Who-ville, who were laughing and singing. Why was Who-ville celebrating Christmas without boxes, packages, or ribbons?

The wicked Grinch ultimately concluded that Christmas means more than traditional toys, gift-giving, and store-bought packages. And you know the rest of the story: The Grinch's heart grew three sizes that day, and he returned every toy, package, ornament, and Christmas tree to the children and families of Who-ville.

Simple truth: the Grinch learned the meaning of Christmas.

And every year the same challenge arises.

If every good thing were suddenly whisked away from us, would we, too, agree with the people of Who-ville? Could it be that the joy of Christmas really is found not on the inside of stores, but on the inside of our hearts?

Family "HisTree"

For the Mighty One has done great things for me;
And holy is His name. AND HIS MERCY IS
UPON GENERATION AFTER GENERATION
TOWARD THOSE WHO FEAR HIM.

LUKE 1: 49-50 NASB

While decorating the Christmas tree at Grandma's house, Helena held up a red tree skirt trimmed in white lace and asked, "What is this, Grandma?"

Grandma smiled and said, "That little tree skirt was a gift our landlady, Mrs. Ratcliff, made and gave us the first year Granddad and I were married. She lived upstairs and we rented the downstairs part of her two-story house."

Helena pulled out an old glass ornament with blue paint peeling off. "Grandma, is this old?"

"Yes, sweetheart, it was one of our very first. We could only afford one box of assorted ornaments, and that is the only one left. That first year Granddad and I strung popcorn and cranberries to help decorate our tree."

A sweater-clad teddy bear ornament sparked another memory. "Helena," Grandma continued, "I sewed a bathrobe for Granddad as my present to him, and he gave me a sweater. We loved each other so much we felt rich and thankful. God's blessings kept us from even considering what we did not have.

"See this basketball ornament?" Grandma said to Helena. "It reminds me of when your daddy played basketball on the high school team and won lots of trophies."

"Here's Mickey Mouse!" Helena squealed with delight.

"Your dad bought the Mickey ornament on a family vacation to Disney World when he was in grade school."

Through sharing family history vignettes, Grandma gave Helena a sense of God's loving faithfulness from generation to generation, decorating HisTree with words of gratefulness and praise.

Some
SPECIAL FAMILY
MEMORIES
I ENJOY
HEARING
ARE . . .

✛

It's a pleasure to share one's memories.
Everything remembered is dear,
endearing, touching, precious.

Keep Your Eyes on Him

Let us fix our eyes on Jesus, the author and perfecter of our faith, who for the joy set before him endured the cross, scorning its shame, and sat down at the right hand of the throne of God.
HEBREWS 12:2

A special
PERSON I SEE

JESUS IN IS . . .

Ginger ran to her mother's room as fast as her five-year-old legs would take her. "Come look; come quick," she squealed.

"What is it, honey?" her mother asked.

"You have to come see."

Ginger grabbed Mother by the hand and led her to the living room. Stopping in front of the credenza, Ginger pointed her chubby little finger to the manger scene.

When Mother had arranged the figures the previous night, the display was properly balanced and evenly spaced. The larger figures were near the stable, and the smaller ones were at the far edge of the walnut top so as to achieve proper perspective. Mother had been pleased with the visual picture. Now the figures were clustered under the stable roof. Each stood facing the manger, as close as possible to the Baby Jesus.

"Isn't that better? Now they can all see," Ginger proudly exclaimed.

"See?" asked her puzzled mother.

"Yes, see," said Ginger, "When I got up, all the men were scattered around. Some of them were so far away that they couldn't see Baby Jesus. I moved them closer so they could see Him."

Can you see Jesus, or do you need to move a little closer to the manger this season in order to see the Savior? Are there those in your life who remind you of Jesus?

By a Carpenter mankind was made, and only by that Carpenter can mankind be remade.

Field of Dreams

Hope deferred makes the heart sick,
but a longing fulfilled is a tree of life.
PROVERBS 13:12

I could
BE MORE
ENCOURAGING
TO OTHERS
IF I . . .

There was nothing special about Randy. Each year his teachers repeated the same words: "You don't want Randy in your class. He's a loser."

But that was before he entered Miss Jewel's sixth grade art class. Until then, only bright red D's and F's adorned Randy's school papers. Test scores plummeted him to the bottom 10 percent of his class.

Miss Jewel saw the sparkle in Randy's eyes when he watched her demonstrations. His huge, rough fingers took to a paintbrush like an athlete to sports. Charcoals, sculpting, watercolor, oils—whatever the project, Randy excelled beyond any student Miss Jewel had ever seen.

She challenged him to take private lessons and suggested the names of several artists she knew. Randy made excuses for not pursuing the lessons, but Miss Jewel suspected it was because of his family's poverty.

The teacher decided to make Randy her special project. Year after year she saved her money. On Randy's graduation from high school, she sent him an anonymous check to cover his college tuition—and the name of an artist who agreed to teach Randy in the summers between his college studies.

One day about ten years later, she received a package in the mail—a beautiful oil painting of herself. And these words: "I will never forget you. I have dedicated my life to helping others grow their dreams like you did for me. Thank you, Randy."

Our words, our time, even our belief in someone's ability could help produce a crop of doctors, musicians, presidents, or simply loving Moms or Dads who will rise in their own "field of dreams."

You cannot teach a man anything;
you can only help him to find it himself.

The Value of Disaster

And not only that, but we also glory in tribulations,
knowing that tribulation produces perseverance.
ROMANS 5:3 NKJV

I want
GOD TO HELP
ME SALVAGE...

For ten years Thomas Edison attempted to invent a storage battery. His efforts greatly strained his finances, then December 1914 nearly brought him to ruin when a spontaneous combustion broke out in his film room. Within minutes all the packing compounds, celluloid for records and film, and other flammable goods were ablaze. Though fire departments came from eight surrounding towns, the intense heat and low water pressure made attempts to douse the flames futile. Everything was destroyed.

While the damage exceeded $2 million, the concrete buildings, thought to be fireproof, were insured for barely a tenth of that amount. The inventor's 24-year-old son Charles searched frantically for his father, afraid that his spirit would be broken. Charles finally found him, calmly watching the fire, his face glowing in the reflection, white hair blowing in the wind.

"My heart ached for him," said Charles. "He was 67—no longer a young man—and everything was going up in flames.

"When he saw me, he shouted, 'Charles, where's your mother?' When I told him I didn't know, he said, 'Find her. Bring her here. She will never see anything like this as long as she lives.'"

The next morning, Edison looked at the ruins and said, "There is great value in disaster. All our mistakes are burned up. Thank God we can start anew." Three weeks after the fire, Edison managed to deliver the first phonograph.

With each new day, we have the opportunity to start again, to start fresh—no matter what our circumstances. Let the Lord show you how to salvage hope from debris. You never know what joys are ahead.

Difficulties are meant to rouse,
not discourage. The human spirit
is to grow strong by conflict.

Look Out for Leah

Thou shalt be a blessing.

GENESIS 12:2 KJV

I am GLAD TO BE A PART OF MY FAMILY BECAUSE . . .

It was the day after Christmas, and Bobby was visiting his older cousin at her family's home. He had received a new bicycle for Christmas and was riding it in the neighborhood. He was a fairly small six-year-old and shy. A couple of neighborhood children decided they did not like having a strange kid riding up and down the streets, so they stopped him and threatened him.

They were around seven or eight years old, bigger then he, and Bobby ran inside crying. His cousin Leah, who was ten, decided something had to be done about the situation. Quickly she marched down the street, found the two young culprits, and as only a ten-year-old girl can do to smaller and younger boys, threatened them with severe consequences unless they were nice to her cousin. Contritely, the two boys apologized. Leah had confirmed what Bobby always knew—she would look out for him and protect him whenever he needed her. It was a very comforting thought.

The joys of the holiday seasons come in many ways. One of these ways is in knowing that we all belong to a spiritual family that is close-knit and caring. Just as Leah stood up for Bobby in the face of trials, we, in God's family, must look out for our fellow believers. Not everyone is blessed with earthly family members who care and love them. But those who are can be ever mindful of the needs of others.

As scripture says, "From everyone who has been given much, much will be demanded" (Luke 12:48). Let's find ways to be a blessing to others. When we do, we are all richer for it.

Blessing others makes you rich.

Black-Eyed Peas

Sing unto the LORD, O ye saints of his, and give thanks at the remembrance of his holiness.
PSALM 30:4 KJV

A special
MEMORY
I'D LIKE TO
SHARE . . .

"Hey, what are you doing?" Eric asked his daughter Cynthia. It was their first New Year's in their new home and they planned on spending the next day with their families. He looked forward to watching football games and munching on a variety of "finger foods" throughout the day: vegetable and cheese trays, bite-sized barbecue sausages, Swedish meatballs, celery sticks with cheese filling, and homemade candy.

In stark contrast to his memories, his daughter was sorting black-eyed peas. "I am preparing the black-eyed peas for tomorrow," Cynthia responded. "It's a tradition I learned about from a friend. We should always eat fresh black-eyed peas on New Year's Day." And with that she promptly dropped a quarter into the pot along with the peas.

"What's with the quarter?" Eric asked.

"Dad," she responded, "it is supposed to represent wealth and happiness in the New Year." She then went on to tell him about holiday stories she had learned from friends about how they celebrate the holidays.

Family traditions and holidays form an essential foundation for our lives. Each holiday season brings with it a wealth of stories that connect us with our families. For our spiritual life to be its richest, it too must include traditions and celebrations that bring to life the stories of our faith.

Take time this holiday season to share your spiritual memories about your life with Christ with one another. Tell the stories of how Jesus became real for you, and listen to the stories of your loved ones as they share the same.

Without tradition, art is a flock
of sheep without a shepherd.
Without innovation, it is a corpse.

Acknowledgments

Latin Proverb (9, 46), William James (10, 174, 206), Mary Gardiner Brainard (11, 30), John Homer Miller (12), Donald Hankey (13), Mother Teresa (14), Thomas Carlyle (15, 40, 154, 259, 281), Thomas Adams (16), Clement of Alexandria (17, 79), Martin Luther (18, 78, 102, 119), Oswald Chambers (19, 128, 131, 203, 231, 347), Meister Eckhart (20), Abba Ammonas (21), F. B. Meyer (22, 240), Gerhard Tersteegen (23), Gerard Goote (24), William Arthur Ward (25, 31, 100, 217), Angelus Silesius (27, 193), Edwin Hubbell (28), Richard Rothe (29), Joseph Addison (30, 99, 164), William Henry Drummond (35, 87, 171, 312), Jean de la Fontaine (34), Jean Racine (35, 247), Ralph Waldo Emerson (36, 46, 62, 76, 80, 215, 238, 324, 333), Mark Twain (37), Lord Chesterfield (38, 232, 341), William Shakespeare (39, 60, 213), Henry Benjamin Whipple (41), Samuel Smiles (42, 117, 148), Chinese Proverb (43, 149, 256, 274, 282), George MacDonald (44, 129, 155, 179, 181, 225), William Law (45, 130, 196), Evelyn Underhill (47, 258), Charles Haddon Spurgeon (48, 353), Miquel de Cervantes (50), Author Unknown (51, 84, 111, 123, 135, 152, 173, 183, 187, 200, 204, 214, 223, 251, 257, 270, 278, 301, 308, 309, 318, 335, 337, 339, 359, 361, 368, 373), Dwight L. Moody (52, 69, 165, 229), Charles Thomas Studd (54), Charles Wesley (55, 163, 184), Vincent de Paul (56, 206), Josiah Gilbert Holland (57, 67, 92, 291), Jewish Proverb (58, 64), Hannah Whithall Smith (59), Frederich Spanheim the Elder (61), Robert Seymour Bridges (63), Mason Cooley (64, 201), John Greenleaf Whittier (65, 350), Horace Greeley (66), Woodrow Wilson (68, 172), William Booth (70), Margaret Sangster (71), Charles Caleb Colton (72), Lucretius (73), Louis Pasteur (74), Lucius Annaeus Seneca (75, 189), William Blake (77), Ovid (81, 235, 292, 330), Søren Kierkegaard (83), Joseph Parker (85), Ian MacLaren (86), Francis Bacon (88), Brother Lawrence (89, 93), François Duc de la Rochefoucauld (90), Epictetus (91), Thomas a Kempis (94, 150, 315, 344), Johann Paul Friedrich Richter (95), Richard Whately (96), Euripides (97), John Bunyan (98, 344), Julian of Norwich (101), Johann Wolfgang von Goethe (103, 156, 161, 202), Charles Dickens (104), Matthew Prior (105), Walt Whitman (106), German Proverb (107), James Hervey (108), Confucius (109), Martha Collier Graham (110), George Herbert (112), Ralph Washington Sockman (113, 307), James S. Knowles (114), Erwin W. Lutzer (115), Henry David Thoreau (116, 191, 338), Napoleon Hill (118), A. W. Tozer (120, 132, 141, 305, 356), C. S. Lewis (121, 126, 266), Helmut Thielicke (122), Helen Adams Keller (124), Henry Wadsworth Longfellow (125), François Fénelon (134), Plutarch (146), Honoré de Balzac (209), William Hawthornden Drummond (210), Basil of Caesarea (211), Greek Proverb (212), Oliver Wendell Holmes (216), Anne Frank (218), Humphrey Davy (219), Bernard Meltzer (220), Robert Herrick (221), Catherine of Siena (224), Rainer Maria Rilke (226), Teresa of Avila (227), William Grumshaw (228), Gotthold Ephraim Lessing (230), Henry Ward Beecher (233, 260, 304), George Muller (236), Richard Henry Stoddard (237), Jakob Bohme (239), Mary E. Maxwell (241), Augustine Hippo (242), William Penn (244, 316), William Carey (245), William Hazlitt (246), Solomon Ben Gabirol (248), Sarah Fielding (249), William Makepeace Thackeray (250), David Belasco (252), Peter Ustinov (253), Conyers Middleton (254), Abraham Lincoln (255), Jane Parker Huber (261), Antoinette Brown Blackwell (262), Amy Carmichael (263), Henry Gardiner Adams (264), Thales (265), English Proverb (266), Danish Proverb (268, 348), Samuel Taylor Coleridge (269, 276, 306), Oswald C. Hoffmann (272), Ella Wheeler Wilcox (275), Herbert Hoover (276), Mother Teresa (279), Robert Burns (280), Thomas Tusser (284), French

Proverb (285), Proverb (286), Aristotle (286), Antoine de Saint-Exupéry (288), Pablo Casals (289), George Eliot (290), Pope John XXIII (293), Don Basham (294), Saint Thomas Aquinas (295), Amish Saying (296), Jean De La Bruyère (297), Evan Esar (298), Marcus Tullius Cicero (299), Charles Fillmore (300), Father Andrew (302), Lord Alfred Tennyson (303), Walter Rauschenbusch (310), William Mountford (311), Maltbie D. Babcock (313), John Kendricks Bangs (319), Johann Tauler (320), Charles Caleb Colton (221), Johann Kaspar Lavater (323), Danish Proverb (325), Inscription over Mantel of Hinds' Head Hotel, England (326), John White (327), Richard Owen Roberts (328), Frances J. Roberts (329), Helen Steiner Rice (332), Washington Irving (334), Jane Parker Huber (336), Sir Walter Scott (340), Benjamin Franklin (342), Christina Georgina Rossetti (346), Francis de Sales (349), Arnold Bennett (351), Barbara Coloroso (352), Pindar (355), Robert Green Ingersoll (357), John Wanamaker (360), Martin Luther King Jr (362), George Washington Carver (363), George Bernard Shaw (364), Dutch Proverb (365), Gotthold Ephraim Lessing (366), James Montgomery (367), Susan Sontag (369), Desiderius Erasmus (370), Galileo Galilei (371), William Ellery Channing (372), Winston Churchill (374).

Endnotes

1 *Knights Master Book of 4,000 Illustrations*, Walter B. Knight (Grand Rapids, MI: William B. Erdmans Publishing Co., 1956), p. 64.

2 *Illustrations for Preaching and Teaching*, Craig B. Larson (Grand Rapids, MI: Baker Book House, 1993), p. 122.

3 *The Diary of a Young Girl*, Anne Frank, (New York, NY: Doubleday, 1952).

4 *Today in the Word*, September 2, 1992.

5 Author Unknown.

6 "Ansel Adams," Morning Edition, November 24, 1997 (National Public Radio).

7 Maugham, W. Somerset, *Of Human Bondage*, Doubleday, Garden City, New York, 1936.

8 Nanette Thorsen-Snipes. Adapted from *Power of Living*, April 1992.

9 *The Finishing Touch*, Charles R. Swindoll (Dallas: Word Publishing, 1994), pp. 186-187.

10 *The Last Word*, Jamie Buckingham (Plainfield, NJ: Logos International, 1978), pp. 169-170.

11 "Won by One," Ron Rand, *The Inspirational Study Bible*, Max Lucado, ed. (Dallas: Word, 1995), pp. 604-605.

12 *Give Your Life a Lift*, Herman W. Gockel (St. Louis: Concordia Publishing House, 1968), pp. 38-39.

13 *People*, March 18, 1996, p. 62.

14 *Artists Who Created Great Works*, Cathie Cush. (Austin, TX: Raintree Steck-Vaughn Company, 1995), pp. 24-25.

15 *A Young Patriot: The American Revolution as Experienced by One Boy*, Jim Murphy (New York: Clarion Books 1996), p. 47.

16 *He Cares, He Comforts*, Corrie ten Boom. (Old Tappan, NJ: Fleming H. Revell, 1977), pp. 29-33.

17 Nanette Thorsen-Snipes, *Southern Lifestyles*, Summer 1996, p. 38.

18 Thomas J. Burns, "The Second Greatest Christmas Story Ever," *Reader's Digest* (December 1989), pp. 10-11.

19 Author Unknown.

20 Kelly McHugh. Adapted from *The Upper Room*, January-February, 1999. January 9, 1999.

22 Gary Johnson, *Reader's Digest*, September 1991, pp. 164-165.

23 *The Last Word*, Jamie Buckingham (Plainfield, NJ: Logos International, 1978), pp. 169-170.

24 *A Moment a Day*, Mary Becurith and Kathi Mills, eds. (Ventura, CA: Regal Books, 1988) p. 25.

25 *Newsweek*, February 15, 1999, p. 47.

26 The Misheard Lyrics Website, www.kissthisguy.com.

27 *The Joy of Working*, Denis Waitley and Reni L. Witt (NY: Dodd, Mead and Company, 1985), pp. 722-723.

28 *The Joy of Working*, Denis Waitley and Reni L. Witt, (NY: Dodd, Mead and Company, 1985), pp. 23-24.

29 *The Finishing Touch*, Charles R. Swindoll (Dallas: Word Publishing, 1994), pp. 186-187.

30 *The Last Word*, Jamie Buckingham (Plainfield, NJ: Logos International, 1978),pp. 169-170.

[31] *Decision*, March 1996, p. 33.

[32] *The Best-Loved Poems of the American People*, Selected by Hazel Felleman (New York; Doubleday, 1936), p. 305.

[33] *People*, March 18, 1996, p. 62.

[34] *Masterpieces of Religious Verse*, edited by James Dalton Morrison. (New York: Harper and Brothers Publishers, 1948).

[35] Linda J. Vogel, *Teaching and Learning in Communities of Faith* (San Francisco: Jossey-Bass Publishers, 1991), p. 124.

[36] Craig B. Larson, *Illustrations for Preaching & Teaching* (Grand Rapids, MI: Baker Book House, 1993), p. 106.

[37] *Reader's Digest* (March 1999), p. 117.

[38] Meryle Secrest, *Leonard Bernstein: A Life* (Knopf, 1995).

[39] "Words of Love By Mother Teresa," *Education for Democracy*, Benjamin R. Barber and Richard M. Battistoni, eds. (Dubuque: Kendall / Hunt Publishing Company, 1993).

[40] *San Francisco Chronicle* (February 4, 1996), p. 4.

[41] Arden Autry.

[42] JAMA (January 10 1996), p. 99.

[43] *The Treasure Chest*, Brian Culhane, ed. (San Francisco: Harper, 1995)

[44] *The Treasure Chest*, Brian Culhane, ed. (San Francisco: Harper, 1995), p. 162.

[45] *Encyclopedia Judaica*, Prof. Cecil Roth and Dr. Geoffrey Wigoder, eds. (Jerusalem: Kefer Publishing House, 1972) Vol. 4, pp. 142-143.

[46] "Leisure," *The Family Book of Best Loved Poems*, David L. George, ed. (Garden City, NY: Doubleday & Co., 1952), p. 261.

[47] Author Unknown

[48] *The Upper Room* (May-June 1996), p. 15.

[49] *The Treasure Chest*, Brian Culhane, ed. (San Francisco: HarperCollins, 1995), p. 94.

[50] *The Treasure Chest*, Brian Culhane, ed. (San Francisco: HarperCollins, 1995), p. 92.

[51] Billy Graham, *Unto the Hills: A Devotional Treasury* (Waco, TX: Word Books, 1986), p. 223.

[52] *Health* (March/April 1995), pp. 48-49.

[53] *Today in the Word* (February 1991), p. 10.

[54] Nanette Throsen-Snipes, *Souther Lifestyle* (Summer 1996), p. 38.

[55] John Baillie, *A Diary of Readings* (Collier Books, Macmillan Publishing Co., NY, 1955) Day, p. 182.

[56] Showalter, Rev. Dr. Douglas, "Nowhere Else to Go," www.heartwarmers.com, 21 December 1999, accessed 2/11/00 from http://dispatch.maillist.com/archives/heartwarmers/msg00490.html.

[57] Galloway, Dale E., *You Can Win with Love*, Harvest House Publishers, Irvine, California, 1976.

[58] *Tales of the Shimmering Sky*, Susan Milord (Charlotte, VT: Williamson Publishing, 1996), p. 47.

[59] *The Treasury of Inspirational Anecdotes, Quotations and Illustrations*, E. Paul Hovey, Grand Rapids, MI: Fleming H. Revell (Baker Books), 1994, pp. 204-205.

Additional Copies of *Quiet Moments with God Devotional Journal for Teens*
and other titles from Honor Books are available from your local bookstore.

Check out these great titles:

Quiet Moments with God for Teens
Glimpses of an Invisible God for Teens

If you have enjoyed this book,
or if it has impacted your life,
we would like to hear from you.

Please contact us at:

Honor Books
An Imprint of Cook Communications Ministries
4050 Lee Vance View
Colorado Springs, CO 80918
www.cookministries.com